Gender and
Werewolf Cinema

ALSO BY JASON BARR

Video Gaming in Science Fiction: A Critical Study (McFarland, 2018)

The Kaiju Film: A Critical Study of Cinema's Biggest Monsters (McFarland, 2016)

Gender and Werewolf Cinema

Jason Barr

McFarland & Company, Inc., Publishers
Jefferson, North Carolina

LIBRARY OF CONGRESS CATALOGUING-IN-PUBLICATION DATA

Names: Barr, Jason, 1976– author.
Title: Gender and werewolf cinema / Jason Barr.
Description: Jefferson : McFarland & Company, Inc., Publishers, 2020. |
Includes bibliographical references and index.
Identifiers: LCCN 2020015002 | ISBN 9781476666389 (paperback : acid free paper) ∞
ISBN 9781476639901 (ebook)
Subjects: LCSH: Werewolves in motion pictures. | Masculinity in motion pictures.
Classification: LCC PN1995.9.W38 B37 2020 | DDC 791.45/675—dc23
LC record available at https://lccn.loc.gov/2020015002

BRITISH LIBRARY CATALOGUING DATA ARE AVAILABLE

ISBN (print) 978-1-4766-6638-9
ISBN (ebook) 978-1-4766-3990-1

© 2020 Jason Barr. All rights reserved

No part of this book may be reproduced or transmitted in any form or by any means, electronic or mechanical, including photocopying or recording, or by any information storage and retrieval system, without permission in writing from the publisher.

On the cover: Benicio Del Toro as the title character
in the 2010 film *The Wolfman* (Universal Pictures/Photofest)

Printed in the United States of America

*McFarland & Company, Inc., Publishers
Box 611, Jefferson, North Carolina 28640
www.mcfarlandpub.com*

Table of Contents

Preface	1
Introduction	11
The Racial Dynamics of Werewolf Cinema	29
The Saga of Larry Talbot	39
The Pre–1960s Werewolf: A Stranger Within Me	50
The 1960s and 1970s: Realizing the Power Within	61
The 1980s Onward: The End of the Tragic Masculine and the Embrace of Power	73
Under Siege: The Wolf Outside the Door	104
Enemy, Mother, Lover, Object: Women in Werewolf Cinema	114
Conclusion	153
Filmography	159
Chapter Notes	161
Works Cited	167
Index	169

Preface

> "There's something very tragic about that man, and I'm sure that nothing but harm will come to you through him."
> —*The Wolf Man* (1941)

At first blush, a film like *The Grey* (2011) isn't a werewolf film. No men turn into werewolves, and they don't wrestle with the shame and terror (or, sometimes, glee) of being a werewolf. But they are attacked and eaten, one by one, by real (at least by Hollywood standards) wolves. The story follows a ragtag band of oil workers whose airplane crashes in the remote Arctic wilderness, where they are immediately set upon by a pack of wolves. Every so often, the men are separated from their own pack and killed by the wolves as Ottway, played by Liam Neeson, becomes the unquestioned leader of the human group. Ottway, whose career in the remote oil plant is to shoot wolves, soon becomes the only survivor, and is locked in a deadly showdown with the alpha wolf that has been stalking him for much of the film.

Of course, there are themes throughout *The Grey* that embrace the basic tropes of werewolf films: one pack against another, the struggle between embracing death and continuing to survive. That wolves are the main antagonist—not zombies or vampires or other fantastic creatures—more closely ties *The Grey* into the werewolf film genre. One of the predominant themes that make *The Grey* more of a horror film than it gets credit for is the slow advance of panic that pervades the camp as, one by one, as in a typical slasher film, the weakest members of the group are picked off, often suddenly disappearing. Howls punctuate the night air, a harbinger of the doom to come, the "unmistakable," "peculiar," and "most eerie" sound (Summers 64) upsetting the gathered humans. This trope—of howls discomfiting people, of disrupting society—has appeared in numerous werewolf films as well.

Yet, the biggest theme that dominates the narrative of *The Grey* is masculinity, and how the opposing perceptions of masculinity affect the relationships of the men in the group. Ottway, the strong but silent type of man, is immediately questioned in his authority by several members of the group, and the film follows their slow embrace of Ottway's leadership as he establishes himself among them mostly by the simple evidence of being correct in his assertions more often than anyone else. He, too, becomes an alpha male, much like the wolf that stalks him, and the duality between the two—wolf and man—is the underlying philosophical structure that propels the narrative arc of the film. Films like *The Grey* closely mirror the fundamental genetic structure of films such as *Dog Soldiers* and *Werewolf: Beast Among Us*, in which groups of men assert themselves against a supernatural werewolf or pack of werewolves while also establishing a sort of masculine pecking order for the characters to follow.

What masculinity truly is, what it means, is a deeply philosophical question. Numerous tropes of masculinity dominate cinema, from the spaghetti Westerns featuring Clint Eastwood to the action-adventures of musclebound actors such as Sylvester Stallone and Arnold Schwarzenegger. Indeed, many of these films (and older viewers can add Charles Bronson and Burt Reynolds and many predecessors to the list), feature incredible amounts of violence, but also redemption. The masculine isn't tied up, entirely, with musculature, but with a particular attitude, a way of carrying oneself. As Chantal Bourgault du Coudray notes, the "excessive masculinity of the werewolf body also exaggerates conventions of masculine representation" (85). In other words, the toxicity of the wolf dominates all, and is often reflected in the sometime feminine or "soft" masculine male suddenly becoming aggressive and stupidly powerful compared to human males. A wronged man makes things right, and is willing to break the law, lose friends, or murder numerous people in order to reset the world according to his own views. At least this is the uninterrogated masculinity that Hollywood often normally presents to its viewers. Indeed, it seems that almost every handsome male lead must appear in an action film at some point in time, just to show that they can follow in the tradition of their acting forefathers. Some have even revived or resuscitated their careers by moving from drama into action.

Yet, the interrogation of masculinity, the attempts to understand what makes an individual a "man," or more ephemerally, "masculine" rarely appears in mainstream cinema. Interestingly, however, a subset of horror films that focuses on werewolves seems to focus almost entirely on questions of gender and masculinity. This is most likely because werewolf lore itself follows the same pattern; the cinematic werewolf, too, has become a "perennial figure of masculine crisis" (du Coudray 80). Within the werewolf film, concepts such as violence, sexual aggressiveness, sexual attractiveness, and an embrace of one's potential (for good or bad) dominates the genre.

The Grey also introduces a concept that is repeated numerous times in werewolf films: the concept of what I call "tragic masculinity." In this iteration, the person afflicted with the curse of the werewolf often truly does not enjoy being a werewolf, and, in many cases, absolutely despises themselves because of their curse (comedies and family-friendly fare such as *Teen Wolf*, *Teen Wolf Too* and *What We Do in the Shadows* have been successful in parodying and inverting this formula). But the various pushes and pulls of masculine identity in werewolf films, from nerdy college student to lascivious sexual beast, from familial outcast to hero, from veteran to victim, often result in the same type of ending. To retain one's masculinity in the face of the curse of a sort of super-masculinity, the person affected must give themselves up to fate, and, often, death itself.

Simply put, the tragic male is one who is unmoored from society, but still beholden to societal expectations of gender; his masculinity is inherently a tragic flaw. Unable to successfully land on one distinct version of masculinity that satisfies himself as well as his social circle, the tragic male is ultimately faced with his own nullification: death itself. The character who is the tragic male, in cinematic depictions at least, often veers wildly from one version of masculinity to the other, never quite finding a center within his own personality. Society and social expectations instead continually confound and box in the tragic male. The tension that this creates in those who are close to the tragic male reveals him as a disrupting force, and, ironically, the tragic male is therefore not only aware of his struggle to find a "center" in his masculinity, but also uniquely aware of how this struggle is damaging those around him. The tragic male alters the space in which he resides, and this alteration exacerbates and heightens the struggle to find a definition of masculinity that is acceptable to him *and to the surrounding social circles in which he moves*. This often, though not always, leads to his eventual destruction, a death wish of sorts that the male character often perceives as the only way to alleviate the all-consuming tension of his own masculinity against what he or others feel is the more "appropriate" masculinity. The tragic male, unable to find a centralized gender identity that pleases them, or provides agency, simply cannot exist in a world where the gender roles of others are so rigidly defined.

Finally, the tragic male has a backstory that only he and the viewer seem to know, understand, and sympathize with. Often, the events leading up to the tragic male's issues in film are ones that are specifically designed to show a specific loss or lack of control: the death of a wife from cancer; the accidental death of a best friend; trauma from previous events; being fired from a job despite being good at it; romantic rejection despite good intentions; being born to the wrong family; simply being in the wrong place at the wrong time. The events that turn a male into a tragic male are those that evoke sympathy within the viewer, even among the males who eventually become "evil" or "bad" werewolves. In other words, the tragedy doesn't stem from the infection or the curse of becoming a werewolf; the precise lack of agency and ability to control one's destiny already exists in the character—the appearance of a werewolf only heightens that tragedy or provides a path out of the milieu of which the tragic male finds himself a part. It is only in rare cases that the tragic male manages to subvert the tragedy he is experiencing.

In *The Grey*, Ottway himself is a tragic male, and, as the narrative unfolds, his basic nihilism is readily obvious—the death of his wife, told in flashbacks, has deeply affected him. He is, by his own admission, a man "unfit for mankind," and as such, has banished himself to a remote oil colony filled with "ex-cons, fugitives, drifters, [and] assholes." Indeed, Ottway understands that he's "stopped doing the world any good," and is merely waiting to die, either naturally or by his own hand. Ottway, at several points in the film, recites a poem that reveals his understanding that his role in society no longer exists:

> Once more into the fray
> Into the last good fight
> I'll ever know
> Live and die on this day

In fact, as the group of men slowly dissolves, the remaining survivors, too, become increasingly aware of their impending doom. Diaz, severely injured, begs to "rest," and the group, knowing that he wants to die, leaves him behind. And, just before the wolves attack the remaining survivors—Ottway and Henrick—Henrick asks Ottway where, at the start of the film, Ottway had gone to when he left the base camp on his own with a rifle. "I never thought I'd see you alive again," Henrick tells Ottway, revealing that he knew Ottway was going to commit suicide. As the film closes, Ottway, his fists wrapped in broken glass, faces off against the alpha wolf, and the ending is presented in such a way that there are two paths: Ottway rejects the nihilism and embraces survival, even with the pain that it brings, or he accepts his death, and the alpha wolf is merely the instrument that allows him to secure his fate, a sort of suicide-by-wolf. The final image of the film—which appears after the credits—shows Ottway's hand draped over the dying wolf's chest. The symbolism here is apparent: through the wolf, Ottway can achieve the primitive nature required to overcome or succumb to the life that stretches out before him. In the final battle with the wolf, he either learns how to survive by defeating a beast, or he dies (or sustains enough damage to be dying), and leaves the world, having reverted to a primitive "eat-or-be-eaten" rubric. The choice is freedom from his past, or death, and there's no other path. The "tragic" masculine that dominates Ottway's character does not change, regardless of if he survives his final battle or not: he is, throughout the film, willing to embrace death, and his survival is borne of necessity or vengeance rather than any true desire to live. This trope repeats itself in numerous werewolf films.

In *An American Werewolf in London*, David is told by the ghost of his best friend Jack, "Kill yourself David, before you kill others," and, indeed, David, after he realizes he is a werewolf, attempts to do just that, but can't quite bring himself to complete the attempt. Ambrose, the cantankerous war veteran in *Late Phases*, faces down a group of werewolves so that he can die with honor. And so on. To cleanse themselves of the werewolf curse, the person afflicted must reject their heightened and often hegemonic or toxic masculinity, and instead embrace their own destruction. For the survivors of werewolf attacks, this means a slow understanding of one's own unease at existing within the world, a heightening of the senses, not just in smell and taste, but in an understanding that they no longer have a viable role to play in society, that they are being rejected by the very people from whom they worked so hard to earn acceptance. Their masculinity, so comfortable in human form, has become as toxic and unviable as wolves wandering through a suburb.

Of course, some films flip this formula entirely. *Howl*, *Wolf*, and *Wolves* focus on male protagonists who are perhaps overly burdened by the expectations of civilization, and their guilt and shame at being "soft" males place them on the lowest and most ineffective margins of masculinity. These "soft" males—as Robert Bly called them—have a "gentle attitude toward life" and are "intrinsically unhappy" (2) because they lack control, and are bandied about by, and, as a result, are often jaded by, the world around them. Yet, upon receiving their "curse," these same men turn into superheroes of a sort, embracing their newfound aggression and powers, their newfound place in the world, where they automatically earn the respect (and fear) they could not achieve previously. Montague Summers described the wolf as having "unbridled cruelty, bestial ferocity, and ravening hunger. His strength, his cunning, his speed were regarded as abnormal, almost eerie qualities, he had something of the demon, of hell. He is the symbol of Night and Winter, of Stress and Storm, the dark and mysterious harbinger of death" (65). Thus, the men who embrace the wolf are subverting the order in which they were formerly subservient: the men who once dominated them now quiver in fear at their approach, if they manage to survive through the entire film, that is. Their "abnormality" does not create a sense of shame in them; rather, it is a source of pride and power.

As one can no doubt tell by looking at the contents of this book, I've made the conscious decision to explore werewolf films that appear emblematic of aspects of masculinity throughout the ages. This book is by no means a complete overview of the entirety of werewolf films,[1] but is instead designed to use films as exemplars of a greater issue. Within these chapters, I attempt to keep the order of the werewolf film chronological, as to reveal larger trends regarding gender and, more specifically, masculinity, within those films. The films chosen for this volume are certainly not the only werewolf films that exhibit an aspect of masculinity and can also propel the discussion further with the evidence that exists within the film. And, to that end, there is no "one size fits all" definition of masculinity. The borders of gender assumption are porous and shift frequently. The idea of masculinity, for this volume at least, is best thought of as a discussion rather than an idea (or ideal). I also want to note that there is no chapter regarding homosexuality in werewolf cinema. As I wrote this work, I felt that the conversation around homosexuality in werewolf cinema was going too far afield from the primary purpose of exploring masculinity in general in werewolf film, and that it was a topic that could not be constrained to just one or two chapters. I do include copious notes on the moments that tend to point toward the possibility of a character being homosexual or symbolizing homosexuality. These notes point toward the possibility, perhaps, of an entire volume on homosexuality and werewolf cinema.

Back to the chronology. To put it bluntly, *An American Werewolf in London* is the final film in what could be considered a more "traditional" werewolf film: a single man (usually) infected with the werewolf curse, battles it with all of his might and attempts to re-civilize himself. In its place came the more "modern" take on werewolf cinema, starting with *The Howling*, which is really the first time that a male (and female) seems to revel in the werewolf curse. This method, I feel, will allow the more casual reader a way of broaching the volume while also allowing for the depth of criticism I feel the werewolf film genre lacks at times. Each individual chapter focuses on an aspect of masculinity and draws on topics and ideas throughout history that attempt to understand masculinity as a driving force behind popular culture.

The "Tragic" Male

Of course, the idea of what constitutes a "tragedy" has continually entertained and vexed numerous scholars and philosophies since ancient times. As Terry Eagleton has noted, there has been no success in the continual search for a "faultless definition" of tragedy (5). As such, it will be impossible to come to any sort of comprehensive version here, either. Instead, it is important to view tragedy in the tropes that are often presented within the werewolf film. In many of the films, people die often brutal deaths, but the character who is most often killed is the cursed person themselves.

The rubric of tragedy is set in place by the first werewolf film to permanently occupy the American imagination: *The Wolf Man*. In this film the formula of the tragedy is set: man romances woman, man gets bitten by wolf, man turns into wolf, wolf meets tragic but often romantic end, wolf turns back into man upon dying. This process requires, also, the presence of two other archetypes to fulfill the tragedy. First, the idea of a tragic witness—someone who has loved or been involved with the werewolf's alter ego, who ultimately is forced to witness their new form and their ultimate demise. In films such as *An American Werewolf in London* or *The Curse of the Werewolf*, that role belongs to a woman who has fallen in love, sometimes improbably, with the human side of the werewolf. In other films such as *The Wolf Man*, the witnesses are the unrequited paramour, as well as Larry Talbot's own father, who also deals the final death blow to his own son.

Werewolf cinema also seems to require the tragic striker: the one who destroys the werewolf (or werewolves). This often occurs if the narrative focuses on the wolves themselves as the antagonists of the story. Larry Talbot's father unwittingly beats his son to death in *The Wolf Man*; Ambrose dies killing wolves in *Late Phases*; Private Cooper survives after killing multiple werewolves in *Dog Soldiers*. These wolf killers sometimes serve double duty as witnesses as well. After Private Cooper leaves the shack at the end of *Dog Soldiers*, for example, a series of newspapers appear on the screen, featuring headlines about werewolves, presumably because he took his story (and photos) to the press.

To continue with *Dog Soldiers* for a bit longer: the film focuses primarily on two male soldiers: Sergeant Wells and his trusted subordinate Private Cooper. As the film progresses, the pair take on different, yet sometimes combined, roles. Early in the film, Wells is attacked by a werewolf, and slowly begins his transformation, symbolized by his quickly healing from evisceration wounds. Wells, then, progresses from a witness to the action to the tragic hero in a long character arc that eventually demands his sacrifice. Wells's own sacrifice also ends the lives of several werewolves and saves Private Cooper. Private Cooper moves from tragic hero, who is misunderstood and, perhaps, overly sensitive, to being a "professional soldier," to tragic witness.

In other words, the roles individual characters play in the tragic masculinity of werewolf cinema can be fluid, and often shift as events unfold around them. At times, the tragic masculinity is based on the sudden inability for the cursed male to "fit in" to modern society; other times, the tragedy is the dissolution or destruction of carefully cultivated relationships, both familial and romantic. Often, the role of the tragic witness is also the role of the tragic striker: Kate in *Wer*, for example, witnesses Gavin's transformation into a wolf, and is also the one that is asked to kill Gavin. This theme is not new—the werewolf films of Paul Naschy routinely mine this territory, and one can trace back the love/death dualism in werewolf cinema all the way back to *The Wolf Man*.

So, it is fair to say that, taken singly, any one of these perspectives: masculinity, tragedy, or horror, shift so much in their definitions that it would be ludicrous to adopt any one perspective, and to a certain extent, this is true. However, werewolf cinema can and does exist at the intersection of these concepts. A werewolf film often shares perspectives on masculinity, from

Ginger's transformation into wolf in *Ginger Snaps* to Bill's transformation in *The Howling*. And, within those perspectives on masculinity often lies the tragedy of the tale.

Of course, although werewolf cinema mines the same territory relatively frequently, it becomes easier to see those same boundaries by looking at comedic or parodic takes on the werewolf film. Works such as *Teen Wolf, Teen Wolf Too, What We Do in the Shadows,* and *Bubba the Redneck Werewolf* allow the viewer a glimpse into the perceived tropes and ideas found within the werewolf films. To parody those tropes, it follows that those ideas must somehow be universally associated with the werewolf film, or else even casual moviegoers would not understand the inherent parody.

Therefore, viewers who see *What We Do in the Shadows* may giggle at the idea of the werewolves not being "swearwolves," but they will also understand, even implicitly, how the film skewers werewolf cinema's portrayal of masculinity. That the werewolf group is comprised of modern, somewhat effete men *is* the joke, and such parody allows the viewer to recognize the absurdity: werewolves aren't supposed to be effeminate, they are supposed to be somewhat masculine, even super-fueled, portrayals of toxic masculinity. *What We Do in the Shadows* is a mockumentary in the long tradition of films such as *This Is Spinal Tap* and *A Mighty Wind*. In *What We Do in the Shadows*, however, the subjects are a quartet of vampires, all hailing from a radically different era, and all trying to navigate their vampiric ways in the modern era. At one point in the film, however, the group of vampires is confronted by a group of werewolves who are, comically, portrayed as "soft" metrosexual males, who are all actively resisting any abrasive or "hard" masculinity. "Remember," goes their mantra, "we're werewolves, not swearwolves." In one of their more memorable encounters with the troupe of vampires, the group of werewolves must openly resist the vampiric taunts. "Don't catch fleas," the vampires jibe, and one of the men retorts by calling the vampires "Count Fagula."

This immediately leads to the werewolf pack—who are all still in human form—chastising one of their own for the slur, who promptly apologizes. Interestingly, the vampires mock the werewolves and their supposed homosexuality, as they are often seen together, in a sort of roving support group. At one point, the vampires trick the human wolves into revealing that they don't smell their own crotches, but "we smell each other's crotches." The sudden confession leads to a quick backpedaling—"it's a form of greeting"—but the damage in this encounter has been done. Enraged, they begin to change into wolves, much to the apparent horror of the vampires—but start to count to ten to calm themselves down. Successful at this, the pack of still-human werewolves tromps away, their domesticated and decidedly non-wild selves almost completely neutered in one simple interaction.

In this simple parody, in which werewolves appear only briefly, the relationship between the wolves and their men is fertile ground for jokes and satire. The idea of the wolf changing men into toxic individuals is flipped around—this time, the men are the ones trying to tame the wolf, and their interactions are ridiculous. The men refuse to swear, shrink from confrontation, and even openly admit to what would be considered homosocial (if not homosexual) behavior, which is essentially the exact opposite of most werewolf tropes that appear in the era of werewolf cinema after *The Howling*.

The payoff for the jokes in *What We Do in the Shadows* is so clear that even the most jaded and uninterested moviegoer can recognize the parody. The idea of the werewolf being vicious, and turning their male hosts vicious, has become more and more imbued in werewolf cinema, with little change, since the 1980s. As a result, the character arc for the male infected with the curse of the werewolf has almost completely inverted: from man trying to avoid the curse and its toxicity at all costs, to man openly embracing the hardening of his masculinity through the wolf. *An American Werewolf in London*, released the same year as *The Howling*, is rather schizophrenic in this regard. David Kessler, after he realizes he is a werewolf, finds out that the physical benefits are not without their charms—he speaks openly about how "athletic" he feels. But, he is also terrified and paralyzed by the wolf's violent and vicious attacks on individuals.

This tension, the swing between varying poles of the masculine (and, much later, the feminine) is what truly fuels most werewolf narratives, but especially film. For this volume to explore these gender roles and their impact, it becomes important to discern the differing forms of masculinity and how they can be found within werewolf cinema.

Introduction

There has been a long-standing relationship between masculinity and beastliness. In many texts that discuss or examine theories of masculinity, the urge to enjoy one's basest desires almost always emerge as something that needs a sort of balancing out. Even in more tepid texts, which acknowledge but do not endorse a sort of primitivism, the idea of a man holding within himself a sort of beast or animal is oft-visited. Take, for example, a passage in *Iron John*, a Jungian examination of masculinity:

> When a contemporary man looks down into his psyche, he may, if conditions are right, find under the water of his soul, lying in an area no one has visited for a long time, an ancient hairy man. The mythological systems associate hair with the instinctive and the sexual and the primitive [...] there's more than a little fear around this hairy man, as there is around all change [Bly 6].

Later: "The Wild Man is not opposed to civilization; but he's not completely contained by it, either" (Bly 8). It's hard to read these words and not think about the mythology of the werewolf. The beast within: sexuality, ancient, primitive, hairy, changes. Stephen King notes in *Danse Macabre* that one could consider stories such as *Dr. Jekyll and Mr. Hyde* as proto-werewolf stories.[1] King writes:

> What we're talking about here, at its most basic level, is the old conflict between id and superego, the free will to do evil or to deny it ... or in Stevenson's own terms, the conflict between mortification and gratification. This old struggle is the cornerstone of Christianity, but if you want to put it in mythic terms, [the ...] split between the Apollonian [...] and the Dionysian [78].

King is partially correct, and, really, any inner conflict that manifests itself internally, as a battle between two opposing poles of consciousness, can be read as a differing take on werewolf lore (or werewolf lore is a differing take on the battle itself). But, there is one vital aspect that King overlooks when comparing modern werewolf films to *Dr. Jekyll and Mr. Hyde*. Jekyll and Hyde inhabit the same body, and much of Hyde's actions are simply immoral ones that even Dr. Jekyll would normally never perform. Additionally, it can be argued that the "strange case" of Jekyll and Hyde is a much more weakened metaphor for the werewolf, "[w]ith his transformation into a murderous beast who prowls the streets to kill and devour his victims only when the moon is full" (Covey 1390). As Bryan Senn writes, the differences between the Jekyll and Hyde dualism and the curse of the werewolf are subtle, but apparent:

> While the werewolf personifies discord between the civilized and the bestial (moral man vs. savage animal), Jekyll and Hyde represent a more sophisticated, more refined conflict (moral man vs. immoral evil). The lycanthrope offers an internal battle between primary forces: civilization and nature; whereas Jekyll & Hyde struggles between the constructs of man: morality vs. immorality [77].

In many cases in werewolf cinema, however, the violence of the werewolf is only occasionally troubling, and people who deeply love or admire the person afflicted with the werewolf "curse" can barely recognize them. In recent years, especially starting with *An American Werewolf in London*, the transformation scenes have become far more spectacular, divorcing in the minds of the viewer the man and the wolf. In these scenes, the male body becomes an object of spectacle. Not only body horror, the werewolf transformation scene reveals the often "abject terror" of a character "witnessing the changes to [their] own body" (Abbott 131). In fact, the films of Paul Naschy, a Spanish actor, writer, and director[2] who placed his own spin on Universal monsters, often featured werewolf transformations that were long and incredibly dramatic. In *Night of the Werewolf*, one transformation scene lasts several minutes, all the while Naschy's character, Waldemar Daninsky, abuses the furniture, slapping aside a goblet, knocking over a set of armor, and kicking a log into a fireplace.[3] Traumatic transformations such as these are designed to keep human and wolf separate; compared to films such as *The Wolf Man* or *The Boy Who Cried Werewolf*, the more staid and placid transformations occur seemingly without the person who is transforming feeling any trauma or pain at the change. In these instances, the character's eyes are closed, the screen shows a series of subtle but ever-deepening changes, and then the wolf is there, often announcing its presence with a feral growl or grunt. These transformations create little separation between wolf and human, and, in many of these films, the idea of a part-man, part-wolf hybrid dominates the narrative. There is little difference between the two, and the wolf remains primarily human-looking, just fuzzier and, in some cases, such as *Wolf* or *Wolves*, can even stop and converse with their victims.

Additionally, the man (or woman) and the wolf are entirely separate entities, and neither seem to understand the other's actions. Hyde, however, is described as being "deformed somewhere; he gives a strong feeling of deformity," although Enfield could neither pinpoint the deformity nor describe the source of his uneasiness in the presence of Hyde (5). Although the basis of interior struggle certainly is reflected in numerous pieces of werewolf cinema, everything else is radically changed. *Dr. Jekyll and Mr. Hyde*, in other words, is only the starting point of the discussion, and many werewolf films have appropriated the themes, and then attempted to creatively address them.

Either way, removing the idea of change and metamorphosis to a wolf, specifically, casts a rather broad net, resulting in a focus that could certainly dilute the critical focus of this volume. Not only would adaptations of *Jekyll and Hyde* have to be included, but so would other films such as *The Haunted Strangler*, among others, in which Boris Karloff's character, James Rankin, discovers that the murderer he's been searching for is actually an evil and somewhat disheveled version of himself. By broadening the definition to fit well into King's thesis, the work would have to necessarily address a slew of films that feature no wolves or werewolves. Thus, for the purposes of this volume, we focus primarily on the change to a wolf (or to wolf-like creatures), with a few notable exceptions. This also allows us to focus on how the metamorphosis to a wolf symbolizes the societal formation and criticism of gender roles.

So, sexualized, primitive, aggressive: these words that can summon forth the image of the werewolf, but most of all, fear, not only the fear that the werewolf engenders in other people, but the fear that the werewolf engenders in the very person themselves. After all, it is hard to think of instances where one embraces the transformation of man into werewolf willingly and is not initially astounded and horrified by the physical changes of becoming a werewolf. Indeed, werewolf films are often judged by many people, but especially horror fans, on their transformation scenes, which, in terms of believability and special effects, can make or break fan and critical response to a film. These "show-stopping spectacles of bone-crunching, skin-stretching metamorphosis" (Abbott 130), are the main draws for most werewolf films of the modern era. Viewers of *An American Werewolf in London*, for example, continue to be astounded by David's prolonged and agonizing transformation into a werewolf, itself preceded by a number of horrifying visions and portents.

Of course, buried within the very definition of werewolf, as we have already seen, lies multiple issues. Critic Leo Braudy defines a monster as

> strange permutations of nature, without any discernable individual agendas, except perhaps survival and revenge against their tormentors. Like the inner sin of individuals that supposedly appeared in the outward shape of malformation or unsightliness, the monster could be an observable indication of evil that was otherwise invisible to the naked and untutored eye [77].

If one adheres to this definition, the contemporary idea of a werewolf has shifted dramatically since Lon Chaney, Jr.'s initial portrayal of *The Wolf Man*.

It is little wonder, then, in a text ostensibly about "monsters" that werewolves get short shrift, ceding most of their critical ground to more easily defined "monsters": vampires, zombies, ghosts, and so on. Indeed, over time, the cinematic definition of the werewolf has no longer been that of a monster per se. Although there is indeed an "outward shape of malformation," the questions are: does the curse of a werewolf make one monstrous, is it the sole source of ostracization from society, and does it relegate the carrier of the curse strictly to evil? Certainly, films such as *Late Phases* and *Dog Soldiers* present werewolves, for the most part, as faceless, almost interchangeable entities. However, other films have worked to "humanize" the werewolf: the remake of *The Wolf Man*, for example, and *An American Werewolf in London* indicate that there are indeed still vestiges of humanity (and human morality) inside the werewolf. Other films such as *Cursed* point to a controllable curse, one that can give people almost superhuman powers, which they often embrace rather than reject. Problematic as the curse may be, it ultimately provides benefits as well—certainly not the more classical definition of a "monster" that Braudy espouses. Yes, the transformation and the body horror remain, but as werewolf cinema has progressed, becoming a werewolf just isn't quite as traumatic or tragic as it used to be. As we see in later chapters, the change in how the werewolf is portrayed in cinema occurs with two films released in 1981: *An American Werewolf in Paris* and *The Howling*. This sudden change mimics the historical narratives of the werewolf, who, over time, have gone from misunderstood individual to prophet to horror as the centuries progressed.

In this sense, werewolf cinema is the latest incarnation of a literary tradition of werewolves, and, as Chantal Bourgault du Coudray notes, the transformation of the literary device of the werewolf has changed dramatically over the intervening decades. At first, in werewolf cinema, the curse functioned as a morality tale, in which the afflicted male would have the opportunity to repent their sins in order to be forgiven (and often die in the process). Then, it reflected a growing (and sometimes misplaced) might or righteousness on the part of the male. The curse then also brought with it the ability to be purely evil and without a moral center, and the male gives way fully, stripped of all humanity and is, simply, an uncaring and vicious beast, unredeemable in the eyes of society.

In many ways, werewolf cinema also borrows heavily from its horror movie kin. One fair comparison is the relationship of werewolf cinema to the typical slasher film. In fact, this kinship to the slasher film—of which there are only a few varieties of the same plot—may be the reason why werewolf films often take a back seat to vampires and zombies in modern cinema. Films such as *Underworld* symbolically depict the difference between vampires and werewolves in terms of how they function in Hollywood: the vampires live in a posh mansion and speak of bloodlines, engaging in backroom power politics; the werewolves live in the sewers and entertain themselves by slashing at one another. As werewolf cinema continues to circle around the same basic plot dynamics, they tend to resemble the "cinematic underbrush" of slasher films (Clover 66). This would explain, as well, how films that feature vampires, for example, have been more successful and attracted broader audiences over time. Carol J. Clover describes the slasher film: "Drenched in taboo and encroaching vigorously on the pornographic, the slasher film lies by and large beyond the purview of respectable criticism. It has also lain by and large beyond the purview of respectable criticism" (Clover 67).

Films such as *Interview with a Vampire* and *Bram Stoker's Dracula* enjoy broad audience appeal, as well as some critical merit. By comparison, most werewolf films that aren't *The Howling* or *An American Werewolf in London* have enjoyed limited success, often going direct-to-video, and rarely get any acclaim or attention from the public or from critics. Although Clover is describing the slasher genre in her statement, the same complaints can be made about werewolf cinema as well, including her pointed assertions that film magazine articles "rarely get past techniques, special effects, and profits" (67) of horror films, while alternatively being dismissed by those same reviewers as camp.

In slasher films, especially in franchises such as *Friday the 13th* or *Nightmare on Elm Street*, the monster terrorizes a series of young people. One by one, the slasher kills them, until one or two remain, and ultimately become the victors in that showdown. Many modern werewolf films follow the same formula for at least a part of the film: beast or monster that kills groups of victims. Some of those victims are random; others are trapped within a confined space. Except, in some ways, in werewolf cinema, the beast and the person who is standing against the beast in the typical slasher film are instead *one and the same*. If they are not wolves themselves, some of those being accosted by wolves, especially male characters, can embody the negative characteristics of being a werewolf. As Mary Hartson is correct to note, "[t]he werewolf is clearly neither 'this' nor 'that,' but rather an amalgamation of the two" (130). The person who is cursed to be a werewolf is both murderer and victim, killer and detective, a supernatural force that is also dismayingly human.

Yet, there is something else inherent in werewolf cinema that makes the genre comparative to the slasher film: the way that masculinity functions. As Nicola Rehling writes, the purpose of the slasher film exhibits "anxieties [...] about contemporary U.S., white, heterosexual masculinity." The "common trope" in the slasher film is the "remasculinization through violence" (Rehling), which is clearly the same trope that appears in many (though not all) werewolf films.[4] Although the "re"masculinization is a bit more problematic, the change for many of the male characters into werewolves, for better or for worse, masculinizes them, often turning them from effete or ineffectual males into assertive males, or, worse, dangerous, toxic males. Like the slasher film, these males often start with an "unremarkable appearance," hidden behind the "universal, anonymous status allotted to white, middle-class masculinity" (Rehling). In the werewolf canon, this holds true for many characters: Larry Talbot, David Kessler, Scott Howard, and Andy McDermott, among others, are all extraordinary in their overwhelming blandness.

If we follow Rehling's ideas forward, specifically the argument regarding the relationship between masculinity in the slasher film and masculinity in the werewolf film, the resemblance still holds. In many cases, the male character's lack of appropriate levels of sexuality or assertiveness matches well with the general discomfort many male serial killers in cinema also enjoy. As in many slasher films, the male—and the male and female victims—interrogate the traditional notion of gender roles, as the murderer and the victim often lack a "coherent sense of self" and stand in stark contrast to "an age characterized by identity critiques." The feminizing forces at play in the slasher film, where American "masculinity circulates as an image," an "oppressive force" derived from "commodity culture" (Rehling) often force viewers and characters to question their gender assumptions. In this regard, too, many of the male figures (at least those that are "good" in the film's formulation) in the werewolf film are torn in two by these combined ideals: the male as commodity (the "socially acceptable" male), and the male as a distinct "hard" identity that is assertive and aggressive. In many cases, and for the purposes of this volume, "hard" masculinity is the deepening of resentment or disdain for individuals or factors that result in "soft" masculinity. A "hardened" male hasn't quite progressed to hegemonic or toxic masculinity—more on those later—but has developed a distaste for displays of "softness" in whatever ways they manifest themselves: from pedicures to polite manners to a full domestic role within a household.

This tension fuels much of the "tragedy" of werewolf film: the interior struggle between gender norms and differing definitions of masculinity is real and realized, and the tension often ultimately ends with the complete and destruction of the masculine. Werewolf cinema, then, like slasher cinema, is often an interrogation of the ideas or ideals of masculinity. Usually, in films with more "effete" and unsuccessful (and even feminized) males, the male experiences becoming a werewolf as a method of embracing one's "primitive" nature, where strength determined the masculine pecking order, and being a werewolf just simply makes one more sexually aggressive, even in human form. In those few films which invert the gender identity of the werewolf, such as *Ginger Snaps*, the same thing results: the woman often becomes sexually supercharged and confident, as well as violent toward rivals.

Buried within the idea of transformation is the common trope of a weak, often subjugated or feckless male wrestling—and either embracing or defeating—the beast that lurks within. Although Robert Bly's *Iron John* concerns itself with the Hairy Man of German legend, the basic notions remain the same. Men who may be considered more fey, such as David in *An American Werewolf in London*, are often confronted with the beast within; it is predictable that David, the coy and boyish man at the start of the film becomes a tortured, but sexually attractive and much more virile male after he becomes a werewolf.

Yet, the parable in many of these films is that the werewolf rarely survives. Films such as *An American Werewolf in London*, *The Howling*, and others, show that an embrace of the aggressive masculine aesthetic ultimately leads to the defeat and destruction of the werewolf. Can it be assumed, then, that the message is one of neutering the supposedly Wild Man within?

Not entirely, for werewolf films tend to follow a myriad of plots, loosely arranged around a thematic structure. April Miller is completely correct when she writes that "werewolf films often avoid originality, preferring to construct variations on the known" (281). By examining the conflicts inherent in the films, it becomes simpler to understand how the werewolf film approaches questions of gender and gender identity. Here are four of the basic structures. Note that there may be some overlap, but many werewolf films outside of parody tend to remain firmly placed in one of these structures. To hearken back to the earlier discussion on modern werewolf cinema's kinship with the slasher film, these categories are partially inspired by the work of Carol J. Clover.

Man versus Wolf: in these films, it is up to one character to somehow discover or defeat the wolf that is terrorizing others. In some cases, the ironic twist is that it is actually the person who carries the werewolf curse that must purge themselves from the victimized society. Films such as *Late Phases* have placed a single "tough guy" stereotype against a werewolf; other films such as *The Wolf Man* have placed the man against his alter-ego, leading to scenes where the afflicted male literally tries to contain themselves by chaining themselves (often with the help of a sympathetic assistant) to walls or in tombs.

Group versus Wolf: *Dog Soldiers* features a pack of men facing off against a pack of wolves. The resulting battle—and the interplay of personalities amongst the men—creates a mirror image between the men and the wolves. For much of the film, the wolves are hidden from view, glimpsed only by the viewers and the characters. In place of the climactic transformation scene is the revealing of the werewolves themselves, who are rarely given much of a backstory other than a possible nod to their origins. Often, the alpha male of the pack of men faces off against the alpha predator of the pack of wolves. The borders of masculinity—especially at the start of the film—are varied among the males in the accosted group; it is only when they are under assault that they begin to define their identities.

The Female Wolf: A relatively underexplored and underappreciated exploration of masculinity lies in the films in which the *female* characters are the werewolves, and, often, those being pursued and hunted are the males. Films such as *Ginger Snaps* and a segment of the horror anthology *Trick 'r Treat* have featured female werewolves often preying on men. The neat inversion within this formula further allows exploration into the boundaries of gender.

Society versus Wolf: In general, the male afflicted with the curse of the wolf is often pressured by, or confronted with, his own inability to function within the world around him. By becoming a wolf, he becomes ostracized from those around him, and from the social circles he once inhabited. David struggles to re-enter society (and maintain his romantic relationship) in *An American Werewolf in London*; a group of men comically try to domesticate themselves in *What We Do in the Shadows*.

Additionally, much of the structure of the werewolf film can be found in *Werewolf of London* (1935), and *The Wolf Man* (1941), long considered to be the first successful werewolf films. Not only is most of the folklore associated with werewolves created in these films—silver damages the wolf, wolves stalking their prey at certain times of the month, a bite from a werewolf passes along the curse, and so on—but most of the thematic structure of the werewolf film originates here as well. The basic structure goes thusly: first, the main character is established as someone who is different or ostracized in some way. Second, that person is infected by the werewolf in an unexpected attack, usually after some portents. The person disbelieves that they are a werewolf until they discover evidence of their own misdeeds: blood on their hands, paw prints in their room, and so on. At some point in time during this sequence is the transformation: the moment when the audience (and the protagonist) sees for the first time the intense changes that occur from man to wolf. It then becomes a choice for the protagonist to either battle the werewolf within, or to try to flee their new reality. In the end, the werewolves are often defeated, or the curse is passed on to a sub-character to create sequels to the film.

To be sure, this is a loose retelling of many werewolf films, and even films such as *Dog Soldiers*, which places the werewolves in the background of the story for a large amount of runtime, still follow this formula, instead massaging the narrative so that the protagonists must fend off an attack by werewolves. In these instances, there remains a character or characters who slowly comes to the realization of the existence of werewolves, and, in the end, either falls victim to them or becomes a werewolf themselves. *Dog Soldiers*, of course, is an extraordinary example of the werewolf film that attempts to eschew this conventional formula, but vestiges of it remain. The board remains the same; it is only the pieces that have moved around.

Alongside vampires and zombies, it's fair to say that the werewolf has slipped quite a bit in the public esteem. Even so, filmmakers and audiences alike are continually drawn to the man and wolf narrative. Films such as *Bubba the Redneck Werewolf* (2017), *A Werewolf in Slovenia* (2014), and *Wer* (2013), exhibit a continued interest in the werewolf, even those these films rarely receive a wide release or any form of public notoriety. Although the werewolf's days as a big-budget blockbuster appear to be far behind us, it remains a fact that the werewolf retains relevance to modern audiences.

Of course, it should be noted that there is no one correct way of examining masculinity. As Todd Reeser writers, "[m]asculinity is dependent on an endless list of other signs that themselves can never be nailed down" (37). Add to this the general complexity of this topic—which seeks to combine a subgenre rather than specific characters or moments in time—and it becomes apparent that there can be no one simple definition of how werewolves in cinema reflect masculinity. Thus, this work takes a much broader approach by examining how masculinity is portrayed on an individual level. This results in themes emerging, and drawing together diverse films that, even in the werewolf subgenre, would most likely not be placed side by side.

Most often, the appearance or germination of the werewolf in a story exposes the theme of masculinity or femininity and how it affects the main characters in the work. As Reeser notes of masculinity in the following passage, the idea of a supposedly "abnormal other" can also point to something that is at once within and without: "A key aspect of power's normalizing effect is the constructing of an abnormal other. For in order to create a norm, discourse must create or invent an anti-norm, which implies that the norm is the norm by opposition" (31–32). The key to examining the werewolf film and its constructions of masculinity, varied though they are, is, unsurprisingly, the werewolf itself. Is the werewolf the "abnormal other," the thing that exists to embrace or embolden the definition of what is perceived as normal? Or (and this appears to be the case in some films), is *the werewolf* the norm, with its host being the "abnormal other" that is ostracized by society or otherwise relegated to the margins as unacceptable?

The dualistic nature of the wolf is unlike any other in cinema, save for the little-explored Jekyll and Hyde tropes. Unlike vampires or zombies, for example, the person who becomes a werewolf *still retains some semblance* of their humanity; they always change back to human, even when killed. Thus, the push and pull dynamic of man (or woman) versus beast is at play in every werewolf film, and the forces of gender identity often provide a supporting structure to this tension.

This dualism—the push and pull of varying definitions of masculinity via the ideas of what is "normal" and "abnormal" powers much of the theoretical underpinning of this work. In each werewolf film (and those closely related to them), the idea of what is "normal" behavior and what is "abnormal behavior" results in narratives in which the werewolf is the hero or the villain, or, moreso, the villain with the sympathetic backstory. In each of these werewolf narratives, the conception of the wolf shifts, revealing how society (or, at least popular culture) depicts masculinity. Additionally, it is important to note that the physicality of the wolf has changed dramatically over time. Larry Talbot's Wolf Man still resembles a human, firmly associating Talbot and his wolf form in the mind of the viewers. However, David Kessler's transformation into a wolf in *An American Werewolf in London* is traumatizing to him and to the viewer; when the transformation is complete, he is no longer human in any aspect. He is a musclebound and vicious beast. Thus, Kessler and his werewolf form can safely be considered opposites, whereas Talbot's close physical relationship to his wolf form indicates that the two are essentially two sides of the same coin.

The phenomenon would also explain werewolves playing the central character in young adult dramas. The *Twilight* film series, as well as the MTV-produced *Teen Wolf* and the British/German television show *Wolfblood* all mine the territory of alienation—rich soil for teenage audiences. In the myth of the werewolf lies the idea of someone who holds secrets that cannot be shared for fear of ostracization. Physical transformations of people into wolves mirror the physical transformations of the human body during the teenage years. And the often-impenetrable teenage angst in regard to cliques and social acceptance can also be symbolized by the "curse" of the wolf.

It should be noted as well that the transformation scene, when shown, has become the *raison d'être* for many werewolf films, and each passing film seems to place a greater emphasis on the special effects wizardry of the metamorphosis, sometimes at the expense of plot. Ultimately, *The Wolf Man*'s special effects—essentially gluing yak hair onto Lon Chaney's frame and slowly dissolving each shot from one to the next—could be considered a product of its time. Perhaps director George Waggoner would have preferred a more extreme transformation to shock audiences. But the idea of Larry Talbot as a "tragic" man shines through in the script as well, especially when juxtaposed with David Kessler's miserable and horrifying transformations. There are, within the very writing of a werewolf film script, multiple clues as to the relationship between man and beast. In considering the entire picture—the characterization and the directorial choices—can we put together a somewhat fuller picture of how werewolves and gender identity meet.

Add to this the idea that the very transformation itself becomes representative of the characters' inner struggles. Some transformations, such as those seen in *The Wolf Man* or *Werewolf of London*, very much result in a mimicking of the human form—the wolf is closer to man than animal. In these ways, one could argue that, as *The Wolf Man* alluded repeatedly, the wolf and man are the *very same thing*, locked in a struggle for that character's sanity. Throughout *Werewolf of London* (and the non-werewolf film *She Wolf of London*), for example, the main character's sanity becomes the consideration upon which their humanity resides. Larry Talbot finds himself ever nearer to being committed to an asylum because of his concerns over being a werewolf, and Dr. Lloyd consistently recommends that Talbot receive psychiatric care.

This form of "mistaken werewolf" is a literary theme as old as the Victorian era, and often focused on an individual suspected to be a werewolf, but, ultimately, their actions can be scientifically or rationally explained (du Coudray 33). This embrace of science is often spurred forward by a forward-thinking detective who risks ostracization by their peers (the most recent and longstanding incarnation of which could be Agent Fox Mulder of *The X-Files* fame), and ultimately reveals to skeptics that a werewolf *does* exist, somewhere between folklore and superstition (du Coudray 42). This process is repeated in several werewolf films, often with the "cursed" male striving to convince skeptics of their own transformation. Much of the film that follows this trope will focus on the cursed person's attempts to get people to understand that *they* are the werewolf; likewise, films such as *Cry of the Werewolf* or *The Undying Monster* follow investigators as they piece together the clues, often reluctantly, that point toward the presence of a werewolf.

Other transformations, however, are designed to provide a sort of replacement for the infected character. In some imaginings of the metamorphosis, the werewolf is a separate entity of sorts, visually and symbolically repressed by its humanness, and thus, when the transformation occurs, it literally pulls itself out of the human body. Films such as *The Company of Wolves*, *WolfCop*, and even the television show *Hemlock Grove* depict a transformation in which the human skin is shed, revealing the beast that resides within, at once a part of, but still separate from, its human host. These transformations are particularly brutal, and often form the narrative core of the film—every aspect of the plot seems to build up to the somewhat grotesque, violent, and painful transformation from human to wolf. Usually, these transformations are an audial and visual assault on the viewer, as the cursed individual screams in pain or cries out for help, and blood and gore, replete with the squishy sounds of muscles and tendons ripping and the crackle of bones giving way.

Much of this stems from thematic needs. Films such as *The Wolf Man* and *An American Werewolf in London* show the transformation of man into wolf, and very few werewolf films "skip" the transformation, even if they are low-budget works. And even though the *American Werewolf* transformation is far more complete—there is no trace of David Kessler in the wolf left for the audience to see—these films have a romantic subplot in which the wolf *needs* to be recognized by their prospective mate, even while in wolf form. Talbot still looks and moves like a human (he even wears clothing), and in the closing moments of the film, his human, "civilized" aspect reappears as a defeated corpse, leaving behind no trace of the wolf. The man, trapped, quite literally, within the primitive form of his curse, bubbles out for just a moment, a flicker of recognition of the woman he loves (though it may be unrequited) in his eyes. Then, the wolf reasserts dominance, and is ultimately destroyed. Thus, closes the loop—the realization that the wolf or primitive force, the very same thing that hypersexualized the male, making him an emblem of toxic masculinity, can no longer exist in civilized society, and must, like a virus, be rejected from the host. Of course, this notion goes under assault almost as soon as it is created—films like *Teen Wolf, Wolf,* or *Wolf Cop* create sympathetic werewolves whom the viewer is supposed to cheer for—or at least identify with—while merging the two, human and werewolf into a new and distinct character.

The idea of transformation itself has shifted over time, and some critics have considered the less-violent and less-special-effects-laden transformations to be a part of a bygone era of horror. Isabel Pinedo writes that "[t]he postmodern genre is intent on imaging the fragility of the body by transgressing its boundaries and revealing it inside out" (21). Pinedo's use of the phrase "inside out" is apropos: after all, many modern transformations involved the ripping and tearing away of the afflicted's flesh in gory fashion. In other words, the horror film, as a genre, has become more and more concerned with the transformation—often traumatic—of the body, and the werewolf film has simply followed suit. The postmodern nature of the horror film, then, reveals an emphasis on body horror and special effects, and in werewolf cinema, the movement from the relatively peaceful transformations to physically violent ones has followed suit. Films like *An American Werewolf in Paris, The Company of Wolves,* and *Late Phases,* among many others, show a "horror film's unquestionable obsession with the physical constitution and destruction of the human body" (Boss 15). This level of gore, too, often extends out to the victims of the werewolf as well. Although Oliver Hammond in *The Undying Monster* is shot repeatedly at point-blank range, his corpse is relatively bloodless; he is captured after rather calmly trying to kidnap his sister while in wolf form. On the other hand, we see exploding geysers of blood, flayed corpses, and broken bones that dominate *The Howling, Wild Country,* or *An American Werewolf in London,* revealing the slow transformation in the perspective and the transformation of werewolf cinema as well over time.

Introduction 23

It is necessary to note that this volume cannot address a complete filmography of werewolf cinema, which consists of hundreds of films. As a result, some may find the films that I have chosen to discuss to be rather eclectic—tried and true classics of the subgenre mixed with comedic interpretations of werewolves, as well as some straight-to-video releases that have been mostly forgotten, even among the most ardent horror fans. Additionally, films with only a tangential connection to werewolf lore, such as *She Wolf of London* (1945)—in which the main character is tricked into believing she is a werewolf—will be overlooked in favor of films that feature the wolf. Other films which prominently feature werewolves, such as *Werewolf: The Beast Among Us* (2012), or the *Twilight* series—once memorably described as "the multi-platform tween juggernaut" (Wasik and Murphy 66)—were excluded simply because the characterization within the film was thin, or the wolves themselves weren't major players in the overall narrative. The *Underworld* series, which is focused primarily on a war between werewolves and vampires, only rarely features werewolves in roles large enough to be of note. In these cases, it would be hard for anyone to pull much meaning from any of the characters, and, as such, they receive scant mention, if any, within this text.

The "tragedy" that is oft-repeated in werewolf film, especially in those works which feature the person afflicted with the curse as a main character, is that the "soft" or passive male is destroyed, often, along the way, becoming overwhelmed by the curse. However, more recent werewolf films have subverted the formula by taking a "soft" male, and rather than having him be destroyed at the end—often by gunfire—the "soft" victim becomes the "hardened" male predator who wins the tacit endorsement of, if not the audience, his female lover. This means that the role of the main character afflicted with the curse is not to be destroyed for his transgressive masculinity, but rather to be rewarded for it. While Larry Talbot lies dead, bludgeoned to death, David and Oliver get killed by police, or Ted passively allows his throat to be ripped out, others embrace their newfound, "hard" masculinity. Will Randall gets a much younger girl and stays a wolf, and Scott Howard wins the girl and, at least, learns to live with the wolf. In fact, after the 1980s, more than a few werewolf films pushed away from the "tragic" aspects of the curse, entering new territory regarding their portrayals of masculinity. Along with films like *Wolf* and *Teen Wolf*, *Wer*, *Howl*, and *Wolves* all portray males who are domesticated or feminized (or otherwise "soft" in the rubric of the film) who become dominant and triumphant soon after becoming a werewolf.

This text focuses on four distinct areas of masculinity. Gender definitions and criticisms sometimes lead to conflicting viewpoints numbering in the dozens, if not the hundreds, and the discussion is ongoing. Yet, the tension between varying poles of masculinity offer the very tension that fuels the plots of numerous werewolf films. This "variation in masculinity, arising from individual experiences, [...] produces a range of personalities—ranging in conception from "hard" to "soft" [...] Conflict arises when society demands that men try to live up to an impossible standard at the hard or gynephobic ends of the scales [...]" (Carrigan, Connell, and Lee 106). The conflict, then, takes on many forms, but is always a conflict: man vs. society, man vs. himself, man vs. others, and so on. In the end, this conflict is fueled almost entirely by the varying definitions of masculinity that are at work within the context of that werewolf film. Rare is the werewolf film (that isn't a parody or comedy, at least) that doesn't center the masculine and hold it up for its characters to interrogate. These various conflicts in masculinity are often nascent or budding at the start of the film, and then explode into the open when the curse is transmitted, and the wolf becomes known.

The difficulty, of course, in writing any text about masculinity is finding the center for the discussion. Although there is some risk for oversimplification, the other alternative seems to be to become so complex as to provide an array of views that confuse and confound. As Reeser notes, "there is no single model everyone turns to in order to define masculinity, but there is no originary form of masculinity either" (18). To be concise and clear, some risk of being overly reductive, and perhaps a little simplistic, must be assumed. For the purposes of this volume, four different types or traits of masculinity, broadly based on Western cultural mores and attitudes, are examined, using the werewolf film as the basis of research.

The "soft" masculine is one that Robert Bly would describe as the male who has "been asked to learn to go with the flow, how to follow rather than lead, how to live in a nonhierarchal way, how to be vulnerable, how to adopt consensus decision-making" (61). This passivity and what Bly calls naiveté reveals a man ready and willing to be wounded by society and the women in his life, going so far as to open "his shirt so that she can see more clearly where to put the lances" (63). The "soft" male is one that is domesticated, embracing his role in the homestead, and seeks input for decisions rather than making decisions. Civilization itself has brought the supposed "wildness" in this male to heel, and, as a result, most of their personality is conformist and avoids direct conflict.

The ideals of domesticity may also factor into soft masculinity as a concept. In embracing the domestic, the male may be "tamed" into playing a role and turned away from the idea of being "competitive and aggressive providers" for the home. Instead, the soft, domesticated male becomes "morally strengthened by women in the private sphere of the home, where they would be influenced by Christian piety, moral resolve, and such sentimental values as sincerity, candor, and faithfulness" (Winter 120). A character like Duncan Marsh in *The Werewolf* (1956) is a clear exhibit of the domestic ideal: he is mentally tortured by his inability to return to his family and re-assume his role as a father and husband. There is also, in this definition of domesticity, the idea that "traditional domesticity and patriarchy [function] as an antidote to cultural chaos," especially "[t]he social and cultural upheavals of the 1960s and 1970s" (Winter 122, 121). *The Werewolf*, in other words, with its idealized depiction of the soft domesticated male in Duncan Marsh gives way to *The Boy Who Cried Werewolf* (1973), in which Robert Bridgestone, a father, is continually nonplussed and irritated by his wife's career aspirations as well as their divorce. Bridgestone continually attempts to reassert the domestic and the patriarchal, even in werewolf form, through the end of the movie.

This means, of course, that the "hard" masculine is almost the exact opposite, and this ideal dominates much of what Bly posits in *Iron John*. The "hard" masculine male is one who is assertive, in touch with their primitive side, and capable of making decisions and taking on leadership roles. "Hard" masculine figures, however, often do not assume the centrality of their masculinity as being dependent on the subordination or subjugation of others, especially women. In many ways, Bly's "hard" masculinity is a simple rejection of the feminine in many ways and reasserting one's dominance in decision-making in the household. Thus, this newfound capability would be akin to a masculine individual suddenly speaking up in meetings and demanding (politely) to be heard. As we will see, the shift from "soft" to "hard" masculinity rarely occurs in werewolf cinema, and this is quite possibly because of the necessity of the genre—werewolves simply don't attend board meetings or write out checks from the family budget. Interestingly, most of the depictions of "hard" masculinity center on the juvenile male experience: films such as *Teen Wolf* or *I Was a Teenage Werewolf* move the male at the center of the narrative from the supposed "loser" (a pushover or failure in life) to a popular "winner" (someone who stands up for themselves and asserts their role in society and relationships). This follows the typical cycle for werewolf cinema, which are often "construed as dramas about men regressing, but also as ones about young men moving forward" (Spadoni 3). Ultimately, for many werewolf films, especially the more violent films, the transformation to "hard" masculinity is a waypoint of sorts for the character to continue to progress to hegemonic masculinity, or, worse, toxic masculinity.

There is a very thin line between "hard" or "hardened" masculinity, but hegemonic masculinity can be seen as a deeper shift from "hard" males. In many cases, the "hard" masculine is in response to those that are considered to be "soft," and all of the social forces they represent. Thus, a male who openly decries men who receive manicures or who decide to become stay-at-home fathers are often doing so because of a perceived effeminacy on the part of the "soft" male. The "hard" male is therefore often completely localized, internalized, and is often reactive to what they perceive as a generalized "threat" to their conception of masculinity. The "hard" masculine identity remains mostly dormant until provoked and may only manifest itself through scoffing at or belittling specific males in their social orbit.

The hegemonic masculine identity, however, is one that tends to assert the dominance of the male. Unlike the "hard" masculine, the hegemonic masculine is an externalized belief system, one that seeks to subtly change and manipulate its environment in order to maintain the power structure of the masculine. This manifests itself, often very subtly, in the thoughts and opinions of men in regard to their perceived roles in society. According to James Messerschmidt, the hegemonic masculine can be split into two categories, "dominating" and "protective" (79). The "dominating" aspect of hegemonic masculinity is one in which men who don't somehow attain a socially acceptable version of masculinity are often derided at best, physically assaulted and bullied at worst. Messerschmidt describes the "protective" hegemonic masculine as one that is "benevolent," pointing out "The [...] identification of 'protective' hegemonic masculinities challenges the notion that hegemonic masculinities are exclusively pernicious and toxic, recognizing benevolent and compassionate ways gender hegemonic relations may be practiced" (81). Messerschmidt adds that the "protective" hegemonic masculinity is also "hidden in plain sight" because the practice of that identity is often "simply uneventful" (81). Not surprisingly, both forms of hegemonic masculinity appear frequently in the world of werewolf cinema, and sometimes may even overlap within the same character. The hegemonic masculine need to protect as well as the pressure to dominate can create a distinct internalized pressure that can ultimately create or otherwise lead to toxic masculinity.

This leaves one more type of masculinity this work explores in the context of the werewolf film: "toxic" masculinity. Toxic masculinity is the nth degree of the hard masculine. In many ways, "toxic" masculinity is the worst of hegemonic masculinity, which R.W. Connell assumes is "the dominant position of men and the subordination of women" (qtd. in Reeser 14). It is the simple belief that "most men benefit from the subordination of women, and hegemonic masculinity is centrally connected with the institutionalization of men's dominance over women" (Carrigan, Connell, and Lee 113). Assertiveness becomes expressions of (or desire for, or demands for) social and physical dominance; leadership becomes demands for unwavering loyalty. The dominant position and centrality of the masculine viewpoint is assumed in hegemonic masculinity, and overlooks, sometimes purposefully, the various roles women may attain in society. Hegemonic masculinity can take on a variety of forms, but a simple example would be a man who automatically feels that all of the housework—cleaning the floors, putting out the trash—is a "woman's job." Conversely, hegemonic masculinity would lead a male to assume that women would be unable to successfully fulfill certain "masculine" tasks, such as changing the oil in a car or repairing an electronic device.

Hegemonic masculinity does not "mean violence, although it could be supported by force; it mean[s] ascendancy achieved through culture, institutions, and persuasion" (Connell and Messerschmidt 832). Very rarely, in werewolf cinema, however, do the shifts in masculinity and gender identity occur without some form of violence—most of these films are horror, after all. As a result, most of the hegemonic masculinity, such as the culture of the wolves in the woods in *Wolves*, soon transforms into toxic masculinity, which, in that same film, leads to the kidnapping and near-sexual assault of a woman. In toxic masculinity, then, sexual and physical violence take the forefront of numerous interactions between men and women, and strains of sadistic intent and desire dominate the toxic masculine's worldview. Taken from the range of "soft" to "toxic," one could move from concepts of overcivilized to uncivilized, from domesticated to completely undomesticated.

Within the rubric of the werewolf film, these versions of masculinity seem to dominate the literal and figurative transformation of both male and female characters. Some male characters are too domesticated, and the curse of the werewolf "corrects" their "soft" natures by making them into the Bly-idealized "hard" male. Other males find every semblance of civilization wiped away from their being, replaced by the dangerous and society-breaking wolf. In some of these cases in particular, these physical and mental transformations are reflective of the sustained mental trauma toward the ever-shifting societal standards regarding what makes a man "masculine." This particular theme is most prevalent in the era of the earliest werewolf films on through the 1950s; the male is accosted with multiple definitions of what is "the right" masculinity, and, as such, experience severe emotional distress at their own internalized, but shifting, masculinities. And, in the cases of films where the female becomes a wolf, those films, too, reveal evolving views on the role of women in society as well, often problematizing the very definitions of masculinity in each and every transformation from woman to wolf.

As we progress through these films, we see how culture and society have impacted gender definitions throughout werewolf cinema, including an in-depth examination of the character of Larry Talbot, the paradigm-shifting films of *The Howling* and *An American Werewolf in London*, and onward to the wolf-positive portrayals of our more contemporary films.

The Racial Dynamics of Werewolf Cinema

To set the background for much of the rest of this book, it is important to consider several salient cultural, political, and racial points about werewolf cinema, and cinema in general. Although this work will focus on gender dynamics and gender roles, the werewolf film, like many other films, both horror and not, are deeply and dramatically influenced by the prevailing cultural sentiments of the time, especially in regard to race and ethnicity. Thus, Robert Bly's exhortations against the "soft man" of the 1960s and 1970s, for example, brought forward as series of heroes and antiheroes who were anything but "soft" in demeanor in the 1980s. John Wayne's death "symbolically represent[ed] the passing of a more traditional, triumphant vision of white masculinity" (Vogel 464), but that vision of masculinity was soon co-opted and exceeded by the various roles of male actors such as Bruce Willis, Sylvester Stallone, Arnold Schwarzenegger, and Dolph Lundgren, among others. In many of the films starring these actors and their respectively over-macho characters, there are only a few nonwhite characters. If they aren't playing villains or street-level criminals, they are often sacrificed so that the white characters may rescue them or continue on in their honor. Films such as *Predator* or *Rocky IV*, for example, do have equally muscled (and, it should be noted, presumably heteronormative) nonwhite characters, but these characters are quickly killed in order to further motivate the white characters to continue on.

The crop of white, heteronormative males that appears in the 1980s have, quite possibly, never been exceeded in their excesses since. The 1980s were a marked backlash to the 1970s emphasis on supposedly sensitive or "soft" men, and, as a result, a return to a form of "hard" masculinity became the norm (du Coudray 104). This "softness," too, is exhibited in their very bodies, musclebound, and, as Richard Dyer notes, are "hard and contoured, often resembling armor. [...] a hard, contoured body does not look like it runs the risk of being merged into other bodies. [...] Only a hard, visibly bounded body can resist being submerged into the horror of femininity and non-whiteness"

(265). This criticism, too, can be applied to werewolf films, except instead of the individual being muscle-bound, their alternate identity of the wolf provides the "hard, contoured body" that remains immune, for better or for worse, to alternative identities. Rare is the individual who turns into a wolf who isn't marked by extraordinary strength, sexual lust, and a thirst for destruction. All throughout werewolf cinema, the impact and importance of a character's masculinity, and where it falls on the scale of prevailing social acceptance, informs many of the plots we will examine. Soft males turn into hard males, those who have Bly's "warrior mentality" (Vogel 464), or hard males turn into soft males, and females, too, find their gender identity shifting in werewolf film.

If one watches a series of werewolf films in succession, it would be impossible not to notice how much they are dominated by the perspectives and ideas of straight white males. This is, most likely, because, as Monica Rehling notes, the overall slasher genre (and, horror cinema in general) remains almost entirely white and highly masculinized. Like many horror films of their era, *Werewolf of London* and *The Wolf Man* joined the overall template of a supernatural (or superhuman) man endangering faceless and nameless civilians, but, more importantly, a woman (or women) in distress. As early as the 1970s, films such as those starring Paul Naschy featured a supernatural creation (Yetis, vampires, and the like) quickly dispatching male victims, but lingering on the often nude or semi-nude female victims—a clear progenitor of later horror franchises such as *Friday the 13th*, where (for much of the franchise) a supernatural man terrorizes young women, many of whom are depicted, literally, in the flesh, before being efficiently and cruelly dispatched.[1] The wolf, in many ways, is a manifestation of hatred toward locals, folklore, and anything considered an Other. As du Coudray notes, the wolf is much more of a beast, "correspond[ing] to the same racist and class-prejudiced conventions that mark out the villain in other films" (85–86).

Yet, the emphasis on the straight white male gaze as centrally located in the narratives of werewolf films becomes especially problematic, as, often, the werewolf and werewolf lore in that plot stems from the beliefs of Others. As a result, when viewed through a postcolonial lens, we can see several uncomfortable tropes emerge. In some instances, the presence of the Other within a white male must be extinguished, for it corrupts his whiteness. In other instances, the presence of the Other also disrupts white "society." And, in many cases, the only way to remove the "curse" of being a white man burdened with the presence of the Other, deep within, is their often gruesome death, a public sacrifice where the miscegenated and corrupted white body is placed on display for crowds to see. In still other cases, the white male is corrupted by the influence of the Other, and often turns from meek, "civilized" male to a more "primitive" state.

Of course, the werewolf legend in folklore mirrors the function of the werewolf curse in cinema. The supposedly "primitive" or "savage" individuals are the source of the folklore (du Coudray 36), and are the "believers" of the curse, and, as such, are often the progenitors of the curse. They are the colonized somehow befouling the often-skeptical colonizers with folkloric tradition, often shorn from science.[2] This can be interpreted in a variety of ways, and few of those explanations would be complimentary to native peoples, or at least the depictions of native peoples in werewolf folklore. The rubric of the werewolf film often centralizes the normative perspective and blames the non-normative native peoples for the travails of the hero; after all, "the heroes are also not usually indigenous inhabitants of the land in which the action takes place" (Dyer 266). The white heteronormative male is victimized by his interactions with a supposedly disruptive influence, even "corrupted" by its influence, and, like a contagion, disrupts the white society he returns to. Like the supernatural murderer of the prototypical slasher film, the "comfortable, safe communities" become assaulted by "a lurking murderous presence" (Gill 21) that no doubt finds its dream of safety harshly destroyed.

Werewolf of London didn't establish many of the ground rules that cinematic werewolves now follow—that standard-bearer is *The Wolf Man*—but it did create one very distinct theme that unfortunately persists through much of werewolf cinema: the Other as a source of evil. In *Werewolf of London*, Dr. Glendon, a botanist, and his assistant, are in Tibet, searching for a rare flower. The viewer's first glimpse of the gathered Tibetans is confusing, as many of them simply speak gibberish (though a few do speak Cantonese). Dr. Glendon speaks with them, insisting on hiring a guide for his adventure, but the gathered Tibetans flee in terror—from a Catholic missionary. "You're the first white man we've seen in three months," Glendon tells the priest. In an odd game of one up-manship, the priest responds, "You two are the first I've seen in forty years." Of course, while in Tibet, Glendon is exposed to the werewolf curse, which is the start of a trend that dominates werewolf cinema for the next several decades: the "curse" is an inherently foreign—and corrupting—influence on the victim. The white explorer, often engaged in a true and helpful activity designed for the betterment of society, is often destroyed by their interaction with another culture.

This rings particularly true in *Werewolf of London*, as Dr. Glendon's obsession with the flower that derives its energy from moonlight has long strained his marriage. However, upon becoming cursed by the werewolf attack, Glendon's obsession becomes catastrophic, and his wolf form (which can represent his Other-ness in a form of miscegenation) wreaks havoc on the London streets, sending police and citizens into a panic. If the werewolf (and foreign) presence is not contained, then London will turn "into shambles" under the new and frightening force.

It should be to little surprise, then, that those xenophobic forces at work in early werewolf cinema follow the same cycle, and that various "homages" through the ages sometimes can't help but do the same to pay appropriate respect to earlier films. Thus, the white man goes abroad or otherwise encounters an Other. The Other often carries, or is at least aware of (and by extension, complicit in) the werewolf curse. The white man becomes sullied with the "curse," and echoes of miscegenation result; the same white man's character suddenly becomes radically different, either frantic with worry (Lawrence Talbot) or even more unreasonable than before (Dr. Glendon). The murders begin, almost always of stalwarts of white society—attractive young socialites, police officers, or the wealthy.

The "there's something out there" moment of panic depicted in *The Howling* is a long-common element in werewolf cinema. *Before* the murders begin, even just a few moments before, the locals are often upset or startled by the sudden and alien howl of a werewolf. The wolf represents "a threat to the social body" (du Coudray 46). "No, not in London, it wasn't a wolf. You can be sure of that," the locals are told in *Werewolf of London*. Yet, the locals in Vasaria in *Frankenstein Meets the Wolf Man* are quick to note the presence of a wolf in an almost everyday manner: "A wolf, that's his cry, let's get him," goes the exclamation, without much of a hesitation. In other words, the very act of a wolf howling is enough to announce the presence of an "outsider" in a predominantly normative area, and the initial belief is that the howl could never happen in a city, where civilization is at its apex. The howl is indicative of a "primal carnality that must be contained and eradicated before the societal status quo can be restored and reaffirmed" (Spadoni 3). Thus, the howls announce not only the presence of werewolves, but also the presence of a disruptive Other that must be expelled so that order may return.

Much of the time, the afflicted victim of the curse awakens in a stupor, sometimes back where they started, other times in a completely different location. They have "reset" back to their original form (without the Other), often symbolized by their disheveled look or outright nudity. As Robert Eisler points out:

> As the naked "hairy hermit" of the St. Onuphrius type represents the ascetic return to the atavistic animal "state of nature" and the "in-nocence" of the "naked savage" of a Paradisic age, the adoption of clothing to cover a nude, hairless body is generally believed to constitute the essential advance from sub-human bestiality to civilized humanity [39].

In this regard, this means that the process of becoming *human* is often partially played out on screen, and is somewhat anticlimactic, especially in regard to the drama of the transformation from human to wolf. The bestial roaring and agony associated with turning into a wolf is juxtaposed with the simple acknowledgment of one's disheveled, nude, and/or weakened state. In many cases, for the male, this means that their body is somewhat on full display, in a weakened or infantile state. The emphasis, then, lies on the physicality of the masculine when they are "reset." In *Frankenstein Meets the Wolf Man*, for example, after Lawrence Talbot kills a police officer, he is found in his pajamas, draped face down over his hospital bed, sweaty and confused. David in *An American Werewolf in London* awakens, completely nude, in a new and strange place, after his transformation. Will Randall awakens in a clearing in *Wolf*, leaves and twigs in his hair, his formerly prim clothing torn and untucked. In this sense, the one afflicted with the curse is condemned to vaguely remember their explorations as an Other, and to be reborn, often quite literally, with that knowledge. Although there is usually some guilt over any killings or maimings that occur, much of the guilt the "cursed" individual feels stems from the very fact that they are an Other. It isn't them that did the killing or caused the destruction: no, it is the Other being that exists within them.

The process begins anew throughout the film, with a slow, dawning realization that the curse must be lifted for the white society to not fall into "shambles." Although this can, at times, take on the guise of the cursed individual trying to save themselves, the reasoning is that the individual who carries the Other within themselves is ultimately a destructive force. "I want to die," Lawrence Talbot repeats. "Kill yourself, David," Jack advises in *An American Werewolf in London*. "Thanks for the bullet," Dr. Glendon says after getting shot in *Werewolf of London*. Karen arranges to be shot and killed on live television in *The Howling*. And so on.

In the *Underworld* franchise, there is a werewolf named Raze, played by Kevin Grevioux, an African American actor. However impressive Raze's physique and presence is on the screen, however, he is relegated to a bit character in *Underworld*. Although the main character, Lucian, is impressed by Raze's abilities and makes him a sort of lieutenant in the werewolf army, it's also important to note that Lucian's patience with Raze often wears thin. In fact, Raze is quickly and unceremoniously dispatched by the powerful vampire Viktor in an anticlimactic face-off sequence. Thus, despite Raze's presence, the plot and the narrative often move ahead without him; he is often sent on missions at the behest of Lucien, and, in spite of his power, is quickly overpowered and killed by Viktor. Raze is indeed unusual in werewolf cinema for being a non-white werewolf, but he is, at best, a secondary character in the *Underworld* franchise, appearing only twice in five of the films.

The lone exception to this rubric is *The Beast Must Die*. Bahaman Calvin Lockhart plays Tom Newcliffe; African American Marlene Clark plays Newcliffe's wife Caroline. Newcliffe is a wealthy businessman and hunter, and he spares no expense in hunting a werewolf. Ironically, his search leads to

Caroline's infection with the curse, and although she is a wolf for less than a minute of the film's time (Newcliffe shoots her almost immediately), Caroline occupies a unique place in werewolf cinema: an Other that isn't an Other. What can be made of this unusual twist?

Quite simply, *The Beast Must Die* is an outlier. According to IMDB, Robert Quarry was originally cast to play Newcliffe before being replaced by Lockhart; in other words, the role could have gone just as well to a white actor. Bryan Senn adds that "the producers went with Lockhart instead to capitalize on the then-current blaxploitation craze" (36). That said, however, one of the simplest and most elegant reasons why werewolf cinema remains almost wholly white is that it is a part of a much larger homogenous genre: the horror film (and the slasher film subgenre) itself. In many ways, the slasher film exhibits an "odd nostalgic yearning for a traditional family and traditional family values" and focuses on "[t]he prosperous middle-class family in their comfortable well-appointed house" (Gill 20, 26). Outside of a damningly small number of actors from underrepresented populations, werewolf cinema, slasher films, and the horror film remain white, middle class, and focus on the "promised comfort and contentment of a loving, supportive bourgeois family" (Gill 17). *The Beast Must Die* is a rare, almost accidental outlier that removes familial connections and class almost entirely from the traditional tropes of werewolf cinema, itself so heavily influenced by the slasher film genre.

Another reason why the werewolf film remains so dramatically white is that it continues to reflect American culture and values, where the white heteronormative male (and often conservative or traditional) viewpoint reigns supreme. It is little wonder, then, that the 1980s were considered the "boom" period for American werewolf films. Films featured white muscle-bound actors like Sylvester Stallone and Arnold Schwarzenegger, whose solution to any problem was often awe-inspiringly simplistic: kill everything that disagrees or disrupts. In much the same way, the conservative mindset of calling back to a simpler time (inspired, no doubt by Ronald Reagan's leadership),[3] can be found in films such as *Rambo* or *Commando*: there are good guys, and there are bad guys (most of the women simply wait to be rescued), and the good guys have to punish the bad guys for their misdeeds, usually by simply killing them. The moral and societal ambiguity that was established in genres such as film noir was completely wiped clean by the 1980s.

Little wonder, then, that films such as *An American Werewolf in London* and *The Howling* appeared: the symbolism of the werewolf was very much in play. Young, white, heteronormative[4] males are forced to confront their inner beasts in such a way as to realize their own tragedy for audiences. The subtextual warning is dire: "soft" men such as David or Bill are doomed to failure. Their "soft" natures create an inner conflict or turmoil that ultimately will lead to their destruction. They cannot—or will not—fathom their sudden agency, and, as such, are destroyed. In comparison, a film like *Teen Wolf* runs the opposite path: the inner wolf is embraced, and one can exist by asserting oneself. There is no real inner turmoil that Scott Howard faces. His middle-class, heteronormative whiteness is not only his insulation, but also provides him with the ability to enjoy his agency relatively penalty-free. In many ways, Scott Howard eschews the "soft" version of his masculinity and finds himself far more assertive. The werewolf is not the end; it is the pathway.

Often, the afflicted male wolf is or becomes romantically attached to a woman, who must witness his demise (in some cases, like the films of Paul Naschy, the woman not only has to love him, but must also kill him). In this regard, we can assume a wholesale rejection of the Other. To prevent further miscegenation by corrupting the young (and often somewhat wealthy or middle- to upper-class) white woman, the wolf must die. This provokes the tragedy—for the white participants. To further cement this aspect of the trope, the male is killed while still in wolf form, and then reverts to a human, which heightens the tragedy—if only this young white male, the narrative argues, hadn't been exposed to other societies or cultures!

And one reason why werewolf films are simply not as popular as vampires or zombies, for example, is that any deviation from this very basic formula can result in a confusing hodgepodge of tropes clashing with one another (*Cursed* and *Wild Country*, for example), or saddle the film with the "groundbreaking" label, even though the film itself struggles to adopt a new and unique narrative (*Ginger Snaps* and *Dog Soldiers*). In the end, the "rules" of the werewolf film may vary only slightly, but the intrinsic core remains, and modern werewolf films must define themselves by how they will accept or reject those same tropes. It's even become a bit of a tradition for modern werewolf films to "call back" to their predecessors—usually *Werewolf of London* or *The Wolf Man*—by referring to them by name, showing them on the screen, or any number of other subtle ways, such as reciting doggerel (*The Undying Monster*) or simply by reciting lines or mentioning the folklore that was solidified in those early films. Of course, the issue of the issues of xenophobic origins still seems to ensnare many writers of the werewolf film, and its little surprise that more modern films such as *Howl*, *Dog Soldiers*, and *Wild Country* have resorted to an action-style narrative. The use of the "base under siege" narrative in werewolf cinema allows the writers and directors to completely avoid those issues, often by simply placing werewolves outside of a building or structure and letting the mayhem unfold. In other words, almost literally any monster could surround a broken-down train or a small hut, and, save for the moon and the howls, there would be little difference in the narrative.

This process, is, of course, not universal, and many films try to subvert this narrative with varying degrees of success. *An American Werewolf in London*, for example, neatly subverts the narrative of the Other. In this case, the Other are David and Jack, a pair of young and somewhat overbearing Americans walking through the English heaths. When they stop at a village, they quickly fulfill the Ugly American stereotype, asking the wrong questions and making a minor nuisance of themselves. The Americans are the Other, bumbling through the moors and upsetting local villagers, who, like those in *Frankenstein Meets the Wolf Man*, know exactly what is happening, and struggle to convince skeptical outsiders of the danger they face.

In *Underworld*, the first of a continuing franchise, there is incredibly low diversity among the werewolves (referred to as Lycans) and the vampires. Each "side" features a singular individual of African descent. In the case of the Lycans, that individual is named Raze, played by African American actor Kevin Grevioux—also one of the creators of the *Underworld* franchise—who functions primarily as the "muscle" for the Lycan leader Lucian. Raze's presence in the film can be summed up in Lucian's cry, "Where the hell is Raze?" Some of this is, of course, because the *Underworld* franchise unfolds from the perspective of white female vampire Selene, and, as a result, the werewolves often get precious little screen time. Raze's power and presence is quickly destroyed by the ancient vampire Viktor, who calmly breaks the neck of his werewolf opponent with nary a struggle. Thus is the story of Raze in *Underworld* emblematic of many of the roles fulfilled by people of color in horror films: a small role that ends in a rather undramatic death.

In *Wolves*, there is a clear divide between the "pure" wolves and the (apparently) impure wolves. "They're just mutts," a pure wolf says about his human counterparts who have been bitten by pure wolves and are thus hybrids of the two. It's clear in *Wolves* that those "mutts" are unable to handle or control the transformation, and "the wild" "gets into" them, and, obsessed with their newfound abilities, spend "less and less time in human form." Although this could, like *Wolfen*, harken back to Native American lore, *Wolves* refuses to do so, as the lines for the werewolf curse that extend back to colonial times are, apparently, all Caucasian.

Wolfen attempts to tackle this issue of the Other head on, but only with partial success. The murder of the upper-class Christopher van der Veer and his wife provokes a full-on investigation; the murder scene even gets a visit from the commissioner and the mayor of New York City. The lead detective, Dewey Wilson, is tasked with figuring out who murdered van der Veer. The film's script is quite pointed in nodding toward the Dutch origins of New York City, and the settler's rapid displacement of native peoples. In a meeting back at the department house, the homicide detectives discuss the possible suspects, and, interestingly, go through a series of Others: no "psychos" have escaped from the "looney bins," "Filipinos" are responsible for similar crimes, and the "voodoo angle" will be difficult to figure out. The van der Veer bodyguard, himself a Haitian, is large and a former bodyguard for Papa Doc Duvalier, is "one tough son of a bitch," and "worth three normals."

Wilson, at first, rejects the notions that these murders are animal attacks, until he realizes that some Native Americans who were working in construction at the time appear to have witnessed or been present at the murders. Realizing that "wolves and Indians evolved simultaneously," Dewey investigates a Native American construction worker named Eddie Holt, who spent time in prison for killing a "conservative" Native American who was, according to Dewey, "red on the outside, white inside." The duality of holding an Other inside of one's body, then, and the struggles of doing so, is played out in ways that aren't symbolized by massive transformations. It can be an entirely internalized structure, fraught with stereotypes and idealization by misunderstanding (sometimes purposefully, sometimes not) whites.

Dewey Wilson is the reluctant tourist into the world of the Other. In one memorable scene, Wilson himself becomes the Other. Stunned by a wolf attack that injures him and kills his boss, Wilson stumbles to a bar that is populated by Native Americans. Eddie Holt finally realizes that Dewey Wilson is ready to believe in the lore of the wolfen. They feed on the "graveyards of your fucking species," "the great slum areas," where "abandoned people" live. The wolfen, then, function as "scavengers," Eddie explains to a shell-shocked Wilson, who realizes that the van der Veer's planned destruction of a city block to put together high-rent complexes is an affront to the wolfen's "hunting grounds," which they have maintained since the colonial era. Thus, when Dewey is confronted by the wolfen soon after, he smashes a mock-up of the van der Veer complex, leading the wolfen to believe that the land is still theirs. To survive, he must believe, and he must internalize and understand the legacy of the wolfen. He must, in other words, embrace the reality of the wolfen, and, in some small part, cede his identity and his beliefs to Native American beliefs.

Wolfen is an incredibly nuanced—for that era—film and is one of the few in werewolf cinema to give voice (even, at times, if it is stereotypical, and voiced by Edward James Olmos, who is of Mexican descent) to Native American beliefs and customs, while also acknowledging the displacement of Native peoples. The ending of the film, in which Dewey Wilson convinces the wolfen that they can maintain their hunting ground, ends in an unusual stalemate for werewolf cinema. Often, as we have seen, werewolf films end in two ways: a werewolf lives, or a werewolf dies, often with very little ambiguity about the outcome. Of course, Wilson's quick submission to the wolfen is based on his own need for survival, and, after all, he seems more sympathetic, or at least understanding, of the Native Americans after watching his friends get killed by the wolfen.

Does this mean, then, that *xenophobia* and a deep and abiding fear of the Other is part-and-parcel in werewolf cinema, taking the ranks along with the folklore of silver bullets and full moons and wolfsbane? If so, this could explain while many werewolf films continue to circle the same narrative patterns, without much variation. People turn into wolves, or wolves attack, and other people must fend them off, often by killing them. Sometimes people like being a werewolf, sometimes they are traumatized by it. Nuance is not necessarily a strength of the werewolf film, and, as noted earlier, films that even attempt to provide some nuance (even if they fail miserably at it) are often lauded by horror fans, mostly because it is so rare.

With few exceptions, it is simple to see the long tradition of white heteronormative thoughts and fears dominating much of werewolf cinema, and this, too, may be a frequently occurring theme. This starts, quite literally, from the first surviving werewolf film, *Werewolf of London*, and manifests itself over and over again, in different forms. The supposed "spirituality" or "folkloric beliefs" of groups of Others literally lead to what could be considered a depiction of a sort of contamination by the Other that needs to be destroyed, even if it means the "cursed" individual must, too, seek death. Rare would be a non-white normative lead in a film such as *Wolf*, but it is increasingly common to have an Other mystical figure who can explain the events to the "cursed" individual. Even in films where the wolf curse is adored or appreciated by the person who holds the curse, such as *Wolf*, the Other still appears to, at the very least, be completely disconcerting to the white character.

There can be little doubt that werewolf cinema can not only sustain a lengthy critical conversation regarding masculinity and gender, but also a sort of postcolonial lens, focused on the interactions of cultures. From the perspective of werewolf cinema—which has historically, much like the standard slasher film—been dominated by white males, the use and appearances of Others may provide a new line of inquiry into the views and ideas espoused in werewolf film.

The Saga of Larry Talbot

To fully understand how gender and masculinity function in werewolf cinema, it's best to start with not the first werewolf film, but the one that has the longest character arc. *The Wolf Man* (1941) introduced viewers to Larry Talbot, Jr., and because of the popularity of the film, spawned several sequels, each of them featuring an increasingly frazzled, panicked, and gender-confused or gender-questioning Talbot. As Talbot's wolf form, always against his wishes, constantly re-appeared to do battle with mad scientists, hunchbacks, vampires, and monsters, his character changed dramatically, exposing a long, arduous process of attempting to re-establish his masculinity.

Within the saga of Larry Talbot, Jr., lie many of the tropes and ideas surrounding masculinity. His ham-fisted and failed attempts to win a lover, followed by his curse, result in a toxic version of masculinity, which, in turn, suffuses many of his actions as an individual, more deeply alienating him than before. Talbot consistently rejects the advances of numerous women after his curse, primarily because the presence of the wolf requires Talbot to engage in near-wholesale feminization followed by gender negation. If Talbot isn't proclaiming himself a "lunatic" that needs to be locked away, then he's actively trying to kill himself, at one point throwing himself off a cliff. Eventually, Talbot, as he seeks a cure, can again reassert his masculinity. In many ways, small portions of Talbot's appearance have fed the narrative fires for numerous individuals who have been cursed with the wolf in werewolf cinema: insanity, questions of masculinity and feminization, shame, and the burden of being an outcast are all familiar tropes within the early pre–1970s era of werewolf cinema.

At the start of the initial film, it is revealed that Talbot has returned to England after an 18-year stay in the United States. The reason for his return is essentially the same as the reason for his departure: his older brother John. As Larry's father, Sir John Talbot, realizes, "The elder, next in line of succession and so forth, is considered in everything. The younger frequently resents the position in which he's found and leaves home, just as you did." In other words, Larry's secondary place in his own household caused him to flee, to put an entire ocean between him and his family. With John's death in a hunting accident, however, Larry has returned to mend fences and to assert his newly dominant position in the household. Yet, his return reveals to him a deeper alienation. In seeking to remove himself from the rigid hierarchy of his family, Larry can only return to a completely new environment. The house remains the same, with a few "modern conveniences" added, but his friends and family have changed dramatically.

One of Larry's first actions reveals his desperation to fit in, as well as how he is stymied at almost every turn. After helping to adjust his father's telescope, he stares across the street at the young and fetching Gwen Conliffe, who is trying on earrings in her bedroom. Larry's initial reaction is to re-place himself in the new hierarchy by immediately trying to find a bride. He dashes across the street to the Conliffe antique shop and describes to Gwen the earrings that she was trying on upstairs. Gwen, rightfully a little discomfited by Larry's behavior, rejects his advances repeatedly, until she essentially agrees to go for a walk around later that evening. Talbot dashes out the door before she can refuse.

His clumsy romantic actions (and his somewhat disconcerting behavior) causes Gwen to invite her friend Jenny along for the walk. Larry is taken aback by Jenny's sudden appearance, and soon realizes that he is not the charming individual he wants to be. Even so, under some pressure, Gwen agrees to walk a short distance with Larry while Jenny gets her fortune told by travelling gypsies. Larry confesses that he used a telescope to spy on Gwen, who immediately tells Larry that she is, in fact, engaged.

It is not surprising that it is immediately after this sequence that Larry becomes infected by the werewolf that attacks Jenny. The manifestation of his inability to re-join the world around him takes the form of the werewolf, which only serves to heighten his continual shame and embarrassment at being unable to reclaim his place in his family and society. Larry Talbot is now part Other, and he must rely on the help of local Gypsies to understand his affliction. Doing so increases Larry's understanding of his situation, but also dramatically heightens his realization that he no longer "fits" in with the rest of society. At one point, Larry, after a late-night sojourn as a werewolf, awakes to find wolf prints leading to his bed. He wipes them off. This shame at his "other form" reveals his ostracization. Talbot's secret is one that must be hidden at all costs, and the pressure of maintaining that secret makes him unbalanced, almost hysterical at times. Larry's behavior is quickly derided by his own father, John, who dismisses the "superstition" of werewolves, chastising his son, "She's been filling your mind with this gibberish, this talk of werewolves and pentagrams. You're not a child, Larry, you're a grown man, and you believe in the superstitions of a Gypsy woman." John's dismay at his son's supposed gullibility reduces Larry even further; Larry has lost, in the mind of his own father, the last shreds of his masculinity. Larry is reduced to a "child," who falls for the "superstitions" of werewolves. Later, John agrees to imprison Larry so that Larry will realize that his ideas of werewolves are ideas that he's "conjured up is only in" Larry's mind. Larry, in his father's estimation, slips from childlike wonder unbecoming of a "grown man," and slips even further to near-insanity, itself an uncomfortable sign of weakness for John Talbot.

Eventually, Larry Talbot, while in wolf form, is caught and destroyed. The ironic twist is that Talbot's own father beats him to death with Talbot's wolf-shaped (and silver-plated) walking stick. Of course, upon the destruction of the wolf, the man is revealed, and Sir John Talbot and the hunters decide—despite the evidence to the contrary—that Larry Talbot died while valiantly defending Gwen from a wolf attack. In doing so, they manage to restore much of the masculinity that John had stripped from his own son. Larry, in death, is remade from a child suffering from delusion to a hero defending the virtue of a young woman. The reality is quite possibly too sinister for the characters: that Talbot, the lonesome and dislocated man, played host to a being with far darker urges. In the examination of Larry Talbot's consistent emasculation—his multiple rejections by Gwen, his wounding by the wolf, his inability to adhere to his family wealth and heritage—the Wolf Man's destruction ultimately reveals an important and virile (and, to Talbot, shameful) portion of his own character. The wolf, in this regard, was an outpouring of Larry's repressed sexual urges,[1] but also the appearance of repressed masculinity that was slowly stripped from him by his own father.

The Wolf Man is, like Talbot, alone in the world, but this loneliness stems from entirely different backgrounds: the Wolf Man is primitive, and Talbot himself no doubt feels unwanted, uncultured, or feminized in the company of his own father. Talbot, too, is sexually aggressive toward Gwen Conliffe, spying on her and then accosting her in the antiques shop. As it goes, the Wolf Man spends a considerable amount of time peering at the lone Gwen in the woods before attacked, a sort of enactment of Talbot's barely repressed desires. And each time, the attack on Gwen is interrupted. Talbot's initial hopes for a relationship are lightly and then substantially rebuffed by Gwen, but it is only when he leans in for a kiss that the wolf attacking Judy interrupts. That Wolf Man's attack on Judy effectively ends Talbot's courtship of Gwen, and he spends much of the rest of the film in human form simply pining after her from afar and exhibiting jealous at her happy romance.

The bludgeoning death of Talbot should put an end to his story, but, to borrow a phrase from Monty Python, he gets better for the next film: *Frankenstein Meets the Wolf Man* (1943). Talbot is awakened by a pair of grave robbers, and the film reveals that his wolf curse also means a sort of damned immortality. He still suffers from the head wound his father gave to him at the end of *The Wolf Man*, and he is soon taken to a hospital after being found by a good Samaritan. The tragedy of Larry Talbot is heightened in *Frankenstein Meets the Wolf Man*, a film which focuses on "fear and pity" and "a search for life and a longing for death" (Siodmak 270).

In wolf form, Talbot, in the earliest portions of the film, is already responsible for the murder of a policeman, and his realization that he is still a killer in wolf form nearly sends him into hysterics. "You're treating me like a lunatic!"[2] he screams at Doctor Mannering, and Mannering obliges by ordering Talbot strapped to his gurney. In many ways, Talbot is feminized by his treatment, and the call for restraints, coupled with Mannering's somewhat flippant diagnosis of "delusion" despite evidence to the contrary, creates a character who, like Frankenstein's monster, is completely under the control of another. In many ways, Mannering's diagnosis stems from a very Victorian-style diagnosis of hysteria:

> [h]ysterics always functioned outside the norm: wither they were in a state of lethargy and somnolent, or they suffered from insomnia; their organs functioned super-fast or slowed to the point of disappearance [...] So-called dissociation or multiple personality disorder is one of the hysteric's other aspects [Appignanesi 141].

Talbot's behavior lends itself to this definition. Mannering notices that he escaped the hospital room at night, and Talbot, frenzied, explains that he "killed someone" because he turns "into a wild animal." He continues, babbling about Maleva and ignoring Mannering's warnings to "calm yourself." For the viewers of *The Wolf Man*, Talbot's story rings true; for the characters in a distant city, however, they see only a patient who is suffering from a mental illness. Later, Mannering refers to Talbot as "the head injury case that went violent yesterday," further exposing his views toward Talbot as someone who is mentally ill, and quite possibly, suffering from afflictions that Mannering's discipline, at the time, would have denoted as a uniquely feminine malady, especially since "women are key subjects of psychiatric illness as well as the vehicles through which the discipline has taken on its shape" (Appignanesi 7).[3] Talbot's feminization and near-complete loss of masculinity and agency continues unabated, even when he appears in an entirely different location.

In many ways, then, Talbot's adventure through the events of *Frankenstein Meets the Wolf Man* is his slow and steady attempts to re-masculinize himself. Immortal, but wanting to die, he becomes the ultimate tragic male, a disruptive presence in society that is ostracized, and fully aware of the pain he causes others.

The final, somewhat anticlimactic, battle between the Wolf Man and Frankenstein's monster, then, is the penultimate assumption of gender between the two characters, with a classic damsel in distress caught between the two of them. Frankenstein, re-powered by Mannering as a part of his corrupt search for knowledge, immediately attempts to kidnap Elsa, and this provides the impetus for the Wolf Man to, for once, play the hero: he frees Elsa from the monster, and the two battle as the dam above Frankenstein's castle collapses, presumably drowning them both. Ironically, it is Mannering who "saves" Elsa in the traditional sense, literally carrying her away from the carnage. It is, however, Talbot and his "curse" of the wolf that carries the day, saving Elsa from the monster and battling him as the castle floods and falls. Mannering is only there to take Elsa's already safe form back to society—it was Talbot's Wolf Man who did all of the heavy lifting.

Mannering is ultimately corrupted by his search for knowledge, and the various masculine identities that work throughout the film yo-yo wildly in the last few minutes. Mannering, who, as a scientist, wants to "clear the name" of Frankenstein, decides, instead of killing the monster, that "I've got to see it at full power," and charges up rather than discharges the creature, which leads to the mayhem. Thus, Larry Talbot becomes fully hegemonic in his masculinity, moving immediately, as a Wolf Man, to free Elsa. His hegemonic masculinity is clearly "protective" in nature, and assumes that Elsa lacks the agency or wherewithal to save herself. He becomes the hero of the film, his masculine identity fully realized, perhaps for the first time on the screen, and sacrifices himself to save Elsa. For his part, Mannering is corrupted by the power and the science he wields, and he ignores Elsa's warnings to "control" or otherwise gain power over Frankenstein's monster. In this way, Mannering capitalizes on Talbot's actions, "rescuing" an unconscious Elsa from the destruction that his own actions ensured.

If one continues to follow Larry Talbot's misadventures as a Wolf Man, the next film in the cycle is *House of Frankenstein*, which opens, incongruously, with a long section featuring Dracula. The narrative focuses on Dr. Gustav Niemann, who, like Mannering, falls into the "mad scientist" trope, and his hunchbacked assistant, Daniel. Unlike Mannering, who, for much of *Frankenstein Meets the Wolf Man*, can only be accused of being too detached and clinical in his interactions with people, Niemann is immediately introduced as someone who is dangerous, reaching through the iron bars of his prison door to choke a guard and demand chalk. With chalk in hand, he continues to work on his theories toward resurrecting the dead as Daniel watches. From the very start, Neimann manipulates all those around him to get revenge on a group of men who are responsible for putting him in jail. For the purposes of this work, *House of Frankenstein* meanders for a while before Larry Talbot appears. Neimann thaws him out from the ice, and Talbot immediately registers his disapproval. "Why have you freed me," he asks Neimann, "from the ice that imprisoned the beast within me?" Talbot's self-flagellation continues throughout much of the film, and he tells Neimann "only death" can free him from the curse. Like Mannering before him, Neimann promises to find a way to end Talbot's life, and Talbot, as before, immediately agrees to help the doctor. Neimann, however, has decided to put Talbot's brain into the body of one of the men he is seeking to gain revenge on, providing that man with Talbot's curse. Neimann promises his victim that "all your waking hours will be spent in untold agony," showing that Neimann is indeed intimately familiar with the legend of the Wolf Man.

A young gypsy woman, Ilonka, falls in love with Talbot, and is ultimately the woman who delivers the (for now) final blow to Talbot, killing him with a silver bullet when he, in wolf form, brutally attacks her.[4] Before this climax, however, Talbot shows almost no interest in Ilonka, who constantly cajoles him. "Why are you so sad?" she asks, "We've been together for three days and you haven't smiled once." Talbot rejects Ilonka, refusing to tell her the source of his sadness—his curse—and instead strives to die faster by pestering Neimann, making the doctor complain about Talbot's "impatience." Regardless, Talbot changes and begins to kill, and he spends much of the film as less of a person and more of a wolf. Talbot, at this point in his life, having been bludgeoned to death by his father, resurrected, then frozen in ice, and resurrected again, has essentially eschewed gender itself. He is, in many ways, like his former enemy, Frankenstein's monster—so racked with pain and guilt as his "unnatural" state that his primary obsession is with death itself, to the detriment of almost every other "human" concern. Ilonka's love for Talbot is entirely unrequited, as he has, in many ways, repressed his own gender. Compare, for example, his small rebuffs of Ilonka's advances to his more aggressive stance toward winning Gwen's affections in *The Wolf Man*. His toxic masculine side—his wolf—must be destroyed at all costs, and, in his continuing obsession to destroy himself, he is no longer "real" in the truest sense of gender study, for "men are read as 'real' by desiring women" (Wallerstein 62). From a Freudian perspective, Talbot's rejection of Ilonka means more than a loss of his gender identity; it is truly exhibited in his nihilistic demands of death. Talbot's repeated demands—and nearly unquenchable thirst for—a permanent death keeps him from being a "real" person, for his desire toward women is permanently chilled. Talbot knows that any romantic liaison will be doomed to destruction because of his toxic and rabid alter ego. This leads to what can only be termed a "melancholic deadness" (Wallerstein 69) or even what Freud would call a "melancholia," a sort of baseless, self-destructive view regarding oneself. Talbot's desires to die are the result of a nameless sort of loss: he knows he can never quite enjoy his previously "human" identity, but moreover, he has lost the last vestiges of what he perceived as his masculinity. Larry, who pursues Gwen with somewhat reckless abandon in *The Wolf Man*, is diagnosed as hysterical or mad in *Frankenstein Meets the Wolf Man*, and, by the time of *House of Frankenstein*, he has ceased acting on any gendered impulses—his only wish is to die. When Larry, upon his first realization of his curse, is accused of having a "mental quagmire" by his father, he doesn't wish to die, but merely seeks to convince people of his curse, an effort to separate the monster and the human, the toxic and the hegemonic masculinity at war within the same body. As Talbot's film cycle continues, however, he begs to die, realizing that convincing people that he is a wolf is much harder than merely demanding death. Indeed, whenever Talbot mentions seeking a "cure" for his affliction, it is almost always coupled with death itself.

In the final film of the original *Wolf Man* cycle, which all feature Lon Chaney, Jr., as Larry Talbot, the Wolf Man again appears for only a brief time, but during that instance, reasserts Talbot's gender, and, for once, plays the hero of the story. Naturally, this ending in *House of Dracula*[5] required a near-complete overhaul of everything that has occurred over the course of the previous films, including, most importantly, Talbot's death by silver bullet at the end of *House of Frankenstein*. Oddly, *House of Dracula* retains most of the ending of *House of Frankenstein*—Frankenstein's monster is found in an underground pool of quicksand, still clutching the skeleton of Neimann—but Talbot reappears, uninjured and apparently unaware of the events of *House of Frankenstein*.

It is clear, in many ways, that Talbot's final film is an arc in which he recaptures his masculinity, which was originally lost in *The Wolf Man*. His nurse, Milizia, even echoes Gwen's line that there is something inherently "tragic" about Talbot, and, indeed, in his attempt to save people from his wolf incarnation, he throws himself off a cliff. His wish to die, of course, fails, and Talbot must rely on Dr. Edelmann's cure, which is based on pseudoscience regarding pressure on the brain from the skull and self-hypnosis[6] and Milizia's ministrations to make him whole again.

Interestingly, of all the cures that Talbot seeks, this one actually works, and, at the end of *House of Dracula*, Talbot steps into the moonlight, but does not transform. His caution about pursuing a relationship with Milizia instantly evaporates, and they happily embrace. Indeed, the final frame of the film with Talbot features him standing side-by-side with Milizia with the harmless moon hanging in the night air over them. After many attempts at a cure, and in finding a romantic partner, Talbot succeeds in reclaiming his "soft" masculinity that originally manifested itself in *The Wolf Man*. His is a journey across multiple films to reclaim his masculinity and cure himself of the gender confusion prompted by the curse itself.[7]

The more recent remake of *The Wolf Man*, originally intended to be a part of the Universal Monster "universe," re-introduces Larry Talbot in the form of a somewhat fey actor. Talbot, played by Benecio del Toro, is first seen wearing make-up and performing in *Hamlet*. As this version of *The Wolfman*[8] dashes from plot point to plot point, Talbot returns to his home estate in Blackmoor to search for his missing brother. While he searches for the mythical wolf that killed his brother, Talbot stumbles upon a gypsy camp and a group of hunters who are convinced that the camp's dancing bear is the source of the attacks.

Almost immediately, however, it becomes apparent that there is a wolf, a preternaturally powerful one, and it begins to kill those in the hunting party one by one. Here, too, is the most notable difference between the original Lon Chaney feature and this version: alongside the incessant soundtrack, the blood and gore take center stage. As the wolf dashes from hunter to hunter, the viewer is treated to numerous shots of disemboweling, maiming, beheading, and the like, alongside roaming shots of intestines and body parts strewn across the ground. The original *Wolf Man* film focused on the *man*; the remake focuses almost entirely on the wolf. Lawrence Talbot is also a victim during this attack, as the wolf leaps on him and takes a chunk out of his shoulder before bounding off.

After the attack, the usual plot scenario falls into place: the afflicted male, on his path to a new version of masculinity, is nursed back to health by a woman who has previously shown little interest in him. Like David in *An American Werewolf in London*,[9] whose relationship with his nurse (a tried-and-true masculine sexual fantasy that blends subservience and nurturing characteristics in one female figure) becomes romantic almost immediately, so, too, does Talbot's burgeoning relationship with his brother's soon-to-be betrothed, symbolized by close quarters and lingering stares. This version of Lawrence Talbot, with his newfound werewolf curse, is highly sexualized, a far cry from the effeminate actor that the viewer witnesses at the start of the film.

It soon becomes apparent that Lawrence Talbot's father, John Talbot, is the wolf, and during a prolonged speech, he tells Lawrence Talbot how he came to be a wolf. Not only was he bitten by a boy, contracting the curse, but he spent much of his life trying to resist the wolf. His servant, Singh, faithfully and reliably locked Talbot in a tomb[10] every full moon. When Lawrence suggests that the best way to be free of the curse is to commit suicide, John Talbot lays bare his philosophy: "Oh, I can't tell you how often I've considered that. But life is far too glorious, Lawrence, especially to the cursed and the damned. Like myself." John Talbot is the antithesis of the original Larry Talbot's reaction to the curse. To Larry Talbot—both the Chaney and the del Toro versions—death is preferable, imbued with a sort of self-sacrificing nobility. This version of Talbot not only embraces his curse, but he revels in it. Of course, a part of this is John Talbot's station in society: a wealthy landowner can afford to make his own definitions regarding his masculine identity, and is most likely to avoid feeling societal pressure to conform to gender expectations. Not so for Larry Talbot.

Sir John's calculus is one based on his own self-identification as a man. The sudden entry of Gwen Conliffe into the Talbot family's life forces Talbot to embrace his bestial nature. Not only is he clearly attracted to Gwen, but he is also jealous of his son, Ben. Ben and Gwen's coming wedding means that Sir John has no family to rule over, and his social station as a patriarch is bound to collapse. In pursuing and killing Ben while in wolf form, John accomplishes two things: he brings back his "prodigal son" to the estate so that he may carry on the curse, and he also eliminates the competition for Gwen's affections.

That is, until Gwen becomes attracted to Lawrence (which, it is important to note, only happens *after* he becomes infected with the wolf curse). *The Wolfman* is then a bizarre love story of a father, his sons, a father who kills one son and attempts to kill the other and a woman who loves them all. This leads, naturally, to a climactic battle between father and prodigal son, both in wolf form.

Lawrence Talbot's goal is to kill his own father, whom he views as mad with power. Yet, it is interesting to note that Sir John's intention to make Lawrence the "heir" to the curse is a fruitful one: he leaves Lawrence a straight razor to kill himself with, but Lawrence, like his father, rejects suicide as an option—one could assume that the long-suffering original version of Larry Talbot would have embraced this option, especially given his attempt in *House of Dracula*. Sir John's full embrace of his newfound power and infamy is symbolized from the moment Lawrence enters the darkened Talbot Hall: their faithful servant, Singh, is dead, disemboweled and hung from a pillar. The key to the tomb that formerly imprisoned Sir John is hung around his neck. He will no longer be ashamed or de-powered by basic society and morality.

When father and son finally confront one another—with the fresh corpse of a police detective on the couch behind them—Sir John reveals his true intentions of not only allowing Lawrence Talbot to carry the family name, but making Lawrence into his definition of masculinity. When Lawrence tries and fails to kill him with a rifle, Sir John tells him "you were the fragile one" and that, as the full moon approaches, Lawrence will become "the man I always wanted you to be." The "release" of the "Beast" within Lawrence is Sir John's goal, the ultimate rejection of his weakness, and the embrace of his source of strength. In this, Sir John seeks to masculinize his son, to turn him into a worthy "heir" to the Talbot estate.

Eventually, the full moon is revealed, and father and son battle to the death in the estate as it burns down around them. In this battle, Lawrence does embrace his newfound power, eventually kicking his father into the fireplace, setting him ablaze, and then beheading him. Gwen, whose sense of timing is impeccable, arrives to see Lawrence attacking a police officer, and then runs away again. Lawrence chases her through the woods until finally catching her on the edge of a steep ravine. As a wolf, Lawrence quickly dominates her, crawling atop her form; Gwen, however, manages to remind Lawrence of their relationship, which brings forward, for a moment, at least, the man inside the wolf. As a hunting party closes in, however, the wolf aspect of Lawrence's personality rises again, and Gwen shoots him before he can kill her. The tragic male is revealed, as Lawrence, dying from the gunshot wound, returns to his human form, and thanks Gwen for killing him and ending the Talbot curse.

There's little doubt that there is a huge amount of Freudian context that resides on the surface of this film, even more so than its forefather. Yet, in recounting the events of *The Wolfman*, the film seems to share more of its plot structure with *An American Werewolf in London* than *The Wolf Man*. The basic plot beats are all there (and special effects guru Rick Baker created the wolves for both *American Werewolf* and *The Wolfman*): man gets attacked by wolf, woman falls in love with him while he recuperates, suicide is presented as the only option, wolf runs wild, woman manages to bring out the man inside the wolf one last time before he is cut down.

The Wolfman also mimics the state of psychic distress that Larry Talbot experiences. Convinced of his curse, and his active participation in the gruesome murders around him, he attempts to convince others of his more savage nature. "Lycanthropy is a disease of the mind," Talbot is told, and a montage of the various "treatments" for his mental disorder underscores the cruelty Talbot endures at the hands of science: electric shocks, dunks in ice-cold water, and so on, all designed to "cure" Talbot of his supposedly mental affliction. And, like the Lon Chaney portrayal of Talbot, this version of Larry Talbot cuts to the only effective cure he knows: death, at times screaming "kill me!" repeatedly to cut his life short. But, if the tropes of *The Wolf Man* are depicted in the more modern *The Wolfman*, so, too, is the entire process that Talbot endures in his masculinity. From pursuer to pursued, from civilized to violence, from intensely gendered to barely gendered at all (even feminized), Talbot's experience stands in stark contrast to the absolute and utter delight his father takes in his ability to be "savage."

In this formula, however, lies the rejection of the "bestial" male formula, and a clearer rejection at that. In the original version of the film, Lawrence Talbot is essentially the only werewolf in the film, and his father's "civilized" manner is viewed as preferable, so much so that father strikes down the son. The roles are reversed, however, in the more modern retelling, as Sir John Talbot is the one who, after some brief pauses (and, apparently, no small amount of confusion and embarrassment at succumbing so easily to the curse), decides to embrace his role at the top of the food chain. John Talbot's attempts to masculinize his son ultimately fail, even after some initial success. It is left up to the shy and dapper son to eliminate the threat before gratefully accepting his own demise.

In the saga of Larry Talbot, we can see various tropes that will appear throughout the rest of werewolf cinema. Although some of these have become famous, in spite of their overall lack of adoption—an allergy to silver, for example, the issues of masculinity, madness, feminization, and societal acceptance dominate the character arc of Larry Talbot. These themes will routinely dominate werewolf cinema for, if one starts with the original *The Wolf Man,* nearly a half a century.

The Pre-1960s Werewolf
A Stranger Within Me

Werewolf of London features an internal struggle at its core: the struggle of a man and his sexuality. In films such as *The Wolf Man*, there is clearly a woman at the center, someone who is desired by the male and actively pursued by his wolf. In *Werewolf of London*, however, the relationship between the male who is cursed—Wilfred Glendon—and his wife, Lisa, is frosty at best. They are already married, and their marriage is fraught with distrust and outright disgust with one another. "Ever since you came back from Tibet," Lisa says, "I've felt you were planning to divorce me and marry a laboratory." Lisa, coolly feeling neglected, quickly adds that "I'll not only divorce you, but I'll beat you as well" when Wilfred tells her that they are attending a party later that night. Although much of Lisa's comments can be dismissed as stereotypical husband and wife bickering, there is an acidity to them that makes their relationship seem, at best, "troubled and distant" (Spadoni 4).

Thus, the format for the very first popular werewolf film is that of a man struggling against himself. The interior battle is, as Richard Spadoni notes, that of a man who is an "unwilling victim of his own sexual awakening" (3). The true relationship at the heart of the film, Spadoni argues, is Wilfred's attempts to reject his relationship with Dr. Yogami, who not only seeks to cure his own curse through Wilfred's research, but has also infected Wilfred with the curse of the werewolf. "Yogami," Wilfred gasps at the end of the film, "you brought this on me that night in Tibet." His final words to Lisa, however, are so stereotypical as to be rendered in little more than ironic distance: "I'm sorry I couldn't have made you happier," he says, just before perishing.

Although Dr. Yogami neatly plays the foil and opposing man and wolf to Wilfred's wolf, the structure of the movie focuses almost entirely on Wilfred's personality changes. His obsession with botany, followed by his obsession with a flower said only to bloom at night, followed by his need to use that flower to cure his curse, lays the foundation for *The Wolf Man*, in which a man's inner struggle between his supposed civilized nature and his newfound

Otherness, the regression to a primitive state. Interestingly, as we will see, many of the films that focus on the interior battle of man and his curse lead themselves down the same path of gender questioning and wrestling with portrayals of "appropriate" masculinity.

The Undying Monster

The Undying Monster (1942) is an oft-overlooked addition to werewolf cinema. In many ways, *The Undying Monster* borrows heavily from *The Wolf Man*, as it takes place at a huge estate, and the primary character is revealed to be the werewolf, although the appearance of the werewolf does not occur until the final ten minutes of the 63-minute film. *The Undying Monster* even features a piece of poetic doggerel, just like *The Wolf Man*, designed to provide an extra jolt of suspense. The story centers around a brother and sister, Helga and Oliver Hammond, who are victims of a "Hammond curse" in which, when there is frost on the ground and fog hovering over the moor, a beast will come and kill one member of the Hammond family.

There are three males who are essential to the plot: Oliver, the ostensible victim of a werewolf attack at the start of the film; Robert Curtis, a Scotland Yard investigator sent to investigate the attack; and Jeff Colbert, the family physician who knows more than he admits about the attack. In each of these three men reside vastly differing tropes of masculinity. Oliver, who is eventually revealed to be the wolf and the latest wolf incarnation of the family lineage, is initially presented as a victim of the wolf. In the opening moments of *The Undying Monster*, the howls of the wolf punctuate an attack on a young woman, Kate, who is also Oliver's fiancée. Helga and her servants "rescue" Oliver and Kate; both are found unconscious on the shoreline at the base of the estate. Kate is in a coma and soon dead; Oliver struggles to remember what happened, and, as such, is presented as a both mentally and physically fragile being, beholden to Helga's ministrations at his bedside.

Kate's murder, and the large number of murders that surround the Hammond family, provokes the interest of Scotland Yard, who sends Robert Curtis and his comedic sidekick Christy to investigate. Robert Curtis speaks bluntly, his words often shoving aside other comments, and he is instantly distrustful of almost everyone involved with the case, including other police officers. In his own way, Robert Curtis is the "proper man," who has seized control of a situation, and is quick to put people—especially the women around him—in their place.

As Oliver climbs the craggy shore, trying to escape, he is shot at point-blank range by a gathered group of policemen. The wolf transforms back to human. Oliver's refined, "soft" masculinity is ultimately destroyed, recreating the classic tragic hero trope that dominates much of early werewolf cinema. His "hard" masculinity only comes to the forefront in the face of what could literally, given the Hammond history, be a primitivizing force.

There are other, more underexamined, facets of *The Undying Monster*. Oliver, in wolf form, first kills his fiancée Kate. Then, later, when he becomes a wolf again, he targets Helga, his sister, carrying her off to the craggy shore where he had originally murdered Kate. While doing so, Oliver's wolf drops past Christy, *but continues to carry away his sister*. Thus, Oliver in his wolf form is completely unmoored from civilizing forces, including the taboo against incest. As a wolf, Oliver simply sees Helga as another attractive female to be spirited away, despite their sibling relationship. *The Undying Monster* ends on a joke, but the joke, which is admittedly a bit poorly executed, points again toward Oliver's sexual attraction to his own sister. The joke plays out between Robert and Christy. Christy realizes, in shock, that the werewolf could have attacked her, as her bedroom was right next to Helga's. Robert reassures her by saying "wolves will never bother you," a double entendre pointing toward the animal and the slang name for sexually aggressive men. Christy looks relieved and then immediately taken aback, as Robert grins.[1] The joke, clearly at Christy's expense, also reveals that Robert, at least, believes that Oliver's wolf-form was completely engulfed by sexual aggression.

The "wolves," of course, are the "hard" or even "toxic" men that appear on the outskirts of the film: the workers and poachers who appear as very brief red herrings to Kate's murder. In Oliver's case, however, his turning into a wolf decidedly de-civilizes him *even more* than those who occupy social stations well below his own.[2] Thus, the opening of *The Undying Monster*, in which an unseen narrator shares the "age-old mystery" of the Hammond family, a mystery which, "by 1900, had become a legend," aligns remarkably well with medieval werewolf narratives. This alignment thus allows for the potentially incestuous desires Oliver's wolf has for his sister Helga; medieval wolf narratives were often sprinkled with numerous cases of incest, according to William de Blécourt (154–157). In fact, the opening narration of the Hammond "curse" points to the family having a werewolf lineage, again echoing the idea that incestuous relationships lead to the "animalization" of the offspring (155). Oliver's attack on Helga, then, comes from a long line of what could be termed patriarchal abuse: after all, Oliver's first filmed attack is on his own soon-to-be wife, who eventually dies, and is replaced by his wolf-lust with his own sister.

I Was a Teenage Werewolf and *The Werewolf*

In 1957, Michael Landon played Tony Rivers, a young man given to "jive talk" who also had an extraordinary temper. The film opens with Tony fighting another high school student. After the fight is broken up, Tony explains the source of his anger: the other guy bumped into him. We also learn that Tony had previously gotten in trouble for throwing a bottle of milk at a grocery store clerk for going too slowly. Later, Tony lashes out at a friend, knocking him down, when he plays a prank on him by blowing into a horn next to his ear.

Tony clearly has aggression issues. In many ways, he would fit in as a part of any of the films of the era that dealt with delinquent teens. However, what makes Tony's experience so different is that he is, in fact, a werewolf who, strangely, earns the curse via hypnosis from an ethically challenged doctor.

It is important to note that in *I Was a Teenage Werewolf*, Tony's anger and rage manifests itself *before* he officially becomes a werewolf, and he seeks assistance for his rage by visiting a local psychologist, Dr. Brandon. Dr. Brandon represents just the latest manifestation of the "mad scientist" trope that dominated much of Larry Talbot's films, joining Dr. Mannering, Dr. Neimann, and Dr. Edelmann as doctors who unethically experiment on patients, often either exacerbating the condition or simply taking advantage of the cursed male.

In many ways, Tony's struggles represent the tumult of masculinity of his era: his barely repressed rage functions as a response to the "reconfiguration of workplace and home [...] a feminization and domestication of normative, white, middle-class masculinity" (Savran 48). This "reconfiguration" led to "the rebel males of the 1950s [...] a significant challenge to the rigors of normative masculinity" (Savran 48). Tony, in rebelling from the apparent feminizing of the previously established masculine roles, is a perfect subject for Dr. Brandon's therapy.

Dr. Brandon, however, is engaged in a series of experiments designed to "regress" humans to their "primitive" state, which apparently includes turning people into werewolves. After just one of these sessions, Tony becomes a werewolf, and starts a killing spree that terrorizes the town. Every now and again—as Tony's transformations don't appear to follow any incident or time frame—Tony wakes up in the woods and dusts himself off before returning home. Tony, of course, has no truly masculine ideal present in his life; like many men of this era that are afflicted of the curse of the werewolf, he is bandied about from one masculinity to another, and can never quite conform to an ideal. The authority figures work to intimidate him, his father drinks too much, and his girlfriend's father deeply disapproves of Tony's very existence, and, as well, is a perfect representative of the "new" domestic masculinity that Tony is rebelling against. Indeed, most of the sequences with Arlene's parents show Mr. Logan standing next to his wife in a typically outfitted 1950s home.

Here, Dr. Brandon's own theories bear mentioning. He feels that there is a supposedly "primitive" state inside of man, and he is merely exposing that state through his hypnosis experiments. Brandon speaks broadly of returning all of humanity back to the beginning, presumably to "restart" civilization before countries begin to destroy one another through nuclear warfare. In this regard, Tony, the erstwhile juvenile delinquent, is a perfect test experiment, as his "primitive" nature is leading him to buck against the rules of civilized society. Brandon knows that Tony needs only a little push to become a werewolf, and, from Tony's shock and dismay at the death and destruction his wolf form has caused, Tony himself seems to know that the dividing line between his human form and his wolf form is dangerously thin, even before hypnotic experiments. The idea of Tony becoming "primitive" as a werewolf hearkens back to *The Werewolf of London*, especially the homoerotic themes of that film. Richard Spadoni notes that *The Werewolf of London*, when examined through a queer lens, reveals a deeply homosexual undercurrent,[3] often based on the anthropological beliefs at the time that gay men were "so construed to become throwbacks, modern humans returned to an earlier stage of evolution" (6). Applying this idea to *I Was a Teenage Werewolf* would mean that Dr. Brandon, as a 1950s antagonist, purposefully leads Tony toward a path of homosexuality, either to more deeply "corrupt" him or to expose him to the inner turmoil that is leading him to delinquency.

The "wrong side of the tracks" story is given a unique twist by the addition of werewolf lore, but it does also contain a rather searing indictment of violence. Tony is no doubt the "good kid" with temper issues (his principal even notes his frequent honor roll appearances), but his upbringing, presumably without a mother in the house, has hardened him greatly, and as a result, he perceives almost every action or loud noise as a personal slight, one that must be met with impressive force.

Interestingly, Tony's first transformation into a werewolf—at least his first physical transformation—occurs as he watches his fellow student Theresa in the gym. The school is almost empty, and Theresa has apparently taken some time to practice his gymnastics routine. Tony watches (some could say he even leers) at Theresa contorting herself in her leotard. Tony leans up against a wall to watch, seemingly unaware that his head is next to a fire alarm. Moviegoers and critics alike assume that the fire alarm's loud ringing noise makes Tony turn into a werewolf. It's a fair assumption, as Tony, before his curse, attacked a friend of his for startling him during a party. But the transformation occurs, in part, due to his unrestrained lust for his classmate and his newly discovered "primitive" nature. Alternatively, Tony's viewing of Theresa's body provokes or reminds him of his sexuality, pushing him back toward homosexuality as a "primitive" force. Tony's relationship with his own girlfriend, Arlene, appears to be chaste, and is colored by the clear disapproval of Arlene's parents. Tony, too, routinely manages to keep his relationship with Arlene rather frosty due to multiple angry outbursts. Tony is, in his human form, playing a role of which society does not approve, and his teenage delinquency is only one manifestation of that underlying struggle to conform.

Thus, it isn't only the loud noise that turns Tony into a werewolf, but also his growing lust and gender confusion. When he turns into a wolf, he immediately pursues Theresa before killing her in the gym. Dr. Brandon's experiment, in that regard, was a success, for Tony's transformation brings with it all the "primitive" aspects of his masculinity. Tony, who originally found himself in somewhat harmless scraps, is now fully toxic, prone to murderous rage and sexual violence, an overcorrection, of sorts, to a fully aggressive male, unmoored from any of the civilizing presences in his life, including his girlfriend, his circle of male friends, and even his father.

Tony's demise, of course, is somewhat reminiscent of the ending of *The Undying Monster*, where the main character, in wolf form, is confronted by police, who shoot him at point blank range. The very symbols of civilization—the police, representing law and order—violently and graphically remove the offending presence from society in a hail of gunfire, silver bullets optional. This theme appears repeatedly in werewolf cinema, most notably in *An American Werewolf in Paris*, in which David's wolf is shot to death, and *The Howling*, in which Karen arranges her wolf's death[4] to be made public on television. The body must be displayed to reveal to the public that the menace has been destroyed.

In this case, Tony dies at the hands of the police after killing Dr. Brandon in his office. In human form, Tony arrived to ask Dr. Brandon for more help, but discovers that Brandon has been the one who has been manipulating him all along. In the film's (and much of werewolf cinema's) scope of justice, the person who is the cause of the werewolf curse must often be killed, usually by the werewolf themselves. In some ways, Tony's death mirrors the ending of numerous film noir and teenage crime wave films produced during the same era: he is too corrupted (or corruptible) to comfortably live in the world and must be destroyed.

The definitions of masculinity at play throughout *I Was a Teenage Werewolf* focus primarily on just how a young man can "fit" into the world around them. Ideas of violence and lust are strictly forbidden (or, at least, repressed), and numerous male role models abound for Tony. His male friends are a bit rowdy but are ultimately law-abiding and generally "good" guys. Tony's father is a hardworking man who is a bit overwhelmed by his single father responsibilities and is given to alcohol, but still tries to keep Tony's moral compass aligned. And Detective Donovan, who appears at the start of the film to chastise Tony for his violence and "jive talk," is an extension of the law itself. It is Donovan, of course, who, along with a fellow police officer, kills the wolf-form Tony, a clear symbol of Tony's inability to exist in a "modern" world. That so many werewolves are killed by the police (or a deputized mob) in werewolf cinema is no accident: law and order, representing the social fabric, dispatches those who don't appropriately conform.

A year prior to *I Was a Teenage Werewolf*, in 1956, the film *The Werewolf* hit many of the same beats as *I Was a Teenage Werewolf*. The honestly titled *The Werewolf* opens with a young man, dressed in a suit, stopping into a small town's bar. He doesn't know who he is, and he only has a very vague recollection of where he's been. The film's rubric is in place within the first ten minutes, as the mysterious man pays for his drink, picks up twenty dollars' worth of change, and is out the door. A few moments later, one of the bar patrons follows him down the street. It is nighttime, and the patron demands that the mysterious stranger, who is becoming increasingly agitated, give him the money.

Instead, the mystery man transforms into a wolf, dragging the man into an alley. The murder takes place mostly off-screen, with two pairs of thrashing feet clattering about, overlaid by snarls and screams. Yes, the mystery man is, in fact, a werewolf, and he runs from the scene of the crime, kicking off a manhunt (wolfhunt?) that will dominate much of the film.

Sheriff Haines and Deputy Clovey begin the search, and discover, along with help from a local nurse, Amy, and the town's doctor, Jonas Gilchrist, that the man's name is Duncan Marsh. Marsh isn't "cursed" with the werewolf in a traditional sense, and to its credit, *The Werewolf* borrows from science fiction anxieties of the time to depict a new form of werewolf that doesn't rely on the Other as the source of trouble. No, in this case, it is the hydrogen bomb. Two scientists, Drs. Chambers and Forrest, rescued Marsh from a car accident, giving him highly irradiated wolf blood to save his life—but also to complete their experiments. Dr. Forrest is a bit more conflicted than Dr. Chambers about the experiment, but Chambers feels that the inevitable nuclear annihilation that will occur will send most humans back to a primitive state, the same sort of ideas that Dr. Brandon espoused in *I Was a Teenage Werewolf*. Chambers and Forrest want to create a serum that will prevent their change, and then they can rule the world (or what is left of it). Marsh's werewolf form isn't brought on by moonlight, but by emotional distress, namely, fear, neatly inverting the by-now formula of a werewolf being the sole source of fear.

Unlike Tony in *I Was a Teenage Werewolf*, Duncan Marsh *is* the newly feminized and domesticated man of the 1950s. Duncan Marsh is far from a rebel, and the film continuously reminds the viewer of this fact, as he spends much of his time, even as a werewolf, wearing a suit and tie. At one point, while Duncan, in human form, hides in the woods, the police bring out his wife and son. Duncan's wife, Helen, calls to him through a megaphone, "we want you to come home," adding "Chris [their son] is here with me, and he wants you to come home, too." Duncan is almost the exact opposite of Tony.

He doesn't rebel against his newfound domestic role, and, in fact, wants to embrace it, but Duncan is very much aware that he cannot reclaim that role. Upon appearing to Helen and Chris, he asks them to be taken away, for fear that his wolf form would harm them.

Of course, for a low-budget feature, *The Werewolf*'s transformation is a simple one, and harks back to *The Wolf Man*: a series of still shots showing the slow progression from wolf to man. The transformation, however, is not a complete one, in that the wolf form itself is closer to *The Wolf Man*'s bipedal form than the full-on descent into wolf in films such as *An American Werewolf in London* and *Wolf*. In fact, the werewolf is just a hairy face, some fangs, and some hairy hands—much of the wolf's neck is human, and the wolf wears a suit as well (at one point in time, it even appears that the wolf calmly took off its shoes and socks to complete the transformation). Yet, Duncan Marsh is indeed part man, part beast in the truest sense of the phrase, as he feels guilt over the murders he commits, but is not truly culpable for any of them. In fact, the film works hard to humanize and domesticate Duncan Marsh. He is a werewolf through no fault of his own, and the murders he commits are, if illegal, at least mostly self-defense and understandable. Amy, Sheriff Haines, and Dr. Gilchrist all agree to do their best to capture Duncan alive and find a cure for him. The portrait of Duncan, then, is that of an average Joe gone mad by circumstances out of his control, and his character's depiction is unusually sympathetic in the werewolf canon. At one point, when Marsh is cornered, he asks "What have I ever done to you?" before transforming into a werewolf.

Marsh is controlled by a series of events well beyond his control, and like Tony in *I Was a Teenage Werewolf*, is completely overwhelmed and almost entirely flaccid in his interactions. Marsh is reduced to clutching his head and begging people to help him, or, alternatively, trying his best to isolate himself from the townspeople. Marsh, who was most likely a successful male in the conventional 1950s sense: breadwinner for the family, more involved domestically, a strict but loving father, is completely shunted aside after he becomes a werewolf. In the place of the nuclear family version of Marsh is a man who is completely emasculated. It's no surprise that his two hunters, Sheriff Haines and Deputy Covey, are bastions of that era's differing definition of masculinity, a masculinity that rejected the domesticated lifestyle of Duncan Marsh. Haines is played by Don Megowan, who spent most of his acting career playing lawmen, cowboys, or outlaws, all rugged, often hegemonic archetypes. And the actor who played Covey, Harry Lauter, is much the same: his career, too, is peppered with numerous roles as sheriffs, deputies, outlaws, or military men. Sheriff Haines towers over every other character in the film, and he makes it clear that the law "doesn't have a choice" sometimes when subduing a person (or werewolf).

The finale of *The Werewolf* follows the pattern of many werewolf films during this era. The lone wolf, cornered by a group of lawmen and vigilantes, wanders about before getting shot multiple times. As in *The Undying Monster*, Marsh, cornered, wanders about in wolf form until he gets close enough to be shot to death, and like Oliver, the final sequence is the wolf turning back into Marsh before dying. The animal becomes human again, and in those final moments, returns to purity, freed of the curse, but at the cost of their life.

The only true antagonists in the film are the scientists, Doctor Chambers and Doctor Forrest, who conduct illegal experiments, plan on saving themselves first in a nuclear holocaust, proclaim their ability to rule the wastelands when the holocaust occurs, and then, maddeningly, decide to put Duncan Marsh out of his misery. Chambers even proclaims to the conflicted Forrest that killing Marsh would be "an act of charity." Of course, the scientists are eventually killed by their own creation, as they break into the surprisingly lightly guarded jail and attack Marsh, upsetting him enough that his wolf form takes over, and he quickly kills them both. Again, this follows the usual trope in early werewolf cinema, because *The Werewolf* puts together an almost entirely sympathetic vigilante. After introducing Duncan Marsh's werewolf form by killing a local thief, the film bookends the sentiment by having Marsh's wolf murder a pair of deeply unlikable and unethical scientists. Indeed, Marsh is killed, with some regret, by Sheriff Haines who looks over at Covey with an expression of regret as the wolf flails about for nearly a full two minutes as it gets shot multiple times.

What expressions of masculinity occur in *The Werewolf*, then? There are multiple, positive expressions. Haines and Covey are willing to listen to science and agree to curtail their desire to kill to capture Marsh, and only engage in shooting him with some notable reluctance. Marsh himself is an extraordinarily sensitive male, horrified by his alter ego's actions, even if they are justified. When he is first captured, for example, and still struggling to remember his identity, Marsh readily admits to Doctor Gilchrist and Amy that he most likely murdered someone the night before. His ready confession is balanced by his sudden escape, but even that is because he can feel his own emotional state fragmenting, which, he knows, can lead to a transformation that would ultimately end with Gilchrist and Amy being injured or killed.

There is some balance that occurs in the depictions of masculinity in *The Werewolf*. Unlike Tony in *I Was a Teenage Werewolf*, Duncan Marsh is not a juvenile delinquent trying to, at least at the behest of those around him, "go straight." He is a family man in the truest sense of the 1950s, and the marker of his status remains even in wolf form: his business suit reminds the viewer, constantly, that the wolf is in fact a successful, domesticated male. And, unlike Oliver in *The Undying Monster*, or Lawrence Talbot in *The Wolf Man*, many of Duncan Marsh's victims are cast as completely unsympathetic, and the wolf's actions in killing them come from self-defense rather than randomized killing and terror. Oliver, for example, while in wolf form, attacks and kills his own fiancée, and attempts to do the same to his sister Helga as well. The werewolf form of *The Wolf Man* terrorizes the town, killing a gravedigger and attacking his friend/prospective mate Gwen. And Tony, in *I Was a Teenage Werewolf*, kills two of his friends in wolf form before killing the hypnotist who was manipulating him.

In many ways, then, *The Werewolf* may have created one of the most nuanced portraits of masculinity in werewolf cinema. The story focuses on a man who openly struggles with his "curse," actively protects his family[5] and "innocent" people, and only reluctantly, in wolf form, kills or attacks people who have attacked him in some way. Duncan is incredibly sympathetic throughout the film, and even the lawmen, many of whom are depicted in werewolf cinema as cold-blooded killers or otherwise inept, work to save Duncan's life. Sheriff Haines and Deputy Covey exhibit marked restraint, especially if one compares the ending of *The Undying Monster* to *The Werewolf*. Oliver, in *The Undying Monster*, is shot repeatedly as he clings to a cliffside by what seems to be a small armada of police officers and vigilantes, many of them shooting him at point-blank range. In *The Werewolf*, the sequence drags on as the assorted townspeople and lawmen fire a shot, watch, and then fires again, all while clearly regretting the action. Of course, the difference between these two scenes speaks to the difference in how these two werewolves are depicted. In *The Werewolf*, Duncan dies, alone, and is not attacking anyone. He is merely trying to escape. Oliver, of course, has kidnapped his sister, Helga.

The blurring of these boundaries most likely occurs because of the origins of the wolf in *The Werewolf*. Like Tony in *I Was a Teenage Werewolf*, Duncan is essentially kidnapped by a mad scientist who engages in unethical experiments to get him to transform to a "primitive" state. Tony, however, has a long, well-established record of delinquency, whereas there is no indication of this with Duncan. In other words, the introduction of a "primitive" state to Tony enhances what is already there: his nascent toxic masculinity, which involves assaulting cashiers and other minor crimes, is enhanced to murderous impulses, aggression, and homicide. In Duncan, the fault lies squarely on the doctors, and, in part, the hydrogen bomb, which, in combination, turns Duncan into something he is not: a toxic male. And, even in the appearance of his werewolf form, Duncan is still identifiably Duncan. He still wears his suit, he still looks mostly human, and he still, at times, resists the urge to attack people, or even to transform. Duncan's reliable and steady masculinity is overrun by the introduction of the toxic aggression of the werewolf, and Duncan resists the toxicity at almost every turn in the film.

In this regard, these films follow much the same pattern. A male who is mostly domesticated or otherwise seeks the comfort of domestication is afflicted with a curse that disrupts those desires. Families, friends, and social circles are ripped apart by the sudden aggression, lust, and hatred brought on by the curse. There is, in these worlds, no place for the toxic male. As a result, the tragedy of a man who has already achieved the "correct" path of the idealized head of the family, or the man who desires to place himself in that path, is that their desires will be ripped away from them. This simple equation means that there is, quite literally, no place in the world for the toxic male: their curse causes them to perform actions which alienate themselves from others as well as their own desires. In this simple rubric, the only path forward for these men is quite simply death: a complete negation of their existence.

The 1960s and 1970s
Realizing the Power Within

A subtle change occurs in the films immediately after *The Werewolf*. As the popularity of the creature in cinema starts to wane, new ideas and definitions seem to come to the forefront of werewolf narratives. Men who were "cursed" with the werewolf were still ultimately tragic in nature, often meeting gruesome ends in order to end their struggles with their masculinity. However, in this era, the presence and possibility of more aggressive and feral forms of masculinity—toxic, hard, and hegemonic—will appear more frequently, and will sometimes be portrayed in a more positive light. A man who is meek and afflicted with the werewolf curse may not necessarily rue the curse as much as he once did, and, in fact, may at times benefit from the presence of violence or the potential for violence in their everyday lives. Indeed, in each of these films, the often-meek male, when afflicted with the curse, may still imbue aspects of the tragic masculine, but there will be instances where the "curse" itself is shown to have some at least mild benefits. In the end, the tragic masculine plot continues mostly unfettered, save for these detours, where the potential positives of becoming more demanding and more virile take center stage, if only for a few moments.

Curse of the Werewolf

The Hammer Horror film *Curse of the Werewolf* belatedly tells the story of Leon, a young man born with the curse of the wolf. His "curse" comes from a variety of factors, none of them necessarily verified during the course of the film's runtime. But Leon is the progeny of a sexual assault; his father a destitute beggar driven mad by an unending prison sentence, and his mother a young woman who refuses the advances of the same Marques that put the beggar in prison. The same young woman—a mute—is released to "serve" the Marques the very next day, but instead kills him and escapes the manor. She stumbles across Don Alfredo and his servant Theresa, and, several months later, she gives birth to a young boy before dying. This entire portion of the story dominates *Curse of the Werewolf*'s early runtime, and, as such, indicate a creative emphasis on the unseemly aspects of Leon's birth.

All these sinister events set into action the "curse": an unjustly punished and insane father, a mute young woman driven to murder, and the death of both of his parents before he's born. He's also the product of a sexual assault, and, as if that's not enough to spur the curse forward, Theresa even notes that he's born on Christmas day, a sure sign of bad luck. All these things combine into the curse that Leon receives: on the surface, it is the curse of the werewolf, but in many ways, it is the curse of societal stigma. Even though Leon was lucky enough to come into a stable family structure, he was ultimately unable to overcome the stain of his origins.

Thus, the werewolf. It functions as the manifestations of his shamed social class, his sordid familial lineage, and, even though he enjoys a stable household and relatively stable upbringing—at least more than he would have, had his mother not stumbled across the correct household—he is ultimately unable to fully join society. In fact, Leon's "awakening" to his more savage form occurs while hunting with Pepe, a local man tasked with keeping the town's livestock safe from wolves. During their hunt together, Pepe encourages Leon to shoot a squirrel, but Leon's timid, loving nature keeps him from doing so. Pepe shoots the squirrel anyway, and as Leon later recounts: "It was horrible. I picked it up and tried to kiss it better. I kissed it, and I tasted something warm. It must have been the blood, but it tasted sweet. I wanted to keep on tasting it, but Pepe took it away." This almost vampiric-sounding origin indicates a deep internal struggle between the boy who is being raised by Don Alfredo, and the boy who comes from sundry origins. The relationship between his caring nature and his bloodlust is disconcerting to Leon. His recounting of his taste for blood, coupled with the sudden deaths of Leon's kitten and numerous farm animals, as well as Leon's hairy arms and hands, send Don Alfredo to the local priest for advice.

According to the priest, the curse can be prevented in a rather unique way. Alongside the conventional silver bullet, Leon's curse can be alleviated by the simple emotion of love, a theme that is frequently mimicked from this era through the 1980s. Simply put, the sinful parts of life can more readily corrupt Leon, and the positive aspects of life have a more profound impact on his stability:

> "A werewolf is a body with a soul and a spirit that are constantly at war. The spirit is that of a wolf. And whatever weakens the human soul … vice, greed, hatred, solitude […] These bring the spirit of the wolf to the fore. And in turn, whatever weakens the spirit of the beast, warmth, fellowship, love, raise the human soul."

In werewolf cinema, this is a profoundly unique way of introducing the trope of the love or sexual interest. In this regard, the woman who Leon falls in love with, Christina, is the person who can keep him from being a wolf, not by killing him, as in the films of Paul Naschy, but by nurturing his soul, by re-humanizing him and repressing the beast entirely.

Curse of the Werewolf repeatedly attempts to make Leon and the wolf as one; there is little delineation between the two, and simple acts of care and nurturing can put the wolf to sleep almost immediately. At one point, while Leon is still a child, Don Alfredo and Theresa come into his room to find the little boy, partially transformed, pulling at the bars across his windows that Don Alfredo had placed there earlier that day. Alfredo and Theresa grab the boy, who bares his fangs and is much hairier than usual, and tuck him in to bed. As Don Alfredo sits next to the boy and rubs his forehead, he loses all aspects of his wolf form and reverts to humanity.

So, when Leon meets Christina, who is due to be married to another man, he is completely reliant on her to somehow "save" him, and, indeed, during her initial introduction to him, she seems decidedly unbothered by Leon, even though he is clearly poorer (he works as a bottler at the vineyard while she is the daughter of the wealthy owner of the vineyard). However, even though Christina's love for Leon is redemptive, Leon's love for Christina, to him at least, is unrequited, and thus, destructive. For the first time since he was a child—at least, the film seems to point in that direction—Leon turns into a werewolf.

This happens, no less, in a brothel, where his friend and co-worker, Jose, has taken Leon to lift his spirits. Yet, Leon, who spontaneously proposed to Christina only to be rejected because of her prior engagement, is uninterested in the prostitutes who continually solicit him. Soon, Leon, feeling unloved, returns physically and symbolically to his cursed state. He transforms, murdering a prostitute and then a drunken Jose, before leaving. The next morning, Leon awakens in his childhood bed, his hands covered in blood.

In many ways, Leon's transformation in *Curse of the Werewolf* depicts an inner struggle in how his masculinity functions. Originating in a much lower caste, Leon is constantly faced with the burden of being a more "cultured" male like Don Alfredo, who can be fairly described as a "learned gentleman." And, indeed, Don Alfredo is mostly successful, but the deeply masculine adventure of hunting is the moment when Leon's masculinity frays forever, between the loving child who wants to kiss a dead squirrel to bring it to life, and the beast who is aroused by the taste of the squirrel's blood.

Thus, Don Alfredo and Teresa have a delicate balancing act, and the movie is most likely wise to skip past Leon's teen years and straight into Leon's young adulthood. There are hints, however, that Don Alfredo feels that Leon's "loving" household also has the capacity to suffocate. As Leon gets ready to leave the home, Teresa begs Leon to stay, telling him to work for his father, but Don Alfredo immediately nixes the idea, telling her that "it is only natural that he should want to make his own way in the world." In other words, Don Alfredo has worried, possibly, that Leon's continued existence in the household could possibly civilize him *too* much, and Leon could lose vital shreds of his masculine identity.

It's little wonder, then, that Leon's first stop is to work in manual labor. Leon is not only "making his way," he's searching for some lost components of his masculinity. It's clear—especially when Leon is juxtaposed with Jose—that Leon is uncomfortable with supposedly "hard" masculinity. It's only natural, then, that love itself would keep him complete, as his baser instincts, in which he fully embraces the class structure that belies his origins, manifest themselves in lust and base drunkenness, as well as poverty. It's little wonder, then, that Leon's discomfort at the brothel—the domain of the hegemonic or even toxic masculine—leads to his violent, wolf-based rejection. Even though the "curse" of the wolf is borne from those sundry origins, it functions as a way of spurning those origins as well. The violence inherent in his origins is part and parcel of his existence among those sundry individuals who led to his curse.

In the end, however, Leon follows the usual path forward, begging at first to be jailed, and then, when jailed, begging to be killed. "You must have me executed," he cries out, "I have already killed three people!" Leon's bravery shrinks a bit, however, when he's told the execution method is to be "burned alive." Don Alfredo asks for Leon to be placed in a monastery—presumably to receive spiritual rather than mortal love, but their efforts are for naught, and Leon turns again, killing the man that shared the cell with him, and then escaping the prison, just as Leon and Alfredo had feared.

And thus, the tragic cycle in *Curse of the Werewolf*: Leon is unable to escape his origins, sometimes literally, and cannot truly exist in the world. The woman he loves cannot cure him, and there is no way out but death, and a very public one at that. And, in fact, the love that ultimately "cures" him is that of his adoptive father, Don Alfredo, who sadly and reluctantly shoots his foster son after realizing that he can no longer be retrieved and made human. Throughout the film, Don Alfredo fails to recognize that the deck is far too stacked against Leon, and the few slivers of love he receives only delays the inevitable transformation that lurks underneath. Alfredo's killing of Leon with a single silver bullet saves Leon from his curse as well as a potentially far more brutal fate at the hands of the townspeople. Leon's inability to discern and then embrace a particular form of masculinity is represented by his struggles with his wolf form. Like Talbot, he is ultimately unable to adhere to the multiple standards and definitions of masculinity that appear in front of him, and the pressure he receives, from society, from his father, from his friends, and from his potential mate, disrupt his masculine identity so severely that he has no role in the world.

The Boy Who Cried Werewolf

The oft-overlooked 1973 feature *The Boy Who Cried Werewolf* focuses on a reclaiming of masculinity through the werewolf curse. The film, quite correctly called "slapdash" in a contemporary review (Thompson), focuses on a recently divorced father, Robert Bridgestone, as he attempts desperately to connect with his young son, Richie, and his ex-wife, Sandy. Robert's attempts to spend time with his son are regular trips to a cabin located in the woods, which, naturally, contains a roving werewolf. Within a few minutes of runtime, Robert is bitten while protecting his son, and the viewer is exposed to the dynamic of Robert trying desperately to recapture his masculinity. A telling exchange occurs when Robert drops Richie off at Sandy's house. "No more concern for poor ol' Dad?" he simpers, chastising his ex-wife for not caring enough about him. As they talk about Robert's encounter with a man—and his later self-defense killing of that man, who is the werewolf—Robert blames Sandy for not being there, after she says none of this would have happened if she were at the cabin to help. He mockingly describes her as the "coming genius of the publishing world," who, in her career aspirations have joined a movement he, with furrowed brows, seems incapable of understanding. "Women of the world unite and all that garbage," he scoffs. His hegemonic masculinity is clear in his sneers and his deriding of his former wife's desires to earn some form of economic and social independence from her husband.

In fact, many of Robert's exchanges with Sandy exhibit a less-than-friendly repartee between the two, with Sandy explaining to Robert that she has a career, and Robert sulkily snapping back at her about alimony, motherhood, and so on. At one point, Sandy reminds Robert that he should be reassured about his wounds, because his "chauvinistic brain is still functioning." It should come as little surprise then, that the wolf form of Robert strips away his barely concealed civility. At the climax of the film, Sandy is asleep in a chair in the cabin, with Richie asleep in the next room. Robert, in wolf form, sneaks quietly through the window, observes his ex-wife sleeping, and then kidnaps her, picking her up and carrying her away bodily. Eventually, when Sandy escapes, the wolf Robert grabs his son and spirits him through the woods. Here, Robert's anxieties and discomfort with the pressures of the new societal standards of masculinity come to the forefront. In wolf form, he doesn't have to negotiate with his wife. There are no legal settlements, there are no careers (for Sandy) that are in the way. They can simply be a family again, even if he must literally pick them up and take them away.

Robert conceives of himself as the alpha male in the relationship, the breadwinner whose role it is to protect and provide for his family. This notion, even in 1973, was somewhat antiquated. Yet, Robert continues to cling to this hegemonic notion of masculinity, and his werewolf form is a logical extension of that more brusque and violent masculine nature. The narrative oddly wends its way to the ultimate showdown between the werewolf and a wandering hippie/religious commune; this final sequence reveals that Robert's version of hegemonic masculinity is preferred. Within *The Boy Who Cried Werewolf* is a titanic clash between two cultures and two different versions of masculinity, "The dominant culture [that] prizes rationality, logic, the rule of law, sobriety, technological advancement, wealth, and occupational stability, [and] the counterculture [that] celebrates the irrational emotional, lawless, psychedelic, pre-industrial, impoverished and transient" (Savran 115). In this regard, Robert's werewolf form is "primitive" only in that it is being challenged by a new set of standards that are arcing through society like an electric jolt; that same new set of standards is an affront to Robert himself as well. As a human, Robert continuously struggles to cope with the societal forces that are appearing around him; as a wolf, he hunts and attempts to destroy the very symbols of those countercultural forces. The cycle of the previous werewolf films, where the wolf is a danger to society often crushed by law enforcement, has completely flipped. In Robert, the wolf *is* the law, the apparatus that rejects the hippie lifestyle in favor of order and tradition.

Tellingly, when Sandy relates to Robert their son's suspicion that Robert is a werewolf, Robert's response is to reassume his role as the disciplinary lead in the relationship. "Can't you handle the boy?" Robert mockingly asks. In this regard, Robert, as a human, views himself as resistant to the dissolution of the "traditional" family unit. Yet, Robert, as a werewolf, is endangering the family entirely, blissfully unaware that his unwavering tie to tradition is manifesting itself in destruction. The difference between Robert's perceptions of his masculinity can be found in his own home. Now separated from his wife, he is sequestered away to a cabin in the woods, reverting, symbolically, to a much more primitive form. The cabin is relatively spare, and a poster of a matador—an icon of masculinity—hangs by the front door, an everyday reminder of his ideal version of masculinity, which he clearly feels is under assault by the changing social forces that surround him.

Ironically, Robert's werewolf form eventually tangles with the hippie cult that wanders through the town. In one of the oddest scenes in werewolf cinema, Robert's lupine form dashes through the camp as the hippie troupe finds cover in a variety of vehicles. This cult is emblematic of Robert's worst fears of masculinity, combined: a group of men who have been feminized in the pursuit of a new form of masculinity. The hippies whom Robert's wolf form attacks "don feminized adornments" (Savran 122) and espoused "a more fundamental change in attitude toward gendered differences" (Savran 123). Additionally, the "hippies" of the era were forming a new form of masculinity, unmoored from marriage and capitalistic employment, employing "a significant rejection of sex roles as repressive cultural artifice" (Hodgon 112–114). In *The Boy Who Cried Werewolf*, then, this confrontation of a professional, career male in a camp of people encouraging him, as he transforms from wolf to man with phrases such as "freak it out" is emblematic of a larger cultural struggle, one between two definitions of masculinity. Robert, on one side, representing the traditional, more buttoned-down "breadwinner" stereotype, who finds masculinity in being able to care for his family through gainful employment, and the hippie cult, who reject that version of masculinity, and instead focus on "the true necessities of life," including a "metaphysical oneness with God and the universe" (Hodgon 113). The hippie leader, Brother Christopher, and his girlfriend, who can't find shelter, confront Robert's wolf form, and, as the sun rises, declares victory, seeing the wolf turn back into man, as they recite Biblical passages and try to cast out "the demon" they see in Robert. The wolf, in this film, at least, now represents social stability rather than subverts it.

Robert's fate matches the end of the men in films such as *An American Werewolf in London* and *The Undying Monster*, among others. As a wolf, he is shot to death, in an absurdly long hail of bullets. The posse (of somewhat sketchy legality) that corners Robert and shoots him seems to fire so much not only to wipe the wolf out of existence, but to mutilate and maim Robert's body as well. He reverts to human form, but not before falling on a piece of wood that punctures his chest. There, the true tragedy plays out, of a man whose masculinity was formerly accepted by society and then brutally rejected, as his wife and child mourn over him. *The Boy Who Cried Werewolf*, though, ends by revealing that Richie was bitten by Robert, and, thus, the "curse" continues onward into the future. Within Richie now lies the struggle of a young man trying to find an acceptable masculinity for society to consume and regulate.

Interestingly, unlike many werewolf films, the werewolf is introduced at the very start, even during the opening credit sequences. This may be a result of special effects budgeting, or directorial choices, but the emphasis on the physicality of the werewolf from the very start of the film, coupled with the transformed werewolf's readily human nature, forces the viewer to overlay, rather than juxtapose, the characters of the werewolf and Robert. The werewolf, which stands upright and wears the clothing the human was last transformed in, is a slightly more animalistic version of Robert. There is little mystery for the viewer as to the identity of the werewolf, and, as such, the viewer is encouraged to draw a straight line from Robert's hegemonic form of masculinity—which desires, or rather, demands, an orderly household centered on his patriarchy—and his wolf form, which lashes out violently, attempting to kidnap his family members and beheading multiple people.

Thus, Richie's inheritance of Robert's curse signals a struggle with the young man's own masculinity. Generationally, Richie is once removed from the turmoil that plagued Robert's expectations of the role of the woman in the domestic household, and, indeed, as it can be assumed that Richie will live with his now-single mother, Richie's own masculinity will no doubt become central to his identity. In the ending, *The Boy Who Cried Werewolf* does, in fact, focus on the boy, rather than the man, and it begs the question of the viewer as to what form of masculinity is burgeoning in Richie's psyche, especially given the numerous versions on display to him as a child.

The Beast Must Die

Amicus Productions made its own foray into werewolf cinema with *The Beast Must Die*. In this film, a renowned hunter, Tom Newcliffe, decides to capture and kill a trophy he's never come across before: a werewolf. To do so, he invites a group of suspects to his mansion, which he has rigged with a series of cameras and microphones. Each suspect may be a werewolf. Arthur Bennington is a diplomat, who although he was "cleared" of ghastly murders, was expelled from his post. Jan Gilmore is a concert pianist who is under suspicion in several European countries, as, everywhere he performs, someone dies a grisly death that night. This, too, means that Gilmore's wife (and former student) Davinia is also under suspicion. Lastly, the final suspect is a former medical student, and now artist, Paul Foote, who left medical school after being caught cannibalizing a corpse. Along with Newcliffe, there is also Professor Lundgren, who provides Newcliffe with "scientific" theories on why werewolves exist, and Pavel, a Polish man who oversees maintaining Newcliffe's surveillance systems. Rounding out the group is Newcliffe's long-suffering wife, Caroline, who becomes increasingly concerned with her husband's behavior. Newcliffe, of course, is the centerpiece of the film, and his character moves slowly from a hegemonic masculinity, deigning to manipulate every guest, including his wife, to a more toxic status, which ends in multiple deaths, including his own.

And, indeed, the "beast" of *The Beast Must Die* can be multiple things. Obviously, on the surface, the werewolf, but also, more symbolically, Tom Newcliffe's ever-growing obsession and mania over determining which of his houseguests is the werewolf. Many times, throughout the film, the camera zooms in on Newcliffe, who has concocted a new test for the group (grabbing a silver candlestick, inhaling wolfsbane pollen—or both), only to watch each test fail. Newcliffe, who initially attempts to cajole and charm his guests—

who also aren't allowed to leave his estate—becomes more distrusting of each of them, vandalizing their cars, yelling at them, and casting each one with additional suspicion, all while sweating profusely and gritting his teeth. In several instances, Newcliffe yells at the guests, as his various tricks and ideas are slowly disproven, and he simply seems to believe that endlessly berating individuals will get them to reveal their cursed status.

Another aspect of the "beast" beyond the werewolf itself are the members of the party. Other than Caroline, the gathered group are mostly bizarre and unlikeable. Paul has a macabre sense of humor and uses a whip to make his art. Of course, Paul didn't seem to think much of his dismissal from med school for eating a part of a corpse, either. Professor Lundgren is overly passionate about his research into werewolves, and thus, in one memorable scene, completely disgusts the gathered party as they attempt to eat dinner (Newcliffe, in another test, had raw meat with blood served to the guests). Jan and Davinia seem utterly confused by everything around them, and Arthur spends much of his time grousing about every aspect of the estate and his stay there.

The werewolf, which, due to the low budget of the film, is a dyed German Shephard, appears suddenly, and, on Newcliffe's first attempt, completely outwits him. The wolf zips past Newcliffe, who squeezes off a few ineffective shots, and quickly runs back toward Pavel in his command center. The wolf then successfully throws a wrench into Newcliffe's plan, and now the two adversaries must meet as equals. It's little surprise, then, that Newcliffe, without the benefit of his cameras and microphones, is at a loss to keep up with the wolf, as it kills the family dog and Arthur Bennington with ease.

Of course, because of the budget of the film, the transformation from human to wolf and back again in *The Beast Must Die* is a complete one. There are no humanoid wolves walking around and talking in *The Beast Must Die*. One moment, the person is human, and the next: a wolf, with little transformation involved other than some hairy hands and a few quick cuts. This is somewhat symbolic of the complete loss of identity that this film's werewolf "curse" brings. *The Beast Must Die* does adhere, mostly, to the standard tropes of the werewolf genre: wolfsbane, silver bullets, and full moons are all a part of this, even though, in one long speech, Professor Lundgren works hard to explain each of these tropes scientifically, discussing diseases of the lymphatic system as a culprit.

For the mystery to truly work, the human must be only vaguely conscious of their lunar activities, and, as such, they all suspect one another. This loss of identity leads to the film's tragedy—in a room, the film hearkens ahead to a scene in *The Thing*, where the gathered guests are asked to submit to another test to prove their humanity. Newcliffe, in a fit of poor planning brought on by his growing mania, gives each of the guests one of his silver bullets to put in their mouths. One by one, they do so, until it is Caroline's turn. She is *a* wolf, but not *the* wolf. Even so, Caroline's wolf form attacks wantonly, without intent, and Newcliffe shoots, distressed that he not only shot his wife, but that he didn't understand that she was a werewolf.[1] The blow to his ego is apparent. Professor Lundgren, however, posits that Caroline picked up the curse by handling the tainted wounds of the family dog, who had been mauled by the wolf. In this regard, Lundgren not only assuages the conscience of Newcliffe, but he also allows the audience to more effectively sympathize with Caroline, a woman who, through her husband's folly and obsession, sat through a dinner party with a group of suspected werewolves, only to accidentally become one herself.

The *real* werewolf is Jan, the concert pianist, who successfully kills everyone but Davinia, Lundgren, and Newcliffe by the end of the film. Jan, ironically, is the most confusing picture of the masculine. Played by Michael Gambon, he cuts a soft figure, who vacillates between simpering or mocking the proceedings. Compared to the distinguished and upper-crust Bennington, and the fey but vicious Paul Foote, and especially when compared to the muscular and successful hunter Newcliffe, Jan is the very definition of a "soft" male. Although he appears, along with Newcliffe, to be the only married male, Jan's marriage to Davinia is immediately cast as suspect by Newcliffe, who points out that Davinia was, at first, Jan's student before they married. In this regard, Jan's marriage is one of convenience, as he takes advantage of his power relationship in a student/teacher role to be romantically successful. It would be no surprise that Newcliffe, a hunter, and the very definition of a "hard" male, would scoff at this relationship, as he successfully "hunted" and "captured" Caroline to win her hand in marriage. Newcliffe did not need any sort of prior arrangement or relationship in order to be romantically successful.

Thus, Jan's slow progression through the ranks could be read, quite literally, as Jan's wolf form climbing the ladder of masculinity. The "beast" within Jan kills his rivals one by one, and as he does so, he grows from the man who tried to escape the estate[2] to one who grouses and complains about the "sport" aggressively. Eventually, Jan subverts the order that Newcliffe had placed upon things: not only does his wolf form destroy Newcliffe's technological advantage, it also kills the family pet *and* infects Caroline, leading to her demise as well. As "the beast," Jan is ultimately shot by the lone remaining silver bullet, transforming back to his human form as he dies. Newcliffe returns to Davinia and Lundgren, tells them the news about Jan, and Lundgren points to Newcliffe's wounds. His obsession has led Newcliffe to being "curse" with the werewolf as well. In the calmest manner he displays during the entire film, Newcliffe walks into his home, sits down, and shoots himself.

That Jan, the somewhat fey musician who drives a small sports car, is the werewolf is no doubt the gender-based swerve the creators of the film were searching for. Playing on decades of masculinized werewolves, the assumption that the werewolf would be the stern diplomat Arthur or the somewhat depraved artist Paul. Arthur is suspected in the murder of two diplomats; Paul is a part-time cannibal fresh out of prison. Jan, however is just as much of a suspect as his former student and current wife, Davinia, in a series of murders in various European capitals. Jan's relative refinement and "soft" masculinity—although tinged from our modern perspectives with his use of power in creating a sexual relationship with a student—is designed to throw the viewer off his scent in the unfolding mystery. The irony, then, is that the "soft" masculine Jan is ultimately the one that is toxic in wolf form, and he brings forth that toxicity to Newcliffe, leading to the hunter's demise.

The wolf is therefore adding little to Newcliffe, but his sudden curse does make him suddenly aware of his growing mania. In one of his calmer actions throughout the course of the film, Newcliffe realizes that he, too, will become a werewolf, heightening his understanding of the toxic way in which he has conducted his "experiment," and steps inside the home to kill himself. It is important to note, in a twist very unusual for werewolf cinema, that the toxicity that is often bestowed upon an individual through the curse is, in this case, used only to bring forth awareness of an already existing toxicity. Newcliffe does not act out and destroy others. Newcliffe is responsible for the deaths of many; his "curse" only accelerates his awareness of the destructiveness of his actions.

There is no doubt that the ending is a bit pat: hunter becomes hunted, then discovers he is just like what he is hunting. There is a moral to the story, but it is muddied by the unusual script. Essentially, from a perspective that considers gender, Newcliffe's literal pursuit of the alpha male position is the same one that eventually destroys him. He wants to be an alpha male, the leader, and he enjoys haranguing the guests, but not at the cost of the destruction of his marriage and, ultimately, himself.

In these films, the cracks in the façade of the tragic male appear. The narrative of the afflicted male's alienation from society, friends, and family based on their newfound curse and the subsequent toxicity it entails remains much the same. In fact, in many of the films, the narrative arc that requires the afflicted male to perish, often at their own hand, or, at least, to give themselves up willingly to a mob, continues to persist. However, there is a new and subtle twist in these films. In the stories of men like Duncan or Larry in the earlier films, they ultimately hate their toxicity and the violent power it brings to them; they derive no joy or benefit from their curse. However, in this next wave of werewolf films, the males (and females) afflicted with the curse often revel in their newfound toxicity and are ultimately destroyed in spite of the curse rather than because of it. This new perspective on masculinity in werewolf film begins with two films released in the same year: *An American Werewolf in London* and *The Howling*. In these films, the characters afflicted with the curse no longer regret the curse entirely; nor do they only temporarily enjoy some of its aspects. In many cases, the cursed character openly enjoys—and benefits from—their curse.

The 1980s Onward

The End of the Tragic Masculine and the Embrace of Power

With the appearance of what may be the two most well-known werewolf films in all of cinema, *The Howling* and *An American Werewolf in London*, the concept of the tragic masculine as a narrative device begins to disappear completely. In these cases, although the man afflicted with the curse may suffer or die, and may be unable to find his "real" masculinity that earns the approval of himself and his surrounding social circle, the cursed man also enjoys the benefits of the werewolf curse, often to a level unseen in werewolf cinema to this point. An embrace of violence, sexual arousal, and dominance appear in numerous male characters who are cursed, and for those male characters who attempt to stop them, they, too, must resort to violence and toxic forms of masculinity in order to survive. And, in a unique twist, gender itself changes, and films such as *Ginger Snaps* unironically embrace this new narrative as well, with female werewolves also enjoying the newfound power and violence that the curse brings to them. Why conform to what society expects of your gender, these films seem to ask, when you can simply demand, instead of a personal change, that society itself change instead?

An American Werewolf in London and *The Howling*

An American Werewolf in London is, outside of *The Wolf Man* saga, the most popular example of the struggle within. David Kessler and his friend Jack are attacked in the English moors by a werewolf, and Kessler's slow transformation into a wolf fuels much of the narrative. After the attack, David's panic and frequent nightmares—most famously, an image of a Nazi zombie—point toward an inner conflict within David, between his softer masculinity and his burgeoning hegemonic and, then, toxic natures.

That's not to say, of course, that David is completely without aspects of hegemony—early in the film, he and Jack speak in somewhat dim terms about women—"I'm talking about a girl you want to fuck," David says as they discuss Jack's infatuation with a woman named Debbie. Jack's response, that "I have to make love to her [...] she has no choice really," exposes, at the very least, Jack's hegemonic nature, but David's disgust with Jack's comments has little to do with mocking sexual assault, and much more with the fact that Jack is smitten with a "dull" woman. In other words, for David, the equation is quite simple: Jack's comments would be more forgivable or in line with David's own masculinity if Debbie were simply a more interesting person. Then, apparently, Jack's desire for "explicit" "love-making" with a woman would be more understandable.

Interestingly, after the attack, David's masculinity becomes a focal point for the staff at the hospital. As he sleeps, Nurse Gallagher tells Nurse Alex Price that she thinks David "is a Jew." When Alex asks why she thinks this is the case, Gallagher smiles and says she "looked." Alex Price gently admonishes Gallagher, saying, "I don't think that was very proper," but is otherwise smiling, too. Later, as David awakens from a nightmare, Mr. Collins, the American ambassador, chides David, telling him, as he struggles, to "try to refrain from hysterics" and "try not to excite yourself." Like Larry Talbot, sprawled on the hospital bed in *Frankenstein Meets the Wolf Man*, David is instantly objectified and then feminized. His "hysterics" point toward a lack of mental capacity to handle his stress, and Collins refutes Dr. Hirsch's[1] argument that David has "had quite a shock" with an almost hand-waving dismissal.

Soon, however, David reasserts his masculinity, at first reveling in his supposed subservience to Alex as she attempts to feed him. David flirtatiously pretends to not want the food—a scene immediately preceded symbolically by Alex attempting to get a small child to take his medicine—and Alex coyly tricks him into eating. Later, as Alex sits next to a sleeping David in his bed, David's childlike demeanor instantly slips away. As soon as he awakens, Alex quickly moves from mothering role to a potential mate for David, and his comment to Alex, "You're a very beautiful girl," reestablishes David's masculinity, as Alex immediately goes, quite literally, from matriarchal role to a "girl" in his mind. She is no longer a caregiver, but a potential romantic companion.

Not long after, David remarks to Alex that they have "a perfect relationship," because "You don't know me, and I know nothing about you." Alex immediately calls out David on his sudden flirtatiousness, asking him, if all she is "is a sex fantasy, then?" David can only admit his embarrassment and doesn't deny his sexual attraction to Alex. The movement from child to "man" comes full circle when David has his next (waking) nightmare, this one featuring the progressively rotting corpse of his friend Jack. Alex runs into the room, and David forcefully kisses her before realizing, out loud, "I'm a werewolf." The passionate (and unsolicited) kiss juxtaposed with David's admission fully symbolizes the werewolf's toxic nature in their newfound relationship, and although David, as a human, struggles with his masculinity, swinging from soft to hegemonic for the rest of the film, his toxic masculinity resides within the wolf itself. David's inner struggle, then, in many ways reflects the inner struggle of Paul Naschy's Waldemar Daninsky—he must be loved, but that same love will be a requirement for him to be killed. Love and death are tied into one entity, and David and Alex's sudden acceleration in their relationship—Alex invites him to stay at her apartment after he is discharged from the hospital, and they immediately have sex—only hastens David's eventual demise.

Of course, much has been said about the now-classic transformation scene in *An American Werewolf in London*, with its seriocomic but seamless special effects execution. But the transformation itself is important in werewolf cinema because it is truly one of the first times in the genre that a transformation appears on screen in all its brutality. In the past, even when the transformation between man and wolf was complete—in other words, there is no physicality of the human remaining—it was depicted as a series of slow dissolves, or more simply, the clever panning away of the camera from the human actor and the return of the camera to a wolf (most often played by a dog). In prior sequences, the transformation does indeed depict the divorce between the two, human and wolf, but in this instance, the wolf is quite literally within David. As he screams and writhes, his legs extend, a snout erupts forward from his face, and hair erupts from every pore of his skin. The scene is long and dramatic, and the gendered "soft" David, who, from the perspective of almost every other (living) entity in the film is struggling with mental illness and would prefer to stay at home, is in direct and painful conflict with his more hegemonic or toxic masculinity. The very ripping apart of his bones and flesh as he screams hearkens back to numerous moments in the film where David seems to wrestle with his own masculinity—does he approve of Jack's somewhat perverse desires for Debbie, or is he upset by Jack's statements because, in David's mind, Debbie isn't worth the effort of sexual conquest? Does he prefer Alex to function as a mother or a lover? Does he view the "ghostly" Jack as an indicator of his own mental stability, or does he truly believe in the fact that he's to become a werewolf? David, no doubt, pinwheels from point to point in his masculinity, and the wolf, in response, asserts itself in the most brutal fashion. While David attempts to find out if his human nature is soft or hegemonic, the wolf within him has no such conflict; its toxicity is on display even in its near-ritualistic abuse of David's body, and is quickly followed by the wolf's carnage.

David awakens, naked, in a zoo, and attempts to get away from various onlookers. Although it is played to comedic effect, David's attempts at covering himself end with him stealing a woman's bright raincoat with a fur-lined collar. He is, again, feminized, and the quizzical looks of the various people on the bus exaggerates this feminization. Thus, the cycle begins anew, the same movement as in the first half of the film, as David becomes objectified and feminized, and then works to eschew that characterization. When he returns to Alex's apartment—still wearing the woman's raincoat—he exclaims that he feels "terrific" even though he's "out of [his] fucking mind." He follows this up with a lingering and forceful kiss, and David has managed to reassert his masculinity. Soon after, however, it becomes apparent that the actions of the wolf have integrated themselves into David: "I feel like an athlete" he says happily, and notes that his "body feels alive, alert." David's glee at his newfound masculine power is quickly balanced by his discovery that six people were brutally murdered the night before. Thus, his enjoyment of the wolf's benefits—a sense of power coursing through his body—is quickly paired with the knowledge that that very same power is what allowed his wolf to murder multiple people.

All of this leads to the penultimate scene of David's wolf form rampaging through Piccadilly Circus at night. Immediately prior, David is unable to kill himself, and sits in a slightly crowded adult film theater, surrounded by Jack and the victims of his prior rampage. Each of them continues to encourage David to kill himself, but he's unable to do so, or at least unwilling to do so, before his next transformation. His wolf form bursts out of the theater and wreaks havoc before being confronted by Alex. Temporarily confused, the wolf pauses, and then lunges, before being gunned down by multiple police officers. In the end, Alex is left to weep over David's naked body.

In the end, then, David cannot reconcile the varying degrees of masculinity within his own person, and the conflict is something that he exclaims is driving him "mad." He is haunted by his prior victims, but revels in the physicality of killing. He exclaims that he is going insane but seeks out domestic bliss with Alex. He seeks out a mother, and then a lover. He says goodbye but can't commit suicide. And he at once loves Alex as David, but attempts to murder her as a wolf. The multiple contradicting masculinities set up within David are in a near-continual conflict from the very start of the film, as soon as the conversation turns to the mythical Debbie, and David's "curse" only heightens his anxiety regarding which form of masculinity is the "correct" one. Is he the aggressive lover? The young man fit to be mothered? The guy who endorses forceful sex, but only if the woman fits his stereotypes? Is he the person who enjoys the sudden athleticism and body-centric physicality? Or is he the sensitive and shy lover? In each of these instances, David swings wildly, almost from moment to moment, as he struggles to resolve these warring definitions, and when he receives the "curse" of toxicity, which leads him to both be disgusted by his acts, but also enjoy the power that allows him to commit these acts, David becomes suspended between these varying poles for the rest of the film.

In this regard, *An American Werewolf in London* follows a long werewolf genre tradition of the tragic male: the man who, unable to find a masculine center, can only be eliminated from society. This moral, although quickly abandoned by films such as *The Howling* and those that follow, resembles works such as *The Wolf Man*, *The Undying Monster*, and *I Was a Teenage Werewolf*. In each of these, the man afflicted with the curse must deal with trying to find a central location for their masculinity. The curse assaults their prior notions—either soft or hegemonic—regarding their gender, and, as a result, throws everything into tumult. And this chaos within the individual leads to that individual male's brutal destruction, often symbolically by a hail of gunfire from a collected group of townspeople or police officers. In many ways, *An American Werewolf in London* functions as the best, and last, example of the "traditional" werewolf film, at least regarding how it approaches masculinity. That same year, however, another werewolf film, *The Howling*, would manage to radically change the storytelling possibilities within werewolf cinema, and the tortured psyche of the man afflicted with the curse changes dramatically into a dramatically new version of masculinity and gender.

In *The Howling* (1981), the narrative focuses on Karen White, a prominent news anchor. At the start of the film, Dr. George Waggner, a psychiatrist, is being interviewed, and his words foreshadow the remainder of the film, and bookend Karen's final speech:

> We've all heard people talk about animal magnetism, the natural man, the noble savage, as if we'd lost something valuable in our long evolution into civilized human beings. There's a good reason for this. Man is a combination of the learned and the instinctual, of the sophisticated and the primitive. We should never try to deny the beast, the animal within us.

Waggner—who is later revealed to be the head of a cult that worships the werewolf and the supposed benefits the curse brings to the human—echoes Robert Bly, and this is crucial to understanding the ending of the film.

White is traumatized after being attacked by a serial killer-cum-werewolf, and at the urging of her psychiatrist, goes upstate to a rehabilitation colony with her husband, Bill Neill, to recover. Although the narrative continues to follow Karen, her husband, Bill, is the one who undergoes a transformation. At the start of the film, Bill is left to fret helplessly while Karen puts herself in danger. He is not there to protect her from the killer, Eddie Quist, and, as a result, she is nearly killed, not only by Quist, but also when a police officer haphazardly shoots several bullets through a closed door.

Bill Neill appears after the shooting and is unable to help Karen. Her trauma leads her to rebuff his advances, which sexually frustrates him. Bill, by this point in the film, is portrayed as a somewhat effete male, what would, in today's terms, be considered a metrosexual. He has a keen sense of fashion and is a vegetarian. He is overly careful with Karen's emotions and accommodating to her career aspirations, repressing his concerns for her safety.

Thus, when Bill is finally bitten by a werewolf at the retreat, he becomes hypermasculinized, embracing the toxicity that Eddie Quist reveled in. Although Karen is unable to satiate his growing sexual lust, he can find an outlet for that with Marsha, a fellow werewolf and Eddie Quist's sister. He consummates his growing lust for Marsha in an unusual scene where they both slowly turn from human to wolf in the act of having sex, just one of many examples in the film where "*The Howling* contains 'a surfeit of sexual imagery'" (du Coudray 84). The wolf is the very manifestation of sexuality, and moreso, often deviant sexuality—Quist turns into a wolf as he watches pornography that depicts a sexual assault; his cabin at the retreat is filled with pornographic images and news stories about his murders; Bill and Marsha turn into wolves when they initially have sex.

Bill's new personality allows him to eat meat, become somewhat slovenlier in his appearance, and, at one point in the film, when Karen argues with him, he backhands her, sending her sprawling onto the mattress. Bill's wolf side has turned him into a dominant, toxic male, and his previous attempts to be accommodating, or even "soft," have fallen by the wayside. He has moved from the meek pronouncement "I try not to eat meat" to "I get hungry enough, I'll eat anything." He has, in his violence, shattered through his domesticated, soft nature and fully embraced his toxicity.

Interestingly, Bill's final act as a wolf is to pass the curse on to Karen. Karen's immediate reaction is to reject her curse by allowing her transformation, and her death by silver bullet, to occur on-air. The existence of werewolves becomes "real" to those watching. She rejects her "monstrous mutation" who has "violent natures." Her primary recollection of this "violence," however, is Eddie and Bill, and, in some ways, she may not be away of the apparent ameliorating effect of femininity that seems to appear in *The Howling*. Marsha is not necessarily violent but is highly sexually aggressive throughout the film. That said, Karen's final statements before she transforms devoutly rejects Waggner's opening speech (and, thus, Robert Bly's formulations about masculinity): "From the day we're born, there is a battle we must fight. A struggle between what is kind and peaceful in our natures and what is cruel and violent. That choice is our birthright as human beings and the real gift that differentiates us from the animals. It is as natural to us as the air we breathe." In these words, Karen summarizes her rejection of her curse, and the physical and sexual violence it brings. Yet, these words are rendered null by Marsha, who is seen sitting at a bar, and happily asking for a hamburger, "raw." These two opposites—between the supposedly "civilizing" forces that emasculate men and overly feminize women and the "cruel and violent" forces of the werewolf that makes men violent and women highly sexual—is the primary struggle in the film.

In this way, *The Howling* has remnants of "traditional" werewolf films, except that the struggle becomes externalized. Bill, Eddie, and Marsha, along with many of the other members of the cult enjoy being wolves. This is a firm rejection of the "tragedy" of the curse, and the start of a new perspective on werewolf cinema. The more civilized forces are directly opposed, and, like two warring armies, the battle is no longer internal. There is no singular man and wolf that struggles between these opposing poles, wishing either for a cure or death. There is simply a group that enjoys being wolves, and a group that does not. From *The Howling* forward, werewolf films will begin to focus on those who enjoy being werewolves.

Teen Wolf and *Teen Wolf Too*

The much later *Teen Wolf* takes many of thematic arcs from *I Was a Teenage Werewolf* and turns them into comedic fodder. Scott Howard is a successful, firmly middle-class white teen in a small town, Beacontown, who isn't a delinquent. Yet, the middle-class ennui has fully engulfed him. "I'm sick of it," he tells his female friend Boof, "I'm sick of being so average. And it's not just basketball. It's school, this town, everything. I like Beacontown. I'd like my life to change. I don't wanna end up working for my dad." Of course, a part of Scott Howard's "average" feeling is his inability to be on a winning basketball team (Scott's father helpfully notes that it has been three years since they last won), and his inability to attract Pamela Wells, the school debutante. Of course, it soon becomes apparent to Scott that he is, in fact, a werewolf. A long strand of hair grows out of his chest, which he quickly plucks, and he soon finds his hearing and eyesight reaching superhuman levels.

Scott's confidence begins to skyrocket, and he soon threatens a local storeowner so that he can get a keg of beer for a local party. In this sequence, Scott's dueling definitions of masculinity are at play: his "hard" wolf masculinity threatens an elderly shop owner, but his soft and still childlike masculinity also adds a pack of licorice to the sale. At the party, he is locked in a closet with Boof, whose crush on Scott has been unrequited. However, the two of them awkwardly tumble about in the closet, a result of a prank by their friends, and Scott begins to change into his werewolf form. He rushes out of the house and returns home, locking himself in the bathroom. When Scott finally turns into a werewolf, he does so in the family bathroom, staring at himself as his skin bubbles and fur sprouts across his forehead. In the decade before *Ginger Snaps*, *Teen Wolf* tackles teen puberty and uses the werewolf as a symbolic rite of passage. Scott's initial and full transformation immediately follows his awkward sexual awakening ("What's it like coming out of the closet?" he's jokingly asked when he's released) and locks himself away for privacy during the change. While his father bangs on the door, Scott yells out, "I'm doing something in here," to stay alone. Yet, when he finally opens the bathroom door, in full wolf form, he is greeted by his father, who is also a wolf. "An explanation is probably long overdue," Scott's father says, and the two discuss the curse of the werewolf, which is genetic, although it "sometimes skips a generation."

Aside from the deeply symbolic near-sexual encounter followed by the masturbatory locking away for privacy, *Teen Wolf*'s initial discussions of the wolf all surround masculinity and changes. Earlier in the film, after Scott plucks a chunk of very long hair from his chest, he goes to see his rather detached basketball coach, Finstock. "I got a problem," Scott tells Finstock, and Finstock, who is supposed to be one of *the* male role models in Scott's life, immediately begins to backtrack on his open invitation to be that role model. "I'd like to help," he says, "but I'm tapped out," before starting on a long nonsensical story about a third stringer who had to leave the team. Scott, nonplussed, leaves the office.

Indeed, many of Scott's male role models have abdicated their position. Scott's father, Harold, has kept the family secret just that: a secret, leaving Scott isolated against the sudden changes that are taking place. Finstock is not only uninterested but, quite literally, afraid of having the "man" discussions with his star player. And Vice Principal Thorne simply abuses his authority over the students at the school. All told, Scott is totally isolated for much of his journey into manhood.

It is important to note, too, that the "change" that Scott undertakes is one that leaves him mostly human.[2] He is fuzzier and more powerful. But he stands and walks upright, talks in normal diction, and still plays basketball and goes to school dances. Unlike Tony's wolf in *I Was a Teenage Werewolf*, Scott's wolf is infinitely more comfortable and civilized. There is little horror in *Teen Wolf*; instead, the werewolf itself is one of the providers of conflict: like a drug, it enhances Scott's masculinity to toxicity, making him more threatening, allowing him to abuse his power, and ultimately, become a bit more violent. Yet, the wolf still gains acceptance among his peers; they even beg Scott to turn into a wolf so that they can win a basketball game. Scott refuses, and his path forward is clear: he has found that his life isn't so bad after all, and that he can be comfortably "a man" by simply being himself.

Scott has two romantic interests in *Teen Wolf* as well: Pamela and Boof. Boof is attracted to Scott's human side, and his "soft" masculinity. He is polite, hard-working, and adheres to societal norms, almost to a default. He takes few risks, in life, and on the basketball court. In fact, the first extended introduction to Scott shows him playing an almost matriarchal figure to his teammate Chubby, gently chastising him for keeping copious amounts of junk food in his locker. Later, Scott even tells Boof to "say no" to friend, but con-man, Stiles, and she immediately follows along. Scott has even embraced his matriarchal role to his workplace, where he helps his father run the hardware store.

In embracing, but then rejecting his wolf form, Scott cycles through the various levels of masculinity until he finds an acceptable level of assertiveness in his softened masculinity. In resisting his team's calls to turn into a wolf, Scott risks their chance at a win (his wolf form is a dominant basketball player) over their objections. He does, however, understand that Boof is his soul mate, and he ultimately rejects the status he seeks in earning the affections of Pamela, who is attracted only to his aggressive wolf. *Teen Wolf* is a film all about moderation, unlike, for instance, the extreme ends of *Wolf* (where hard masculinity is the ideal) and *The Wolf Man* (in which soft masculinity is the ideal). Scott moves from "I'm average" to realizing that being average, and not necessarily rocking the societal boat, is perfectly fine. Scott's wolf form is always with him, but he's managed to seek out acceptance among his peers in human form. In a final act intended to show how "okay" he is with his relatively soft masculinity, he realizes that Boof, not Pamela, is the young woman most deserving of his ardor and ultimately turns away from Pamela as the source of his affection.

The same themes and structures play out in *Teen Wolf Too*. In this instance, Scott's cousin is the wolf, and most of the same plot plays out, only now with a college boxing tournament. All the beats are still there: discovering his wolf, using it to get ahead, realizing that being a wolf is problematic at best, embracing being human and still winning at life.

The subtlety and overall endorsement of embracing oneself—even if you are a nerd or soft masculine—in *Teen Wolf Too* is almost completely abandoned. Bryan Senn is right to note that the werewolf as a "metaphor for the difficult transition from adolescence to adulthood" in *Teen Wolf* turns into "a symbol of Todd's inner jerk" in *Teen Wolf Too* (203). There's little doubt that Scott, especially when he first discovers his lycanthropy, uses his newfound powers for less-than-ideal purposes, including threatening a shopkeeper to get a keg for a party. But, where Scott eventually decides that the wolf is a supplement for his original personality rather than a replacement, Todd embraces every aspect of his inner wolf, including misogynistic comments and an overreliance on the powers that the wolf gives him. Indeed, whereas Scott decides to win the final basketball game for his team without the wolf, over the protests of his coach, teammates, and fans, Todd leans on the wolf for his penultimate boxing match.

There is only a little time that has elapsed between the two films: *Teen*

Wolf was released in 1985 and *Teen Wolf Too* only two years later, in 1987, so it would be difficult to argue that there was some sort of massive cultural shift regarding views toward masculinity. More simply, *Teen Wolf Too* was an attempt to cash in on the first film's success, and the basic re-writing of the plot without the finer details is a clear indicator of this. However, *Teen Wolf Too* could be viewed as one of the first werewolf films where the protagonist, in this case Todd, actually embraces the hegemonic and toxic nature that the werewolf often brings via the curse. The shift represented by the *Teen Wolf* franchise, itself inspired, in part, by *The Howling*—that maybe being a werewolf isn't so bad after all—will start to dominate werewolf cinema from here forward.

Bad Moon

There can be no more 1990s-style horror film opening than the first five minutes of *Bad Moon*. It has it all: uncomfortable stereotyping of native peoples, copious amounts of (mostly) female nudity, a sex scene, a gory attack, and an exploding head.

This is all the set-up for the rest of the film, as Ted is clawed by a werewolf during his lovemaking session (apparently to celebrate the final day of a film production) and is thus infected by the curse. *Bad Moon* plays with the standard rules of werewolves. Ted realizes almost immediately, for example, that werewolves do not require silver bullets to be killed; the close-range shotgun blast to the first werewolf's head proves that. But, by the time Ted reaches the United States again, another modification to the typical lore becomes apparent: he changes into a werewolf *every night*, not just during the full moon.

This change moves the narrative along at a breezier pace, and the total timeframe for the film seems to be less than a week. Ted, depressed by his newfound curse and the werewolf-related death of his girlfriend Marjorie, all depicted in that opening sequence, takes to living in an Airstream trailer in the woods. Every night, he goes out to the woods and handcuffs himself to a tree, with varying levels of success. Ted eventually contacts his sister Janet, a single mother and attorney, who lives with her son Jake, and their massive and preternaturally intelligent German Shepherd, Thor. Janet lets Ted move his Airstream into the backyard. She is obviously concerned about his mental health, and rightfully so.

In this film, although the physical battle is between Thor and the werewolf form of Ted, the true battle resides entirely within Ted himself. Ted refers to his "shadow" near the start of the film, and it's an apt metaphor: his entire life is informed by the presence of the wolf, and he can't seem to gain any traction. Jake, while snooping through Ted's trailer, uncovers Ted's obsession with his own curse: a small closet is filled with microscopes, blood samples, and phlebotomy equipment, along with a very old book on werewolf lore. Despite his efforts to uncover a "cure," Ted is quite simply stuck with his other half, and, in his desperation, he contacts Janet to see if "family love" is a potential cure for being a werewolf. Although Ted never spells this out, it appears that he is hoping that his human love for his family—and, as we will see, especially his sister—will somehow prevent him from turning into a wolf, or, alternatively, prevent him from murdering while he is a wolf.

The theory fails. Thor's omnipresence outside of Ted's trailer irritates him, and the German Shepherd is the first character to piece together Ted's werewolf form. At one point, Thor even urinates in front of Ted's trailer, sending the clear signal to Ted (and the audience) that an alpha male battle for dominance is about to ensue, and that the massive German Shepherd is betting on himself. Ted, even in human form, understands this, and is irritated with Thor's attempts at dominance.

Yet, Ted's constant wrestling with his "shadow" manifests itself in what some critics have derided as Ted's constant personality shifts. His personality *does* change, as he moves from gleeful to oddly flirtatious to demanding to pleading to threatening, all within the span of the film's rather short 86-minute runtime. These character changes are stemming from two distinct creatures in the same body: Ted at one point demands that Janet keep Thor and Jake in the house at night to keep them safe, but, as his werewolf form slowly starts to dominate his personality, Ted schemes to rid the house of his nemesis Thor and gently threatens Jake. In one of the odder aspects of the film (and one that is strangely underexamined), Ted's relationship with his sister Janet becomes much more flirtatious and tinged with the repressed sexuality of an elderly married couple. The two gently joke, hug, and openly profess their love for one another in what, on the surface, seems to be a deep and rewarding sibling relationship, but, in the context of most werewolf cinema, becomes a sexual minefield. Ted's sexual aggression, much like Hammond's in *The Undying Monster*, points toward his own sister.

Ted's plan to remove Thor from the equation is mostly successful, as the negative aspects of his personality manage to coax Janet (with some assistance from the local sheriff) into believing that Thor is an inherently dangerous dog and must be impounded. In one of the odder scenes in a film full of them, Ted, in human form, mocks Thor as he is dragged away by a pair of animal control officers. Thor lunges and snaps at Ted, who stands behind Janet and Jake. Ted, for his part, grins at Thor, and waves goodbye, before putting his arms around Janet. After Thor is put into the back of the animal control van and is driven away, Ted walks to the back of the house and urinates in Thor's doghouse. By this point in the film, it should be clear that the "wolf" portion of Ted's personality is now fully in control.

Of course, this scenario ultimately ends with Ted's destruction. With Thor gone, Ted tries one more time to handcuff himself in the forest, but this time, Janet stumbles across him. In what could be an homage to any number of adaptations of the Jekyll and Hyde legend, Ted pauses in mid-transformation to talk to Janet. His countenance is plainly human, but strained, with eyes turning color, and fangs in place. He refers to his wolf form as his "private affair," his "mistress," and it becomes clear to the audience and to Janet that Ted, in the failure of his "family love" experiment in seeking a cure, has decided, quite simply, to embrace being a wolf.

This sequence, of course, leads to *Bad Moon*'s physical showdown: the large German Shepherd against the bipedal werewolf. Thor, rescued from the pound by Jake, rushes to Janet's rescue, and together, the three of them severely wound the werewolf. Thor, injured, manages to track the wolf to a clearing in the woods, but, by the time he does so, the wolf has reverted to Ted's human form. Ted encourages Thor to "finish it," and the always obedient German Shepherd does so, killing Ted, and, presumably, ending the curse.

Like most males infected with the "curse" of becoming a werewolf, Ted must meet his unhappy, ultimately tragic end. The likeable, somewhat scarred Ted that is introduced at the start of the film, a man who is vulnerable and at wit's end, turns into a man who is aggressive, sexually (and inappropriately) flirtatious, and revels in his newfound power. This reversion to the toxic masculinity is ultimately unsustainable, and Ted realizes this. His end is less a result of his wounds, and more of a willingness to accept that his curse cannot be cured, and that his continued toxicity cannot be accepted by his family or by broader society. He is an outcast, doomed to failure in almost every avenue of his life, and his final human command to Thor to "finish it" is tantamount to suicide, hearkening back to Larry Talbot's attempts to kill himself. Ted commits suicide by German Shepherd.

Ted's tragedy is his slow transition away from his humanity into guilt and then toxicity. He realizes that he is no longer a part of society—his toxicity has earned him shunning from his sister and his nephew. In the end, *Bad Mood* manages to embrace the same parables as films such as *The Wolf Man*, although there can be little doubt that, for just a little while, Ted does enjoy his newfound powers. It is only when he understands that his "curse" is truly a curse, costing him the only remaining valuable human relationships in his life, does he realize that his existence is expendable.

Wolf

In the Jack Nicholson vehicle *Wolf* (1994), the viewer witnesses the idealization of aggressive, "hard" masculinity. Nicholson's character, Will Randall, is an aged editor-in-chief of a major press that is about to be bought out, and his job is in danger. As the film opens, Randall is driving back to New York City from Vermont, when he hits a wolf, and thus the cycle begins. Randall pokes the playing-dead wolf with a sharp stick a few times before it bites him[3] and runs into the woods, where it joins its pack. Randall drives away, panicked, as the pack eerily looks on.

We soon, however, see that Randall is not an idealized male, at least in the context of *Wolf*. When he arrives back at his apartment, the viewer discovers that Randall's purpose in Vermont was to land a new client for the publisher. His wife, Charlotte, asks if he used his "charms" to persuade the client to join the publisher, but Randall corrects her: no, he says, he simply "begged" the client to sign. Later, on his way to work, Randall, stoop-shouldered and clutching his bags, walks past an opposing symbol of his masculinity: a loud and boisterous construction crew, profane in their interactions, and uncaring about how others perceive them. The juxtaposition is even more jarring when Randall enters his studious and otherwise quiet office complex.

Randall's primary nemesis in *Wolf* is his protégé, Stewart, who successfully angles with the new owner of the publishing house to take Randall's job. As if this betrayal wasn't enough, Stewart also convinces the new boss, Raymond Alden, to force Randall either to resign or to be shunted off to a low-paying job in Eastern Europe. Stewart even cuckolds Randall by having an affair with Charlotte. Within the first half of the film, as the curse slowly progresses, Randall's emasculation is completed. Every aspect of his masculine identity is shown to be "soft" and unable to cope in this new world of unfettered lust and capitalistic drive. As if to drive the point home even further, Randall's new boss, Raymond Alden, points out that Randall's main characteristics—"taste and individuality"—are "actually something of a handicap" in the modern world, and that the new characteristics for survival are "drive and 52-carat ambition," which the human, "soft" Randall simply does not have—until he starts to turn. In the formulation of Robert Bly—who was an unofficial consultant for the film—Randall is the "domesticated, emasculated" male who is no longer "in control of the small orbit" of his life (Vogel 464). *Wolf* is a film that is, without a doubt, "self-consciously positioned as a film about masculinity," thanks, in part to director Mike Nichols's consultations with Robert Bly (du Coudray 108). We see this lack of masculine control everywhere, from work to home, in Randall's life. He is simply unable to respond to events, and has no true agency, being out-manipulated and overlooked at almost every turn before his curse starts.

Thankfully, then, Randall's initial meeting with the wolf becomes his outlet to a new form of masculinity, one that ultimately frees him from the bondage of having to be civilized. Interestingly, in *Wolf*, despite the participation of renowned special effects (and wolf transformation guru) Rick Baker, the transformation of Randall into his wolf form is rather tame: Randall basically grows long sideburns, puts on contacts, and has a fang underbite. Along with a change in gait, this is his entire transformation. As a result, Randall's wolf form[4] begs the viewer to associate the wolf with Randall, and vice versa. At one point in the film, Randall, in wolf form, lopes through Central Park, and is accosted by a trio of African American muggers.[5] Randall turns, and, with long sideburns, fangs, and contacts, has a short discussion with them before attacking. Unlike other films, they are not two separate entities, vying for control of one body. Instead, they are *the same entity*, and both enjoy the benefits of the other.

The film makes no secret of the benefits of Randall's newfound "hard" masculinity. He uses his wolflike senses to his advantage, exposing his wife's affair with Stewart. He castigates a less-than-eager employee for drinking too much. His newfound aggression allows him to strong-arm Raymond Alden into creating a memo that keeps Randall as editor-in-chief, giving him a pay raise and sweeping administrative powers. Naturally, the first thing Randall does upon signing the memo is to seek out Stewart in the men's restroom, where Randall, after informing Stewart he is fired, promptly turns and urinates on Stewart's shoes, explaining that he's "just marking" his "territory." Indeed, Randall's newfound aggression and power brings his wife begging for forgiveness and a restart of the relationship. Later that night, Raymond Alden's daughter, Laura, has sex with Randall.[6] Randall is now clearly in charge not only of his life, but of everyone in his orbit.

The film makes the benefits of being a wolf perfectly clear when Randall visits an Indian mystic and scholar to learn more about his curse. That scholar, Dr. Vijay Alezais, reveals that he is dying, and asks Randall to bite him so that he may become immortal, at one point even trying to shove his arm into Randall's mouth. Dr. Alezais says that he admires Randall for having the supposed curse, because it "feel good to be a wolf [...] power without guilt, love without doubt." Of course, Randall had already, by the time he visits with Alezais, has enjoyed these benefits greatly, but still seems stunned to learn that being a "demon wolf" doesn't lead to "damnation."

As most werewolf films go, however, *Wolf*, too, ends in a climactic battle between the two major characters, and the winner receives the crown of the most masculine of all. During Randall and Stewart's confrontation over Charlotte, Randall instinctively bites Stewart, thus passing along the curse to the much younger man. The symbolism of the mentor-protégé relationship continues throughout the film, as Randall is at first gobsmacked by Stewart's behavior, only to instead completely lay waste to all of Stewart's intricate plans to subvert his own mentor. The showdown occurs on the Alden estate, where Laura has temporarily locked Randall in a horse stall to prevent him from escaping. Randall, who is wearing an amulet that prevents him from turning into a werewolf, watches as the newly feral Stewart attempts to sexually assault Laura. Laura resists, but is eventually overwhelmed by Stewart's aggression. Randall tears off his amulet, transforms, and rescues Laura from the assault. The moment of Randall's decision to remove the amulet replays in slow-motion, a clear endorsement that to beat the beast, one must become a beast. The two men fight to a stalemate until Laura shoots Stewart several times, killing him.

The final few moments of the film play out in a bizarre dreamlike sequence. Randall, now in his somewhat slightly more lupine form, runs away from Laura, tearing off his shirt in the process. When the police arrive, Laura comes out of her house, wearing heavy makeup, and pins the shooting on the now-dead security guard. A montage plays to end the film, with one image zooming in on Laura's eyes, which are now clearly lupine in nature, and an animatronic wolf in the woods.

There are a series of assumptions to be made here. The first is that the wolf curse was transmitted through sex, and Laura, at no point, suffers an injury from Stewart or Randall (and most, if not all, werewolf films, focus on the point of transmission during their narratives). Stewart's unsuccessful sexual assault, then, points toward Randall's hotel room tryst with Laura as the source of her infection. The closing sequence—and Randall yanking off his shirt in slow motion—points to a different logic for the wolf transformation. Unlike multiple other films, where a transformation is complete (and painful) from human to wolf and back again in a short amount of time, *Wolf* seems to have made the turning into a werewolf a long, drawn-out process, where, over the course of several lunar cycles, the cursed human slowly transforms more and more into a literal wolf, possibly never to return.

The finale of *Wolf*, then, points toward an illicit wolf-based affair between Randall and Laura, who will presumably wander the woods forever, fully relegated to their beastlike forms. Even so, there are definable borders between "soft," "hard," and "toxic" masculinity in *Wolf*. Randall, even as a sympathetic protagonist, moves from "soft" to "hard" to rediscover himself. Stewart, however, in his coldly manipulative and backstabbing way, is the antagonist, who never quite leaves toxicity as an identity. In fact, if Dr. Alezais is correct, Stewart's toxic masculinity fuels his bad behavior after Randall infects him: "the demon wolf is not evil," Alezais tells Randall, "unless the man he's bitten is evil." This means that, in the movie's logic, Randall's transition from soft to hard masculinity is much more preferable than Stewart's transition from hard to toxic masculinity. Stewart had successfully manipulated his way to the top of his industry, while elbowing aside his sole rival and, not only that, he is sleeping with his wife. Randall essentially follows the same path, but the difference is that the audience is supposed to cheer for Randall's hard masculinity at the expense of Stewart's own hard masculinity. The difference is that Randall was, in the morality of the film, wronged first; Stewart also manages to be incredibly smarmy and fey in his interactions. His duplicitous nature is in no way portrayed as noble, and, after he becomes a wolf, he swings wildly from one toxic characteristic to another, while Randall attempts only to secure his position in the world.

The "hard" masculinity wins the day, and the film not only endorses this form of masculinity, but it seems to point toward Randall embarking on, quite literally, a completely new life as a result of his "curse." He is freed, in those final moments, from the last civilizing forces of his life. Unmoored from the capitalistic constraints and desires of everyday life, Randall comes to resemble that fabled "wild man," who is shorn of everything but his connection with nature. In this cinematic tale of werewolves and masculinity, there is no real tragedy, only triumph, for Randall.

As an important aside, the treatment of women in *Wolf* is also noteworthy. There are three distinct roles that appear in the film. The first is that of loyal servant, Mary, who is Randall's administrative assistant. She is quite happy to work hard for Randall, and silently yearns for Randall to become more assertive at the start of the film. When Randall, newly infected by the wolf curse, hatches a plan to not only keep his job, but to subvert Stewart, she reacts with barely disguised glee. Mary appears only in her role as Randall's assistant. Conversely, the seemingly supportive wife, Charlotte, is quick to abandon Randall for Stewart when it appears that Randall is about to lose his income, and Stewart is about to become a wielder of power and influence. Charlotte reappears only once in *Wolf* after Randall discovers her affair, and it is specifically so Randall (and the audience) can enjoy putting her in her place. "I never loved Stewart," she proclaims, "I'm begging you to be kind." Randall essentially shunts her aside with barely concealed rage. A few minutes later, Randall is having sex with the much younger Laura.

Wolf's narrative logic indicates that Laura's "demon wolf" curse stems from having sex with Randall rather than a direct bite. Dr. Alezais notes the possibility when he says to Randall "I can't ask you to transform me with your passions," indicating for *Wolf*, at least, homosexuality will remain completely out of the discussion. *Wolf*, then, treats the curse as an STD, something that films like *Ginger Snaps* would explore more thoroughly (and successfully) years later. Yet, Laura willingly submits to infecting herself with the curse, and, in fact, Randall only plays a small part in the seduction. When Laura stumbles on Randall in his hotel room, he has handcuffed himself to the radiator in a tried-and-true method of confining his wolf form. Laura keeps Randall handcuffed (at least for the onscreen portion) during their sexual activity. In many ways, Laura and her rebellious nature—she only initially shows interest in Randall to anger her father—have more in common with the film's masculine-driven ideas than any of the other women in the film. She is, in many ways, presented as the ideal woman for Randall's newfound hard masculinity. She defies authority from men who aren't Randall but is wholly subservient to him. She is sexually available and aggressive, and despite her early misgivings, her youth, and her attractiveness, is simply smitten with Randall, who has neither youth nor (conventional) attractiveness. She is, for a middle-aged man newly discovering his masculinity, the perfect female. In many ways, she is the perfect fulfillment of Randall's middle-aged midlife crisis.

Cursed

Wes Craven took a break from his *Scream* and *Nightmare on Elm Street* franchises to direct his only werewolf film, *Cursed*. *Cursed* is a hodgepodge of plot holes and dead ends, and any interpretation of the film can be fraught. However, the issues of gender and masculinity still bubble to the surface frequently. This can be no clearer than in the character of Jimmy, a teenager who is bullied at his high school. Jimmy has a crush on Brooke, who is dating a school jock, Bo. Bo is quick to dismiss Jimmy, accusing him of being feminine, calling him "a geek on his way to fag town." Jimmy is embarrassed by the accusation and stammers a denial of homosexuality before stumbling away. Later, Bo tries again, but the insinuation of homosexuality is turned back toward him, as Jimmy refers to the "male to male contact" of Bo's amateur wrestling prowess.

This, like many teen movies of the era, plays out the same: homophobia masquerading as masculinity. The supposedly "feminine" aspects of gay males is something to be avoided at all costs. Of course, Bo and Jimmy must have a physical showdown to determine who is the most masculine in the relationship (and to woo Brooke, who seems to be fine with playing both men off each other). This takes the form of a wrestling "tryout" in the school, which, after some initial embarrassment, Jimmy wins rather handily, calling Bo a "fairy" before dropping him viciously to the mat with his newfound wolf strength.

Here is where *Cursed* deviates from the typical formula, however. In most werewolf films with teenage antagonists, the afflicted teen and his bully must battle to determine who is the alpha male in the group. Almost always, the werewolf-affected male, embracing and sometimes even enjoying his newfound physical prowess, overcomes their bully, who slinks away, never to be seen again, or only to reappear for future humiliations. Bo, however, does not disappear, and, in fact, he appears on Jimmy's porch, as the homosocial in film such as *Teen Wolf* and *Teen Wolf Too* becomes subverted, turning the homosocial environment into a homosexual one. "I'm gay," he confesses to Jimmy, assuming that Jimmy, too, is another "gay guy." Jimmy quickly refuses Bo's attempted kiss, and the two reach a stasis in their relationship, with Jimmy and his "unnatural sexual allure" essentially making Bo his newfound friend and follower. The depiction of an openly gay male in werewolf cinema is new in *Cursed*, however, the unfortunate relegation of that same character to comic relief and sidekick status is a trope that exists throughout much of 1990s cinema.

Bo, who showed no signs of homosexuality, repressed or not, outside of the admittedly sometimes homoerotic world of amateur wrestling, is, according to the film's logic, feminized and subjugated by Jimmy's animal masculinity. The two young men remain friends, and, for the most part, Bo disappears from the rest of the narrative, attempting to assist Jimmy only to get knocked out during one of the werewolf battles. Bo's sudden weakness leads to the uncomfortable stereotype of homosexuals as somehow less than masculine, and his desire to follow Jimmy around like a lost puppy is only exceeded by his physical flaccidity. Bo is unable to be a part of the pack, as he is simply too weak to be able to hold his own. Homosexuality is rarely a direct part of the werewolf narrative, with films such as *Werewolf of London* or *I Was a Teenage Werewolf* symbolically addressing (according to critics, at least) repressed homosexuality. The joke of Bo's comeuppance—his homophobic language overcompensating for his burgeoning homosexuality—is indeed rare in werewolf cinema, and Bo's movement from a hegemonic, even toxic male, is replaced by a soft, almost fey version of masculinity. The stereotyping in *Cursed* regarding homosexuality is indeed uncomfortable and falls more in line with societal stereotypes during the era rather than a nuanced gendered commentary on werewolf cinema. In other words, the subversive nature of Bo's sexuality stems not from his transgressive presence as a homosexual werewolf in a critique of horror films in general. Instead, Bo's sexuality plays to stereotypes of homosexual men being somehow more feminine or, at least, less masculine than their straight counterparts. That Bo is played for comedy immediately after professing his homosexual desires only deepens the stereotyping here.

The "plot twist" featuring Bo, however, neatly fits in with the perceptions of masculinity presented in the film. Jimmy is a young man who is a "geek," feminine in nature, and completely asexual, something even his sister notes when she gently points out that he doesn't even "download porn" like many teenage boys. Bo, however, is introduced as the typical jock, replete with his own posse of males and his attractive, if coquettish, girlfriend. In other words, at the start of the film, the oft-repeated pecking order of teenager-based drama dominates: asexual nerd repeatedly bullied by arrogant and popular jock. The inversion, however, is unique, in that Jimmy's burgeoning wolf-form leads to, instead of a comeuppance, a complete turnabout. In many films that feature the teenager nerd versus jock formula, the nerds win, but it comes in the form of a truce or a begrudging acceptance by the jocks on the rights of nerds and geeks to exist. *Cursed*, however, within the framework of its own logic, places Jimmy at the alpha male position, and he quickly subjugates Bo, so much so that Bo becomes his own highly stereotypical and feminized being, free, for sure, of repressed emotions, but also seemingly now burdened with being Jimmy's follower.

One of the casualties of the multiple reshoots that surrounded *Cursed* is any sense of logic regarding the character Jake, who swings wildly from one characterization to the next. Eventually, in the climactic battle of the film, Jake battles Ellie and Jimmy as all three slowly turn into werewolves. Jake at first offers a romance to Ellie, telling her that he can help her "live with" her newfound wolf-based lifestyle, but then almost immediately decides to kill her because she's "not doing a very good job." In the end, the feature battle is mostly Jimmy battling Jake as Ellie occasionally attempts to help. This is, as werewolf cinema goes, the penultimate battle that almost always seems to be required in films featuring more than one werewolf. In this case, Jimmy manages to become the alpha male of the pack by killing Jake, stabbing him with a piece of silverware before helping Ellie cut off Jake's head with a shovel.

The victory relieves both Ellie and Jimmy (and their dog, Zipper) of the werewolf curse. Jimmy, however, manages to retain his status as a newfound alpha male, sexually virile and confident. Bo and Brooke appear just after the battle to return a lost and confused Zipper—who, in his werewolf form, was far more aggressive toward people—and Jimmy offers to walk Brooke home. The pair of them start to walk away, but Jimmy asks Bo if he's coming along. Bo, fully subservient, agrees to walk with the new couple. To clarify: Bo walks back home, straggling behind a couple, the male of which physically dominated him and rejected his advances, and the female of the pair having apparently dumped Bo after flirting with and defending Jimmy for much of their relationship. The masculine pecking order at the start of the film is completely inverted by the end, as Jimmy becomes more confident in his masculinity, while Bo is completely neutered. Jimmy's hegemonic outlook extends not toward the role of women in his life, but also toward the role of his gay friend.

Underworld: Rise of the Lycans

Like *Underworld*, the prequel, *Underworld: Rise of the Lycans*, keeps its focus almost solely on the vampires, and as such, joins the rest of the franchise in being a film centered on vampires that oppose a group of werewolves. And, indeed, the vampires continue the tradition that first came about in the Universal monster series (and later parodied to great effect in *What We Do in the Shadows*): the vampire clan is immersed in matters of governance and debauchery. The werewolves, on the other hand, are relatively uncivilized, aggressive, and clearly lower in the social pecking order in *Underworld*'s formula.

Ironically, a film subtitled *Rise of the Lycans* rarely depicts werewolves. The soon-to-be werewolf leader, Lucien, is trapped in a collar preventing his change for much of the film. Indeed, he appears as a werewolf only a few times. The same goes for his second-in-command, Raze. Much of the film's runtime focuses, again, on the vampires, and the werewolves don't really appear in any meaningful form until well over an hour into the film. Even so, the tension that Lucien feels in his "Lycan" heritage stems from a decidedly human emphasis: he, too, appreciates the merits of civilization and civilized talk, rejecting his werewolf peers who hunt in the forest. "They are mindless beasts," he tells the head vampire Viktor, "No relatives of mine."[7]

In many ways, Lucien's innate "humanity" within his Lycan form is symbolic of how he views his masculinity—the werewolves, the "mindless beasts" who wander through the forest in packs, killing humans and werewolves, are entirely toxic. Lucien's beliefs—evidenced by his love affair with Viktor's vampire daughter Sonja—hedge more toward a soft masculinity. He is deeply in love with her, and many of his decisions are based on her specific wants and desires. For example, he at first refuses to leave his enslavement—and eschewing possible freedom from his growing group of enslaved Lycans—so that he may be with Sonja. When she encourages him to escape, he eventually does so, but only after she promises to follow him. Alas, she is uncovered as a traitor by Viktor and sentenced to death, which leads Lucien on a foolhardy quest to try to rescue her, an attempt which fails horribly.

Lucien's wolf-form is really, in *Rise of the Lycans*, only useful when he interacts with his beastlier wolves, the "mindless beasts" that he derides, but later comes to appreciate. Every other time Lucien becomes a wolf, he is quickly re-subjugated by the vampires, or otherwise harshly defeated. At his most desperate, Lucien decides to lead the Lycans with a rousing speech. "There is a new life behind these walls," he yells to the gathered, enslaved Lycans, and no less than a new life is a new form of masculinity, removed from bondage and no longer subservient to others. The enforced soft masculinity can give way to hegemonic or hard masculinity, where masculine agency is reintroduced. Lucien's first decision is to form an army of Lycans to storm Viktor's castle, and one of his first tasks is to seek out the den where the "mindless" werewolves lurk. In this sequence, Lucien stays in human form and approaches the dozens (if not hundreds) of wolves, who, after a few beats, acquiesce to him. In his most desperate hour, Lucien recognizes that he needs to strike a balance between the often-toxic existence of the wolf and the ideal of the softened domestic servitude with Sonja that he once cherished. Of course, all his decisions in the film are based on his desire for Sonja, but he realizes that he can no longer focus on an idyllic and entirely hopeless ideal; he must adopt violence to win the day.

Even so, Lucien is content to leave the violence to others. He storms the vampire castle to save Sonja in human form—by now his collar preventing his turn into a werewolf is no longer affixed—swinging swords. Ultimately, he does not turn into a wolf, even when captured, until Sonja is dead, and he, enraged, allows the transformation to occur. Even so, his first instinct as a wolf is to grab a token of remembrance from Sonja's corpse and escape, a plan which ultimately fails. He is quickly attacked, stabbed, and speared by the vampires, and, as he begins to collapse, howls for the "mindless beasts" to come and rescue him. Again, Lucien struggles to maintain the balance in his masculinity, and, as the werewolves storm the castle, and the violent battle begins in earnest, the naked and severely injured Lucien—since turned back to human form—can only watch as his army engages in violence on his behalf. Even though his ideal of domestic bliss is shattered, he can only provoke—but not participate in—the violence around him.

Wer

Wer (2013) sets up a somewhat traditional werewolf film narrative: a mysterious stranger who is hiding their dark secret of the werewolf is strangely alluring to the young female character, who, herself, is the source of romantic angst. In this case, young attorney Kate agrees to represent a man named Talan Gwynek after he is accused of mercilessly killing a young family that is camping near his home.

Kate has already hired a young man named Eric as a sort of forensic evidence technician; his main goal is to piece together the, literally, found footage of the attack and murders. But, to help assist with the rest of her case—as she firmly believes that the family was murdered by an animal—she summons an old flame, Gavin, who is introduced as an expert in animal attacks. Gavin and Eric begin a subtle, but steadily escalating, game of one-upmanship to garner Kate's attention. At one point, with Kate out of the office, Eric warns Gavin to cool his ardor for his past lover. Gavin, after clumsily asking Kate out for a drink, and "to catch up for a second," walks into the next room, only to see Eric sitting at the desk, casually waiting for him. Their exchange reveals a lingering jealousy that both have for one another. Gavin tells Eric that he "doesn't know anything" about his relationship with Kate, and Eric, ever the forensic evidence technician, replies with an intimidating, "actually I know a lot about your relationship with Kate." When Gavin clumsily argues that he's seeing another woman, Eric shoots that down, too, with a quick "No, you're not." The two men spend much of the film circling one another, jockeying for Kate's attention, and failing to do so.

Yet, what neither Gavin nor Eric seem to understand is that the primary focus of Kate's attention is Talan, a huge man who is as taciturn as he is hairy. Talan is somewhat smitten with Kate, who, despite her professional veneer, is intrigued by Talan's presence and his background. She is, of course, set to defend him from the murder charges, but ultimately decides to go well beyond just a professional interest. She becomes a private investigator of her own, of sorts, as Gavin and Eric linger about in the background, each one progressively more hegemonic in their outlook toward Kate. Kate visits Talan's family and repeatedly tries to interview him for additional insight into his thought process, at one point asking the police officers to uncuff Talan to build a trusting relationship with him.

Yet, the two men in the background of the story, Gavin and Eric, spend much of their time attempting to assert their dominance over one another as Kate continues her fascination with Talan. Gavin's generally flaccid attempts to win over Kate and dominate Eric falter and fail, repeatedly, throughout the film, but, after Talan bites him, he begins to enjoy a new definition of masculinity. At first, he takes on the role of the martyr, the injured man who simply shrugs off the wound, despite Kate's pleas to the contrary. But, ultimately, Gavin's slow transformation into a werewolf turns him into the alpha male of the film, even more powerful and deadly than Talan. His transformation, like Talan's, is unconventional[8]—he moves from an angry man to a much angrier man. In the process, his climactic transformation essentially consists or shaving his head, snarling, and tearing off his shirt.

As Talan escapes his police escort, however, Eric and Kate are in hot pursuit, rather outstripping their roles as forensic investigator and attorney. As they search for Talan at the edge of the woods—Talan having avoided the police helicopter by dropping to all fours and running away at high speed—Eric is suddenly accosted by the animalistic Talan. Eric's response, and the camera focuses on this, is to start weeping as Talan hovers over him. Trying to save his own life, Eric gives a Shakespearean soliloquy: "Talan, it's okay. Talan, please, come on. None of these people understand you, and they never will. They're scared of you. But I can help you. Please, Talan. Talan. Talan, no. Talan, Talan, please, Talan." But Eric's efforts to somehow identify with Talan ring hollow to both the viewer's and Talan's ears. By the film's logic, Eric is the worst of the three males vying for Kate's attention. He is underhanded, devious, and has spent much of his life, one can assume, talking his way out of situations. His "protection" of Kate from Gavin is little more than a territorial move, for example, as it seems clear that Eric has no particular fondness for Kate, but he does feel that she is somehow "his," or at least enough for him to feel comfortable warning other males away from her without her presence. Eric's hegemonic masculinity duels with Gavin's, as both men seem to claim Kate for their own, a tug of war that she seems to be barely aware of; she's more concerned with the toxic masculinity embodied by Talan. By this point in the film, Eric and his shady past of eavesdropping and strange fascination with Kate's romantic life, is decidedly not a sympathetic character, and Talan seems to agree. Symbolically, he rips off Eric's lower jaw, rendering Eric's false sympathies mute. Eric's one true power—to talk himself free of any situation, or to talk him into any situation—ultimately fails in the face of powerful, toxic masculinity.

Talan's attention then turns to Kate. He quickly grabs her, but instead of killing her, he begins to fondle her. Even in his wolf-life form, Talan remembers Kate, as evidenced by his interaction with the ring she wears around her neck. Earlier in the film, he gives Kate the ring back after she loses it, and the two have a brief bonding moment. Just as Talan's hands begin to work their way down Kate's body, Gavin appears, throwing Talan off her and sparking the climactic battle. Here, we can see the film's slow-building set-up: Eric himself was a red herring of sorts, a faux competitor for Kate's attention. The true romantic tension is not between Eric, Gavin, and Kate, but between Talan, Gavin, and Kate, and moreso, between a newly lupine Gavin and the old alpha wolf, Talan.

As a police helicopter takes potshots at both men from overhead (there is a loosely tied subplot of a reckless and morally bankrupt police officer being exposed by Kate's investigation), the two werewolves clash violently in a riverbed, spraying water about, and clubbing one another senseless. At the end of the battle, however, Talan is brutally vanquished, and Gavin—or his wolf form—rescues Kate. His rescue is short-lived, however, as Gavin inexplicably demands that Kate kill him, kneeling before her. Presumably, he's horrified by his newfound power and masculinity, but it's a melodramatic, "tragic" moment that exists throughout much of werewolf cinema: the male as supplicant, cursed and doomed by the very freedom of full masculinity. Gavin's demands go unheeded, however, and the French police shoot Kate, killing her. This upsets the "tragic" narrative, much as the narrative is upset in films such as *Howl*, in which the "tragic" arc of the werewolf's demise becomes replaced by a full embrace—and almost luxurious bathing in—the fully masculine and feral form. When Kate is wounded by a police bullet, the last truly civilizing force that holds Gavin hostage is destroyed, and he quickly and violently dispatches numerous police officers before escaping into the surrounding woods.

Again, we can see the theme of masculinity appear, in that a man isn't a real "man" until he has rejected his calm, gentle metrosexual domesticization, the so-called "soft" male, and embraced the wolf within. Gavin, formerly a rather forgettable person who meekly and clumsily attempts to romance Kate, can only exist as an unattached male. As the film concludes, Gavin appears once more, as a news item, but again in his Clark Kent–like disguise as a mild-mannered expert on animal attacks. During the interview, Gavin reveals that there have been multiple murders across Europe, all in the guise of an animal attack. This attempt to put together a possible sequel provides the viewer with two distinct conclusions. The first is that Talan survived the battle and is still murdering people in his wolf form, or, far more likely, that Gavin's exterior is just a shell for the inner wolf that is still preying on individuals.

Considering how werewolf cinema copes with the supposedly "tragic" male, the one cursed with being a werewolf, and thus an outcast, in modern society, it is safe to assume that Gavin, is roaming the forests at night, killing at will.[9] The scale of his masculinity, throughout the course of *Wer* slides from uber-domesticated and "soft" male to a fully toxic, almost feral existence, barely covered by his previous life. Indeed, Gavin's physical transformation to a wolf in *Wer* is simple: like Talan, there's little physical change, and although such a lack of change could be credited to a relative lack of special effects budgeting, it does effectively make a point. Gavin's turn into a wolf leaves the man as, still, identifiably Gavin. No glasses, some red contacts, and a little extra fang, along with a hastily removed shirt and shaven head is all that stands between Gavin the "soft" male and his wolf form. Gavin becomes, almost literally, the wolf in sheep's clothing, and his perfection of the "soft" exterior hides—and will continue to hide—his lupine rampages. In this regard, *Wer* follows the same path of numerous films of the late 1990s and beyond—toxic masculinity "saves" the soft male, and he is an object, if not to be adored, then one to be feared.

Wolves

There is an odd normalization of the role of the werewolf in *Wolves*, so much so that the werewolves come across as superheroes of a sort. "Is it a gift or a curse?" Angelique asks protagonist Cayden, and the answer the film presents is clearly: gift. However, *Wolves* is one of the few films that depict differing forms of masculinity over the course of the story. Cayden "tries" a variety of approaches to his new wolf powers, from toxic aggression to hegemonic protection, to a more "hard" outlook that allows Cayden to act in a more violent—but justifiable—manner. Cayden is already a complete "male," at least in the conventional sense, when the film begins. He *is* the jock we meet at the start of *Cursed*, for example. There is, in Cayden's eyes especially, no real need for additional power, because, at the start of the film, he already has it all. He narrates over a scene of himself playing high school quarterback, saying he had "the hottest girl in school" and has life "sewn up and tied." But, as the sequence of his playing football ends, Cayden is provoked into attacking an opposing player. He does so by leaping through the air about ten yards and raining blows down on the opponent, denting the player's helmet and knocking him unconscious.

That's when we discover this film's rules for the werewolf, and they are particularly loose.[10] Cayden is a "pure-bred" werewolf, who descends from one of four major families that have been in the country for quite a while (the film never quite creates a complete backstory). In being "pure-bred," Cayden must control his excitement, including his sexual excitement, lest he turn into a physical manifestation of a werewolf, which itself is incredibly human, retaining the ability to speak and even his hairstyle, a blonde sweep along the top of his head. The "pure" wolf can benefit from a variety of abilities, including super-speed, a keen sense of smell, and super-strength. And all these benefits grow stronger with the full moon.

Eventually, Cayden escapes, at the urging of another "pure" wolf named Wild Jim, to the incredibly aptly named town of Lupine Ridge, where he stumbles into a civil war between "pure" wolves. In the town, and on the farms, are the town elders, who are all "pure" wolves who have successfully managed to control their transformations so well that they "ain't even changed in years." A clandestine love affair splits one "pure" wolf named Connor from the rest of the group, and he raises a group of his own werewolves by biting a group of townspeople and teaching them how to use their newfound powers. To defray the conflict, the elders agree to hand over a young woman, Angelina, so that Connor can impregnate her. Interestingly, Angelina is rather okay with the arrangement, as she thinks it will end the conflict in the town.

In a twist suitable for the teenage audiences the film no doubt targeted,[11] Connor is revealed to be Cayden's father,[12] and, additionally, Cayden and Angelina have fallen in love, setting forth an oddly Oedipal-style battle between son and father over their shared (at least Connor has been promised to have her) love. Connor, the self-styled "alpha" wolf, looks and acts the part, constantly prowling the outskirts of his town with his pack; he is far more animalistic than Cayden in actions and in physical appearance.

Cayden manages to find and embrace his wolf almost entirely because of Angelina. He admits to her, at one point, that his fear of sexual excitement and the wolf within has kept him a virgin: "wait, not never?" Angelina asks.

"No, not never, exactly," Cayden stammers, and he and Angelina have sex, all while turning into wolves, in a scene that clearly pays homage to *The Howling*. This is the exact moment in the film in which Cayden decides to help defend the townspeople—and especially Angelina—from a coming attack by Connor and his gang.

Cayden's arc over the course of the film is a slow movement from "soft" masculinity to a much harder form. He learns to harness his sexual aggression; when he is alone with his "hottest girl in school" at the start of the film, his sexual energy and excitement turns him into a wolf almost immediately, and the specter of sexual assault looms large as he literally paws at her. She manages to escape, but not before having her shirt torn and claw marks dragged across her back. The next time she appears, she is with the police in the front yard of his home. From her perspective, Cayden had committed sexual assault.

This lack of an ability to control his sexual and violent urges means that Cayden, the upper-class white teenager, is toxic in his masculinity. Although the film attempts to apologize for his earlier outburst on the football field, is it violent enough to get the police and the administrators involved. There appears to be no direct fallout from that incident, but it does echo back to *I Was a Teenage Werewolf*, in which Cayden's inner "primitive" nature manifests itself in what could have been called, in the 1950s, at least, juvenile delinquency.

Having been framed for the murder of his parents, Cayden goes on the lam, and develops, within the context of the film, a healthier, harder masculinity, where his violent impulses are no longer morally confusing to the audience. At a truck stop, Cayden is propositioned by a prostitute, but, fearing his change into a wolf, summarily rejects her. Later, he hears her screaming; she is being beaten by a pair of biker gang members. Cayden, in this formulation, and his wolf form are no doubt heroic in his actions. Even though he slaughters the two bikers, he is justified in the film's context for doing so. Later in the film, Cayden even puts forward his own unique mantra for what it means to be a werewolf: "Wolves, real wolves, only kill for food and defense." Cayden's wolf form is indeed super heroic: his newfound powers allow him to defend the defenseless, and he quickly embraces the role, even chastising Connor by saying "Wolves don't terrorize towns, or kidnap innocents, or brutalize women!"

It is important to note, however, that before Cayden can harness his energies in an appropriately violent manner (violence that, at least, is meant to defend or protect), he has sunken to a decidedly soft masculinity. Although the film manages to spend a significant amount of this time focusing on Cayden walking around shirtless, muscles rippling, he refuses most interaction with women, despite his inherent attraction to them. Upon meeting Angelina, he fumbles mightily, even forgetting what his name is when she asks him. His later revelation that he hasn't "exactly" had sex before indicates that he has effectively neutered himself, depressing himself far enough into soft masculinity that he has abandoned all pretense of sexuality entirely. Within the film's logic, then, he and Angelina's hyperactive sex scene, in which both slowly turn into wolves, is deeply symbolic of Cayden finding his own "true" masculinity. He becomes a "hard" male, one given to violence and enjoying his superpowers, but limiting them to only defensive measures, and righteousness. In this context, the film, like many others in the 1990s endorses a more aggressive hardness in masculinity.

Of course, Cayden does murder, often quite savagely, throughout the film, and always in wolf form, but the body count he creates is all for Angelina, as Connor is a direct threat to her safety (or, at least, her freedom to choose a partner). Until Cayden understands this, he embodies "protective" hegemonic masculinity. Cayden's newfound hegemonic masculinity is derived from classical (and decidedly anti-feminist) perspectives of having to guard his home and his mate, *even though Angelina herself is a "pure" wolf*. Angelina, in fact, is integral to her own rescue, and in rescuing her own family, from Connor. In other words, even though Angelina is more confident and exuberant in her wolf form, she still "needs" protecting from Cayden's perspective. In fact, after Cayden dispatches Connor in what the film considers a righteous kill, it is revealed that the machine behind all the events in the film is another "pure" wolf, nicknamed Wild Joe. Wild Joe, to get his revenge on the entirety of Lupine Ridge, has pointed Cayden there, knowing conflict would ensue, and to be sure he arrived, framed him for the murder of his parents. Cayden battles Wild Joe one on one, and quickly gets the upper hand. As Wild Joe is trapped above a fuse that's about to blow up a fertilizer bomb, Cayden's "wolves only kill for food and defense" mantra earns a quick amendment. "I never have killed anyone in cold blood," Cayden says, adding, "but life is complicated." Just as the fuse reaches the bomb, he yells out, in a seriocomic manner, "and you ate my fucking parents!"

At the film's end, Angelina and Cayden decide to explore the world together, and, as they leave, the film gives the viewer one last reminder about Cayden's newfound hard masculinity, which has essentially replaced every other form of masculinity he's tried on during the course of the film's narrative arc. "Big Bad Wolf" by The Heavy plays, with the notable chorus of "I'm the big bad wolf, and I'm blowing down your neighborhood." Through Angelina, then, Cayden discovers that, rather than caring for an individual, protecting them becomes paramount, and he is willing to kill, main, or frighten other people to do so. Like Will Randall in *Wolf*, Cayden not only becomes a wolf, but he does so *and* gets the girl, and they can live together by embracing their inner animal.

Wolves, then, is a figurative descendent of *Wolf* in many ways. Primarily, the tacit endorsement of a much more hardened edge of masculinity. The young male wolves in the film who all battle one another do so violently, and they pursue sex violently as well. The older male wolves have lost almost all their vitality and, really, their will to live. In many ways, they are a generation that has become almost too human compared to their wolf selves; *Wolves* pushes back against this notion by endorsing the full embrace of the wolf, its powers, and its inherent violence. Everything is re-ordered into a more correct pattern for the film's protagonist through violence or aggression, and the benefits are assumed by both the human male and their wolf half.

Wolf Cop and *Another Wolf Cop*

The werewolf film has become ubiquitous enough to bear the true hallmark of popularity: parodies and humorous takes on the genre. Within these humorous takes, which often toil fertile ground by expanding the core concepts of "serious" werewolf films, lies exploded interrogations of gender and gender roles. Thus, more humorous takes on the genre, from *Wolf Cop* to *Teen Wolf* to *What We Do in the Shadows*, lay bare the gender politics that has often confounded critics and aficionados of the genre.

Of all the parodies, however, *Wolf Cop* is not only one of the most absurd, but also one of the most pointed (and graphic) depictions of burgeoning hegemonic masculinity. The appropriately named Lou Garou is a deputy in the local sheriff's office, and when we first meet him, the viewer immediately is made to understand two distinct facets of his personality: he's a drunk and a womanizer. Neither of these are "good" portrayals of masculinity, and he's immediately revealed to be marginalized at work as well. He arrives late, is excoriated by the sheriff, and is immediately compared to his far more capable female counterpart Tina. It becomes clear that the only reason Garou is still a deputy is because his deceased father was a deputy at one time, too. However, the viewer also soon learns that Garou is being left in his position so that the local townspeople—all of them long-lived shapeshifters—can infect him with the curse of the werewolf and then drink his blood so that they can continue their near-immortal lifespans.

After his infection, Lou becomes a somehow *better* (or at least, the film seems to endorse it) version of himself. During his transformation, he literally peels off his human skin to reveal the wolf within. The wolf is more violent, more sexually aggressive, and even becomes more powerful (rather than, one assumes, less powerful) when he consumes liquor and donuts. The wolf version of Lou is still completely humanoid in appearance, however, which seems to be the norm for many parodies of the genre. Lou's wolf form walks upright, wears the police uniform, shoots his service weapon, and speaks, albeit in more guttural, almost indecipherable, words. Wolf Lou, in other words, is better than Human Lou, precisely because he becomes more competent and confident in his masculinity. Human Lou is a near-complete failure at life.

During perhaps the most absurd portion of the film, the Wolf Lou has been placed in a jail cell by his supposed friend Will, so the wolf can't escape and wreak havoc. Eventually, barkeep Jessica shows up, a woman whom Lou has obviously pined for. Jessica dismisses Will, and the Jessica and Wolf Lou have a prolonged bout of lovemaking, complete with slow pans and dissolves in a send-up of the softcore pornography genre. Wolf Lou has, it seems, even managed to capture the love interest of Human Lou with little struggle. This scene is echoed in *Another Wolf Cop*, the sequel, when Lou Garou comes across a woman who is herself a wolf; their sex scene is reversed, with Garou in human form. In this regard, Lou's human form becomes highly feminized, as he becomes subservient to the female wolf, who, in delicate terms, is rather rough with him.

Lou's initial transformation into a wolf in *Wolf Cop*, interestingly, begins with his penis. As in *Ginger Snaps* with the character of Jason, Lou begins to urinate blood in ever increasing volume. His penis (which, for a rarity in all of cinema, is shown onscreen) enlarges and sprouts hair, before the rest of his body follows in transformation. There is little doubt that Lou's wolf form is not only more well-endowed, but also symbolically far more masculine and toxic in his action and his intent. Lou is no longer a lovable loser when he turns into a werewolf: he is a violent sexual dynamo. Lou's penis makes an additional appearance in *Another Wolf Cop*, very early in the film, when he stands up without his uniform's pants on. The penis itself defies description, but his co-worker Tina's response—"You'll poke an eye out with that thing"— reveals a heavily masculinized and sexually aggressive wolf, both mentally and physically.

By the end of the film, Lou is hunted by the combined group of shapeshifters, who reveal themselves to be almost everyone he has known, save for his fellow officer Tina. In a protracted and bloody battle, with many deaths. At the end, Lou is left to face off against his boss, the police chief who has been harassing him the entire film. Of course, Lou is victorious (with some help from Tina), and the two of them walk out of the woods, arms around one another. He has taken his toxicity and turned it into a more protective hegemonic masculinity.

It is important not to mistake *Wolf Cop*'s often amusing send-up of masculinity for an outright endorsement. Lou Garou is a super-sized example of numerous men in werewolf cinema. Like David in *An American Werewolf in London*, for example, Lou cannot consummate a relationship as a pursuer until he becomes infected with the wolf curse. And, like Larry Talbot in *The*

Wolf Man, Garou is an outcast in his own world—shunned by his fellow police officers (or, in the case of Talbot, his family), and set adrift in a sea of barely realized understandings on how human interactions should work.

The sequel to *Wolf Cop*, called *Another Wolf Cop*, is a study in the fine line between parody and homage. The sequel wears its mockery of masculinity on its sleeve, quite literally, as the promotional art—of a Wolf Man dressed in a police uniform and holding a gun against a red background—is a clear send-up of the Sylvester Stallone film *Cobra*. In *Cobra*, Stallone's character, Cobretti (whose nickname is Cobra), is one of any number of Stallone/Schwarzenegger 1980s action film heroes, who solves problems by shooting them, blowing them up, or punching them senseless.[13] The tagline for the film—"Dirtier. Hairer."—references another highly masculinized film franchise, Clint Eastwood's "Dirty Harry" series, whose protagonist, despite his much slighter frame, is still the sort of action hero who would rather shoot bad guys than talk to them. Lou Garou, in the span of two films, moves to a more toxic form of masculinity, modeled after the "shoot first, questions later" mindset of the 1980s action stars, who "represented an idealized image of American heroism and working-class masculinity—violent, independent, white, muscular, and victorious" (Gates 111). Ultimately, *Another Wolf Cop* follows many of the same tropes and plot elements of *Wolf Cop*, but manages to emphasize gore, and may even fail to successfully parody itself, leading to a hollowed-out parody that fails to ring as true as *Wolf Cop* does. Lou Garou appears first in werewolf form and stops a robbery by dismembering and beheading four criminals. The over-the-top sequence, which includes Lou's police car, complete with a stylized W emblazoned on the hood, ends with the local police force investigating the remnants of the bodies in somewhat graphic detail. Lou's savagery is played for comedy, but there's little question that the moral haze that surrounded *Wolf Cop* has been entirely lifted: Lou, despite his faults, is meant to be a hero.

Lou, in human form, had promised now-police chief Tina that he would stay hidden, but he consistently refuses to lock himself away—a clear break from most werewolf males who feel remorse over their actions. By comparison, Lou, who has set up a mini-apartment in a meat locker, is overly pleased with his actions as a wolf, and his newfound toxic masculinity as a wolf bleeds over into his life as a human. Posters of semi-naked women adorn his walls, he walks around without pants or underwear, and drinks heavily—gone is the guilt over his alcoholism that appeared in the first film. Lou, in human form, is still the loser in a lot of ways, but, in *Wolf Cop*, he felt guilt and a desire to do better at everything: romance, police work, combating his alcoholism. In *Another Wolf Cop*, Lou still faces the same challenges, but no longer cares, and, in fact, even embraces the roles he worked hard to eschew in the original film: he's a hard drinker without shame and feels no remorse or surprise at his wolf powers. As a result, he moves from lovable loser afflicted with a sometimes-terrifying curse to an abrasive male whose sole existence, it seems, revolves around the benefits of his curse. He seeks no friendship or counsel, and he delights in his abilities to maim and terrorize. In fact, the film's rubric is clear from the opening moments: despite his uncivilized nature, Lou Garou's wolf form is really the only protection that the citizens can look to. Yes, he is absurdly violent, and yes, he is hard drinking and self-destructive (often hallmarks of the action heroes *Another Wolf Cop* sends up), but, in the end, the wolf is what makes Lou Garou "worth" something. In *Another Wolf Cop*, Garou is not the hero of the piece, and he even plays second fiddle to the true hero: his wolf form.

The interior struggle that fuels so much of the werewolf genre is almost entirely dependent on definitions of gender, specifically masculinity. In many regards, the cursed male must either reconcile themselves with their newfound and uncontrollable wildness, or otherwise perishing as a result. In many ways, as werewolf cinema split in two between *An American Werewolf in Paris* and *The Howling*, two clear paths emerged: the cursed male could be destroyed by their werewolf sides, either by the forces of society or by their own hand, or the cursed male could delight in their newfound and primitive toxicity, learning how to become more of a culturally acceptable man via the wolf itself. That the films that endorsed the more assertive aspects of masculinity that were brought forward by the wolf curse coincided with the growing cultural concerns about the "soft" and more domesticated male is no accident. In the end, these interior struggles between varying poles of masculinity identity remain a hallmark of werewolf film.

Under Siege
The Wolf Outside the Door

Interestingly, the journey to becoming a werewolf (or to stop being one, or to kill one) is often a solitary exercise. In most werewolf cinema, the person with the curse of lycanthropy is on a path of abject loneliness even before they have been cursed, and that loneliness is heightened after the curse. A few friends, perhaps, or lovers, are the only people who appear in the afflicted person's orbit. In *An American Werewolf in London*, for example, David Kessler is supported only by his nurse/lover, Alex Price. Even his friend, Jack, appears to David in a series of nightmarish visions to encourage David to kill himself. In both versions of *The Wolf Man*, Lawrence Talbot receives support only from Gwen Conliffe. Even in films where the werewolf is the exterior enemy, such as *Late Phases*, only one person, in this case, Ambrose, stands against the wolves with only some minor moral support from his son and the local priest.

Dog Soldiers

Yet, some films do address a pack, both male and wolf, and these films will sometimes place a set of wolves and a set of men in opposition to one another. Like many "base under siege" plots, however, the team of men rarely functions well together, often devolving into hyper-competiveness, backstabbing, or outright cowardice as the wolves pick them off one by one. Of this list, the most critically successful film is *Dog Soldiers*. The sparest plot sets up the action: a platoon of soldiers are sent to the Scottish Highlands on a routine training mission. However, they soon discover that the training mission is leading them to a pack of werewolves that are in the woods. Panicked and wounded, the group stumbles across a Land Rover driven by a local resident, Megan, who takes them back to her cabin. There, the standoff begins.

Each man in the unit veers from disbelief to terror as the truth about their situation unfolds. However, each is part of a larger group, a pack of what Jack Donovan calls "simulated masculinity," where "primal gang aggression and gang bonding are directly simulated through precipitation in military service, police service, and similar 'guardian' activities" (97).[1] In Donovan's formulation, the platoon, as they engage in the military exercise are engaged in the basest and most primitive expression of masculinity. Ironically, in the breaks between the military action, other forms on Donovan's scale emerge, and a more rounded portrait of masculinity emerges. Joe and Terry discuss an "important" football match between Germany and England, and their desires to be watching that instead of being on a military exercise. Joe falls silent about "missing the footy," however, when Sergeant Wells reminisces about his former military buddy Eddie, who stumbled across an anti-tank mine, and, in Wells's words, "it really puts things in perspective when you have to scoop your mate up and put him in a bin-bag." The story quiets the group, and Donovan's scale of masculinity moves to, for many of the men, "vicarious masculinity," in which "males watch other males participate in team or individual sports" or "watch other males demonstrate strength courage, mastery, or honor" (97). In other words, the soldiers, introduced to us (except for Cooper) as a group of "hard" masculine stereotypes, slowly reveal that civilization itself, and the act of only being a part-time military member, has kept them, at the least, well within the ideas of "soft" masculinity. Many of the men, except for Sergeant Wells and Private Wells, are everyday workers outside of the military, and engage only in part-time violence, most likely for the pay it brings.

The rubric of *Dog Soldiers*, then, is revealed: to survive the pack of werewolves, the pack of soldiers need to, for the most part, embrace a version of masculinity that seems foreign to them: violent and toxic. As the siege on their tiny house continues, the men not only rely on training, but on hegemonic banter to stay focused. "More like pussies," Terry says about the wolves. Spoon, about to be killed, tells the wolf, "I hope I give you the shits, you fucking wimp." Wells commands Cooper to knock him out, or he's a "fucking pussy." Cooper, as we will see, the most civilized or the least "hard" male of the group, taunts Ryan, asking his wolf form, "Have you tried licking your balls yet?" before quickly adding, "I forgot, you don't have any."

The numerous "macho" quotes only arrive when the men are faced with the werewolf attack, and, as a result, the film seemingly endorses hegemonic and toxic masculinity. At one point, Wells even loses most of his intestines, resulting in Cooper getting him drunk, stuffing them back in, and supergluing the wound shut, in what can only be an over-the-top act of machismo in the vein of Rambo's wound treatments. However, the film's central character is Cooper, and there's a rather large significance to his story and his ending—the film, in the end, rejects the hegemonic and toxic masculinity that many of the men and their wolf opponents engage in. Indeed, Cooper manages to survive by staying grounded and logical, and his bookended story—refusing to kill a dog for a promotion, and saving a dog—indicates that Cooper's version of level-headed, often hard, masculinity is the way to survive.

Private Cooper is a capable and adept soldier, and has earned the respect of his platoon. Yet, what starts as a symbol of weakness for Private Cooper turns into a symbol of strength. At the start of the film, in a flashback, during training exercises for special forces, Private Cooper is commanded by Captain Ryan to shoot a dog. Ryan's commands are little more than an effort to determine where Cooper stands in his masculinity. "I don't need a man of conscience," Ryan sneers, dismissing Cooper's explanation that he "couldn't kill a dog," but "will not kill a dog for no reason." Ryan ultimately shoots and kills the dog in front of Cooper. Later, while trapped with his platoon in the cabin, he takes care of the family collie in between preparations, much to Ryan's chagrin. Ryan chides Cooper as the battle between wolves and men begins to tilt toward the wolves. "You failed," sneers Ryan, "because you didn't take that extra step." That "extra step" is the tilt from Cooper's version of masculinity toward Ryan's version.

Even so, Cooper takes the lead of the troop when Sergeant Wells is seriously injured, and Captain Ryan is captured, and Cooper ultimately is the only soldier that survives the onslaught. Cooper first defeats the assorted werewolves of the family on his own, after cutting a gas line and setting the very air around him ablaze, killing the wolf family. He ends up in the cellar, where he must defeat a freshly transformed Ryan; Cooper does this by deftly using a letter opener as a weapon, before shooting the Ryan wolf in the head. Although Cooper survives through violence, and he also mocks Ryan's "balls" before killing the wolf, Cooper is clearly the ideal version of masculinity in *Dog Soldiers*. He picks and chooses his battles, cares for his men, and only kills out of necessity. Unlike many of the men in his platoon, who seem to enjoy the tension and the battle itself ("You're bloody loving this, aren't you?" Joe asks Spoon), often resorting to bravado, both verbal and physical, Cooper is content to plan things out, ordering the men to count out the bullets and gather assorted brickbats for their own protection. At one point, Cooper chastises Ryan for not viewing the men in his platoon as individuals: "now he's dead along with two other mates I'd have rightfully given my right arm for. Too fuckin' right it's relevant," he says. Cooper is, in the end, the only soldier to survive, and most of this is due to his quick thinking rather than his muscles or his inherent violence. And, of course, as *Dog Soldiers* ends, Cooper's reluctance to kill in cold blood returns, as he symbolically leaves the remains of the house with Megan's border collie in tow.

Howl

Howl, like many "under siege" stories, produces a series of masculine definitions that the protagonist must navigate, all the while fending off werewolf attacks. In this case, the main character is an English train guard named Joe, who, from the very outset of the film, is presented as decidedly de-masculinized. Upon arriving at work, a letter in his locker informs him (and the viewer) that he did not receive a promotion to supervisor; instead, that promotion went to a much smarmier and more assertive man, who immediately assigns Joe a double shift. When Joe balks at the order, the new supervisor challenges him to be "a man," a challenge which Joe reluctantly accepts, if only because his unrequited love interest, a train steward named Ellen, is on the same train. Later, Joe confesses to Ellen that the reason he wanted to become supervisor was so that people would "notice" him, and, indeed, Joe spends much of the first half of the movie sinking into the background and being ignored or castigated by the other members of the cast.

Once aboard the train, Joe's domesticated masculinity becomes more starkly defined. He is good at "caring" for the passengers, Ellen assures him, before rejecting Joe's offer to meet for coffee. Joe abashedly asserts himself to a woman who has lost a ticket, and then cannot stand up to a young teen female, named Nina, who dismisses him as a "perv" before continuing to ignore him. In all corners, Joe finds himself humiliated, or otherwise, under assault. At one point, immediately after Ellen's rejection, another man, Adrian,[2] begins flirting openly with her, which she reciprocates.

There is a moment in which Adrian and Joe spend a few moments together that creates an endorsement of Joe's burgeoning shift in his own masculine identity, and it is also the moment where Adrian as a character moves from slightly insufferable to dangerous and overbearing. Pulling Joe aside, he pulls out two sets of keys. One, he explains, is for the ideal married life: kids, wife, home in the suburbs. The other set is an expensive flat in the city where he can enjoy "discreet" encounters. Adrian uses this to make an unusual analogy: that people do what they must to survive, and he asks Joe to let him leave the train and the two of them will leave behind the "weak" set of passengers to survive. Later, Adrian is confronted by a businesswoman, who was also on the train. Kate remembers him, for she went for an interview at his company, only to have him leer at her the entire time (presumably to set up a "discreet" encounter). He responds that he doesn't remember her, but he remembers her type: one whose femininity and sexuality is essentially lost at pregnancy, who becomes a drain on the company, and one, Adrian alludes, who quickly loses her vitality and attractiveness. By this point, Adrian has clearly become the negative version of masculinity in the film—one in which he is held up in stark contrast to Joe's nurturing leadership, Billy's technical knowledge, and Ged's loyalty to his wife, for example. By the time Adrian takes a wrench from Kate and leaves her for dead, it is clear he becomes the villain of the piece.[3]

Indeed, along with Adrian, there are several masculine identities at play within the train. Adrian's assertive and sometimes sexually aggressive nature is offset by Ged, Matthew, Sam, and Paul. Ged is the cantankerous old man who wants to simply go home. Matthew is the nerdy individual, who, when the train screeches to a halt, is most concerned that he lost his page in the book he was reading. Sam is a small engine mechanic who has immense technical knowledge. Paul is the overweight sports fan who is a bit slow. In each of these characters lies a stereotypical "base under siege" character, all of which are in direct opposition not necessarily to the wolves or the women within the train, but to Joe, whose sense of orderliness and calm is consistently under pressure from their various demands.

It is only when the werewolves attack, disabling the train, that Joe begins to reorder his own masculine boundaries. This process is first seen when he snatches the teenage girl's cigarette out of her mouth and grinds it on the floor. Yet, Joe's transformation moves in stops and sputters—he is upset about the cigarette but refuses to force Nina off her phone. Her constant chattering and singing in the designated "quiet zone" of the train irritates everyone, but Joe lets it slide. In other words, Joe's masculinity is a work in progress, and at the halfway point of the film, he remains more nurturing than commanding—he implores the train passengers to "relax" and "stay calm," temporarily ceding the authority role to Adrian. It is only when Adrian's unseemly toxic masculinity comes to the fore—after his revelations about his multiple affairs, for example—that Joe begins to attack Adrian, which Adrian dryly notes that means Joe has "finally grown a pair" and has become "a man."

But has he? From Adrian's perspective, Joe's turn toward violence, which manifests itself in Joe ordering the passengers to tie up Adrian, and his later punching of Adrian, is a symbol of his newfound masculinity, which has tinges of toxicity. However, Joe is simply speaking Adrian's language in many ways: Adrian trades in violence, both sexual and physical, and he is quick to resort to victimizing others to maintain his place atop the other males (and females) in the train.

Almost every heroic male figure in *Howl* exhibits their masculinity in varying fashions during the final confrontation. Billy, upset that he did not gain admission to an engineering program, manages to fix the train's fuel pump, redeeming himself and his technical knowledge. Matthew overcomes his nerdiness to hack a wolf to bits with an axe, later telling Billy that he "didn't know what came over" him, only to get killed while trying to rescue—on his own—an already destroyed Nina. And Joe not only beats the wolf to death again with a fire extinguisher (apparently, the wolf got better), but also leads the remaining members of the group to safety. Ged is killed by his wife after she turns into a werewolf, his loyalty betrayed, but still loyal to the end. Only Paul and Adrian do not necessarily get their moments of heroism, quite possibly because the film is stylized to assert preference of one form of masculinity over another. Paul and Adrian's deaths are no doubt the results of their own selfish actions. Paul dies because he undoes a gate, leaves the group, and goes to the bathroom, the victim of his own excesses, and Adrian himself eventually dies, punished for his toxic masculinity.

It is the final sequences of the film that problematizes Joe's masculinity. *Howl* simply turns from a standard "base under siege" story and switches to a narrative focusing on Joe's decision to embrace the more violent aspects of his masculinity, or, at least, to reject his previously soft masculinity. After Billy dies ensuring that Joe and Ellen can escape, the wolves quickly track the pair down. In a chivalric move, Joe stays behind the delay the wolves so that Ellen can run. The alpha wolf squares off against Joe, and Joe holds his own, repeatedly stabbing the wolf before finally succumbing. The "twist" in the film, however, is that Joe, in his final battle, is not eaten like the others (the transformation of Ged's wife only occurs because she is rescued before she can be consumed) but is turned into a wolf; one can assume that the alpha wolf has somehow deemed him worthy of joining the pack. Thus, when Adrian, alone and on the run, sees Joe, he is partially metamorphosed: mostly man, but with the fangs and claws of the wolf. Joe attacks Adrian as the credits roll, and thus, Joe takes his place, temporarily, at least, atop the food chain of the humans. The alpha male Adrian meets his match (and then some) in the newly minted alpha male of Joe.

Howl, therefore, seems to point toward the complete embrace of what made Adrian such an unseemly character in the first place. Joe's violent assault upon Adrian indicates that, in Joe, the wolves have found someone who has a propensity for violence and rage in humans, indicating that Joe's meekness is not the result of some new matriarchal or soft form of masculinity, but rather the outward sign of his ability to contain his barely repressed rage. The way he cares for passengers is quickly replaced by his unbridled and murderous aggression. He moves from motherer to murderer, yet the film endorses his sudden toxic, violence-based masculinity as he eliminates his male rival but does so after saving Ellen. Joe's supposed sacrifice is more of an embrace of his curse and follows his continuing desire as a male to simply *be noticed* as a man by those whom he seeks romantic involvement. Unlike many of the male characters in werewolf cinema before him, Joe embraces his curse to further his own notions of masculinity. Presumably, with his alpha male enemy out of the way, he can more rigorously pursue Ellen and enjoy a more commanding (and demanding) masculine profile.

Late Phases

The ongoing saga of Man versus Wolf continues in *Late Phases* (2014), in which a blind war veteran squares off against a werewolf that is slowly killing the residents of an assisted living community. Ambrose McKinley is a rugged individual, taciturn and often sarcastic in his responses to those around him, and he clearly has little patience for the concept of being in a retirement community. His decline, from his perspective, had been poorly predicted by his own son and his daughter-in-law, who constantly cajole him to try to fit in to the community.

Eventually, Ambrose's backstory reveals a man who has, over time, become slowly aware that the world he has envisioned has faded and been replaced by something he no longer recognizes. At one point in the film, he speaks about having to shoot a six-year-old child that had a grenade strapped to his chest during the Vietnam War. This experience was something that severely jaded his views not only of the war itself (although Ambrose consistently introduces himself as a veteran throughout the film, indicating that it is an important part of his masculine identity), but also of humanity. Ambrose returned from the war with "eye trauma," but he was "too stubborn" to see a doctor about it until he had gone completely blind—something which Father Roger Smith wonders aloud is some sort of penance for Ambrose's actions during the war. Ambrose replies, simply, "maybe." Ambrose also speaks frequently of his desire to die ("I couldn't stand to look at the world anyway," he explains to Smith about his blindness), but not in the way, as many of the other character seem to think, of suicide or a slow fading away. The werewolf in *Late Phases* is Ambrose's last chance to die in battle, to embrace a rather vainglorious end rather than an embarrassing one. It is an act of redemption.

Ambrose's desires to kill the werewolf are not necessarily stemming from a desire to help the retirement community (as a matter of fact, he seems to dislike almost everyone in the community), but he rather sees one last chance for a sort of redemption, a way to embrace and reassert a tragic masculinity. Ambrose's odd decisions throughout the film, decisions that his son, Will, considered as potential indicators of senility or just being a mean person, have been made with a plan in place. For example, Ambrose's long, slow digging of his guide dog Shadow's grave, even going so far as to leave Shadow rotting in a tarp next to the grave, and then his incongruous decision to spend a significant amount of money on a headstone, is Ambrose's rendition of a pit trap, which partially works: the werewolf falls into the grave and gets hit by the headstone, pulled over by Ambrose. Ambrose's townhouse looks unkempt, full of boxes never unpacked, and messy, and Will chides him for it, but the boxes and materials have all been moved so that Ambrose has any number of hiding places and places for cover, all of which he has memorized by counting out loud as he walks. Ambrose is fine with seeming senile, so long as he can enjoy a distinct tactical advantage.

It's also important to note that Ambrose is really the only person in the film to put together the presence of the werewolf—he feels the claw marks on the wall, hears and smells the creature as it attacks his next-door neighbor—and move to kill it. His blindness is less of a disability, and more of a different way of "seeing" things. Although he is quickly dismissed by almost everyone as a man who is not whole—someone who needs assistance with everything, and who is lost without that help—Ambrose is truly the most complete male in the film. Ambrose is an action star for the male of the 2000s. No longer muscle-bound, now elderly, and relying on help, he is still cagey, perceptive and resourceful. In many ways, Ambrose is John Rambo[4] or John Matrix aged forward a few decades. Wounded, elderly, but still dangerous, and much more perceptive and able than anyone else in the film.

James's transformation reveals a dualism in Ambrose and the werewolf. Whereas James has turned to religion in an attempt to sate the beast, Ambrose has simply turned away from everything. As he tells Will in a phone message, Ambrose had let "something black" grow within him, a process which divided Ambrose from his family and essentially ruined every stage of his life. It is not surprising, then, that when Smith begins to transform into a werewolf, he does so from the inside out. His shift to a wolf involves the usual growing of nails and claws, but also the peeling away of his own flesh. The human body is a cocoon for the wolf within, just as Ambrose had successfully created his own hard shell for protection.

In the final act, then, are two "black" entities battling one another: Ambrose, who dons his old Army uniform for the final battle, versus the wolf. Each of them is now free after years of attempts to keep their own traumas within, and, especially in the case of Ambrose, the only true way to overcome the "black" nature of their existence is simply to assure their death. For Ambrose, his only option is to die a heroic death; he cannot exist any further in the world. He knows that his battle with the werewolves will quite possibly lead to his demise, or, worse, his own infection, and it seems like that holds true early in the standoff when he gets severely injured. Ambrose, however, has ensured his own destruction: he has purposefully taken an overdose of pills in a delayed suicide of sorts. His redemption is tied in with his impending death. Thus, the tragedy at the core of *Late Phases*: neither man nor wolf can wholly exist, and the meaning they find in each other (Ambrose seems more active and moves with more purpose when he is preparing for his battle) leads to the battle that ultimately causes their destruction. Both find purpose in the final battle, and the final battle must also end with their demise.

At least, that's how Ambrose sees it. In the days leading up to the final battle, he makes amends with his son, puts the house (literal and figurative) in order, and feasts on nostalgia, going so far as to, as stated previously, put on his old uniform from his youth. At one point, Ambrose cloyingly tells his son "I wasn't just blind in my eyes, I was blind in my heart." Ambrose's newfound sense of purpose, as Jeanette Catsoulis writes, means that "Ambrose was resigned to death's waiting room; now, he has a reason to work out." Ambrose's hard masculinity, then, revives itself one last time, and he becomes, once more, the "warrior" male that Robert Bly fondly remembers, but, in a retirement community, there is no room for warriors, and Ambrose senses this. His battle is self-contained; final. He has no plans to survive the battle, and he dies sitting on a chair, like some sort of ancient king who survived a war but did not live long enough to see the peace. Ambrose successfully embraces and then exterminates "the black"—here, represented by the wolves who show up at his door—and his primary hope is that his final heroism and his embrace of a more natural "warrior" masculinity, which includes the hegemonic protective care of his family—can purge the memories of his toxic masculinity, all of the bad decisions he made as a father. Ambrose acknowledges that "the only thing [he] was good at was being a soldier," and therefore, he falls back on this version of masculinity—violent and toxic—one last time, but this time, it is to save the townspeople from the wolves.

The final battle, then, is symbolic, and, if one removes werewolves from the equation, Ambrose's "black" could be any symbols of toxicity, really: physical or mental abuse, drug dependence, and so on. Ambrose "tries on" multiple masculine identities: his initial domestic, "soft" form, which is reliant on others for help, gives way to some mild toxicity in the way he treats other around him—a toxicity that his family would acknowledge informed many of their dealings with him. His desire to stop the wolf is born of a protective hegemonic masculinity—if no one wants to stop the wolf, it's left up to him, and the battle itself shows a more hardened perspective on life, including Ambrose's lack of place in the more modern world he finds himself in.

In many ways, *Late Phases* refuses to let Ambrose appear to be anything but superhuman at times. He hears and senses things that other people cannot. He is, although this defies reality, decidedly not a skeptic when it comes to the possibility of werewolves, and his embrace of his theory is immediate and unyielding. Not only does he concoct a forward-thinking plan that no one else in the housing development can anticipate, but he manages to kill several werewolves, not just one, when James manages to infect three others immediately prior to the film's climax. All the oddities in Ambrose's behavior—his refusal to bury his dead seeing eye dog, his purchase of an extraordinarily large stone for the dog's memorial—are all revealed to be traps he has set for the wolf, and he often proceeds with his plan despite the opprobrium of his neighbors. His "blackness" has given him the ability to "see" what others cannot, and, in embracing it, he also embraces his own demise. He redeems himself, and, when his son, Will, fires a round from Ambrose's rifle in his honor, has repaired all his relationships.

Enemy, Mother, Lover, Object
Women in Werewolf Cinema

One of the possible reasons that the werewolf has struggled to diversify its depictions of gender is the cinematic history of the wolf when compared to other monsters. Alongside Dracula and Frankenstein (or, for purists, his monster), the werewolf has rarely progressed to address issues of gender. This is simply a matter of a philosophical inquiry on the matter of being human. In many ways, vampires, for example, allow for a deeper questioning of the distance between life and death, between human and undead. The same holds true for other monsters such as Frankenstein's creation: the question of what makes one "human" is the very centerpiece of *Frankenstein*. As a result the source novels of *Dracula* and *Frankenstein* have been well examined for their roles in questioning and examining often tenuous gender boundaries in their work and have long been well within the literary canon; there, conversely, remains no culminating central source for werewolf lore, as the wolf remains the crux of a hodgepodge of folklore and legends, and, as such, is somewhat distilled by a lack of a cohesive "origin" point around which numerous authors, artists, and filmmakers can gather.

One need only consider how little time elapsed between sympathetic portrayals of women in the other franchises when compared to the cinematic adaptations of werewolves, vampires, and Frankenstein's monster. A more nuanced portrayal of the feminine and masculine identities appears just four years after *Frankenstein* in *Bride of Frankenstein*. In 1936, five years after *Dracula*, *Dracula's Daughter* appeared, and critics have repeatedly examined the gendered identities in that film, especially the lesbian overtones (which will come to dominate depictions of female vampires in the 1970s forward).[1]

Yet, for *The Wolf Man*, whose gender identity is even centralized in the title, no such quick turnaround exists. Three years after *The Wolf Man*, the film *Cry of the Werewolf* depicts cinema's first female werewolf (Senn 57), but the depiction is one that is fraught with less-than-subtle criticisms toward female sexuality, unlike *Bride of Frankenstein* and *Dracula's Daughter*, which both addressed gender identities within their narratives, and have received increasing critical attention in the past few decades. Both *Dracula's Daughter* and *Bride of Frankenstein*, for example, carry "homosexual undertones" including "homosexual or bisexual vampires" or "queer" relationships between males (Benshoff 47–48).

In *Dracula's Daughter*, for example, there is substantial use of imagery and coded language regarding gender identity, specifically, in this case, lesbianism. Those watching the film in the 1930s, writes Elizabeth Erwin, "would easily equate normalcy to heterosexuality" as Marya, the vampiric woman, seeks to "be cured of her inner conflicts" (18). *Bride of Frankenstein*, too, explores gender roles and gender dynamics; the Bride contains within her form "notions of desire, perfection, and spectatorship" (Hawley 224) and is successful in "deploying characters in new ways" (Hawley 229). In the end, both *Dracula's Daughter* and *Bride of Frankenstein* were new, fresh interpretations that allowed for new critical interpretations; the Wolf Man, alongside other Universal monsters such as The Creature, The Mummy, and even The Invisible Man, all suffered from a lack of meaningful sequels that struck new ground on their initial narratives.

Thus, even though Lon Chaney, Jr., centered Larry Talbot as a semi-immortal Wolf Man for several films, the aspect of the werewolf was concentrated so much on the masculine experience that while other creatures entered cinematic lore, the werewolf was soon consigned to the same dustbins as *The Creature from the Black Lagoon* or *The Mummy*, reappearing in fits and starts throughout Western cinema, and never quite enjoying such vigorous critical renewals and reinterpretations as those related to *Frankenstein* or *Dracula*. The werewolf, unlike the vampire or Frankenstein's monster, is, even in folklore and literature, often shorn of nuance, embodying "the ancient dichotomy of the dog—between the intuitive, loyal companion, and the savage, potentially rabid beast—with each pole of the dualism merely ratcheted out a notch" (Wasik and Murphy 74). In fact, most critical interpretations of werewolves only really lead toward two conclusions: the wolf as "admirable and superhuman or as malignant and subhuman" (Bernhardt-House 160). There also seems to be precious little that would separate the werewolf from any number of other relatively alien or faceless monsters in cinematic history: "Werewolves have been consistently portrayed as outlaws, not only because they transgress the laws of society and stand outside of its boundaries, but because the ordered logic of society is unable even to account for, classify, or assimilate their existence" (Bernhardt-House 179). If, for example, one looks at the Universal horror series, it's little wonder that films such as *Frankenstein* and *Dracula* remain long-lived concepts. Not only did these stories come from an esteemed place in the literary canon, but they also focused, almost exclusively, on what it means to be "human," complete with motivations that help viewers identify, even if only in passing, with vampires and creations sewn together from corpses. The werewolf has little to offer in this regard. They are either human or they are not; they are either good or they are feral (bad). There is precious little depth to the characters, and thus, *The Wolf Man*, in spite of the original popularity the film enjoyed, spawning numerous sequels, slipped away from the mainstream, joining other non-human creatures as *The Creature from the Black Lagoon*, *The Mummy*, and *The Invisible Man*.

Additionally, the werewolf, in the literary canon, barely appears on the radar, with the most notable example of werewolf literature being the lowbrow penny dreadful novel *Wagner the Wehr-Wolf* by George W.M. Reynolds, a novel known, perhaps, only to the advanced English literature student. This is the issue: the man is the man, and the wolf is the wolf. The separation of the two doesn't allow for much nuance or questioning of what makes one "human."

In fact, werewolf cinema will go a very long time without what viewers and critics would accept as even an attempt at a rounded depiction of female werewolf: almost 60 years will elapse between *The Wolf Man* and *Ginger Snaps*. Werewolves, in whatever form or gender they take in cinema, have long resided as a sort of backbench monster, giving way to the Frankenstein and vampire tales; indeed, most narratives with vampires *and* werewolves, such as *House of Dracula*, *What We Do in the Shadows*, *Twilight*, or *Underworld* focus almost exclusively on the vampiric perspective. Shorn of most nuance, or with the nuance already presupposed through a large back catalog of folklore, the werewolf simply has not been able to maintain a sustained critical interrogation, and, as a result, female werewolves are rarely seen; the commentary of the wolf as masculine has simply dominated and otherwise stifled the narrative potential.

It should come as little surprise to horror fans and critics alike that women have often been depicted at the margins of werewolf cinema, a trend that has extended from the earliest silent horror films to the height of the 1980s slasher cinema. Like most horror films, women in werewolf films are often relegated to romantic interest status, victims, or marginal observers of their own story. Their primary purpose in many early werewolf films was to be a forsaken love interest for the man afflicted with the werewolf curse. Take, for example, the role of Jane in *Silver Bullet*, who narrates the story of how her uncle and her younger brother defeated a werewolf (also a male), often by recounting events that she was not present for (she is also "saved" by the duo). Since 2000, however, multiple films have started to feature women in more prominent roles in werewolf cinema, often by casting a new light on the werewolf itself—in these cases, such as in *Dog Soldiers*, *In the Company of Wolves*, *Trick 'r Treat*, and *Ginger Snaps*, the woman becomes the werewolf, neatly inverting the usual narrative and problematizing the traditional gender roles that have come to dominate werewolf cinema. The historical import of female werewolves is somewhat problematized by literary tradition, however, and can lead to radically altered interpretations of films such as *Trick 'r Treat* or *Ginger Snaps*. According to du Coudray, "Demonic women were usually young, beautiful, foreign, and dangerous, intent upon the deception and destruction of husbands, lovers, and other unsuspecting men. In the literature of female lycanthropy, such representations were recapitulated so frequently that it is possible to identify a cliché developing..." (47). But there's an issue that is deeper here. If masculinity is the key to male werewolves, then how does a female werewolf function in cinema? The question alone results in gender-bending possibilities, not the least of which is masculinized females, and vice versa. In this case, the idea that a masculinized female is the result of a "disembodied phenomenon, existing on its own outside the confines of a given type of body [...] without regard for the sex of the body possessing them" (Reeser 131), aligns well with the basic concept of the werewolf. After all, the curse is indeed a "disembodied phenomenon" that could strike almost anyone at random in nearly any location (although nature is usually the setting for the transmittal of the curse), and is a concept that often does occur "outside the confines" of the body, as the transformation almost always renders the human, if not completely invisible, then radically changed. Even though Ginger, for example, is still somewhat recognizable as Ginger during her slow change to a complete wolf, her overall appearance changes dramatically over the course of *Ginger Snaps*. Indeed, the young woman who transforms often seems to lose their identity more often than male characters. In films such as *Wolf*, *Werewolf* (1956), *Teen Wolf*, and *Wolves*, among many others, the male often remains closely identified with their human side, even when fully a wolf, often walking upright, wearing clothing, and conversing with others. This occurs far less frequently when a female becomes infected with the wolf curse. In films such as *Ginger Snaps*, *Trick 'r Treat*, and *The Company of Wolves*, the female body becomes entirely given over to their feral wolf form, unrecognizable as a human in almost every way. This could be interpreted as almost entirely symbolic of the loss of the female form, and the overtaking of masculinity as a new identity. Every symbolic representation of the female body is given over to a completely new form. In this regard, "female masculinity needs to be metaphorically male to function or to complete itself" (Sellers 136). Indeed, the young women who become infected with the curse of the wolf will often transition completely to wolf form by the end of the film, becoming that metaphorical—and problematic—masculine.

In this regard, the films that feature women who turn into wolves could also be fairly considered as gender bending. The young woman who becomes a wolf can be considered as one who, willingly or not, adopts primarily masculine characteristics. These gender conflicts manifest themselves in a variety of ways beyond the transformation into a wolf. Ginger in *Ginger Snaps*, for example, becomes sexually aggressive; Brigitte, in the same film, functions as the masculine Final Girl, overcoming her own sister's transformation; the young women in *Trick 'r Treat* are sexually assertive and aggressive, luring men to their often-bloody doom. Again, du Coudray has a salient observation, noting "Unrepentant hedonism and physicality of such female werewolves can be contrasted with the psychological torment experienced by their male counterparts" (du Coudray 55). Whereas Larry Talbot or David Kessler fear their wolf selves, Ginger delightfully proclaims, in contrast, "I'm a goddamned force of nature," and the female wolves in *Trick 'r Treat* likewise revel in their power. In many ways, this transformation can be read as a part of a long tradition of women seeking to earn new perspectives or power by adopting masculine traits. As Todd Reeser writers,

> a woman [who adopts the guise of the masculine] might be attempting to be a batter man than a man can be, one who displays traits coded as non-masculine or non-phallic such as intimacy or intuition. This response to masculinity may be a way to construct or to contribute to a new type of masculinity that a woman wished existed more commonly [139].

Reeser adds that the goal of creating a more masculine "presentation" is "not to reach masculinity [...] but to [...] subvert it from within" (139). In this regard, films that feature female werewolves do indeed subvert the expectations of the genre, but also do so by embracing the often-typical conventions of the masculine. In much the same way that films such as *Sleepaway Camp* problematize and question typical genre conventions for slasher films, this rather small set of films with female wolves often do the same, and, sometimes in the process, become problematic in their depictions of women as well.

Many critics and film reviewers have lauded *Ginger Snaps* for creating a "radical model" of broaching subjects of femininity and sexuality (in particular, menstruation) (Miller 281). Some of this gender confusion regarding women in werewolf cinema, of course, from the fact that werewolf cinema, as a part of the larger horror genre, is, as Peter Hutchings writes, "a 'male' genre, produced largely by men for a predominantly male audience and addressing specifically male fears and anxieties" (84). However, Hutchings continues, noting that even though horror films have long been accused of "compensating for feelings of inadequacy on the part of the male spectator" (84), they instead "puts the male spectator in the best position to witness and empathize with the victim's powerlessness" (87). In other words, films such as the *Ginger Snaps* trilogy may be less about creating a reasonable "twist" in a tried-and-true trope, and more about getting the still predominantly male audience to think a bit more about the issues facing women in horror and, in society. That's not to say that all of the films with female characters are perceptive; in fact, the opposite holds true, and, with the exception of very few films, including *Ginger Snaps*, *Trick 'r Treat*, and *The Company of Wolves*, struggle to incorporate female characters in any meaningful way, relying instead on the tropes of enemy, mother, lover, and/or objects throughout.

If this is the case, then, the question of how a female werewolf is depicted remains problematic. The difference lies, as usual, in the interpretation. As Barbara Creed notes, there are two distinct possibilities in many horror films in which women take lead roles: the phallic woman and the castrating woman. In Creed's words, to the male audience, the phallic woman is a "comforting phantasy of sexual sameness," whereas the castrating woman is "a terrifying phantasy of sexual difference" (158). Within these two very opposite poles are the roles of the female werewolf: they are either masculinized, embracing aspects of the masculine, or they are sexual predators, out to destroy the male. It is important to note, however, that regardless of the role of castrator or phallus, the horror film is "usually a sympathetic figure" (Creed 123), and this holds true in many werewolf films. Female characters routinely find themselves subjugated by society or the men in their lives before becoming werewolves, which often grants them some degree of terrifying (to themselves and to others) freedom and strength. When the women in *Trick 'r Treat*, for example, decide to prey on the men, dismembering them, the film works to make the viewer sympathize with the female wolves—after all, the most recognizable victim is a male serial killer, responsible for a few brutal deaths earlier in the film.

In many cases, female werewolves that are clearly objectified throughout the course of a film, as in *An American Werewolf in Paris*, would be a clear-cut case of a rather uncomfortable portrayal of a female character. Yet, if one accepts, for instance, that a female werewolf is, too, a curse, then films such as *Ginger Snaps* and *Dog Soldiers*, which feature female werewolves as capricious and cunning predators, are not the feminist-style icons that many reviewers declared them to be. Instead of sexual empowerment in *Ginger Snaps* or *Trick 'r Treat*, for example, the female werewolves are quite possibly more of the same, pulled from a tradition where the male is the inherent and hapless victim to the predations of female sexuality. Although April Miller, for example, argues that *Ginger Snaps* and its sequels focus on depicting the female experience in a radical and sympathetic light, her language when describing Ginger and Brigitte's werewolf forms shows the subversion, as typically male werewolf characteristics come to the forefront of their experience. Miller writes that the "status as werewolf" gives the cursed "considerable power," (296), and that Ginger is "bloodthirsty, sexually aggressive" (288), and derives "pleasure from killing" before being "eventually consumed by her violent sexual potency" (298).[2]

The "sympathetic" view that Peter Hutchings adopts simply does not hold, as, in many cases, the female werewolf is the killer, and, in many ways, she exists to portray a world (or gender) that is unfairly maligning masculinity in almost all forms. Thus, the appearance of Ginger's period[3] in *Ginger Snaps* becomes less of an allegory about female maturity, and more about how Ginger will now progress to damage the men in her life. This is the true "feminizing experience" (Hutchings 91) of the female werewolf: the presence of a female character who becomes a werewolf provides an often-steady threat to men by inverting the stereotypical gender roles of the film. The women adopt masculine traits, and the men become feminized, the pursued become the pursuers. In *Trick 'r Treat*, the female werewolves gather random strange men upon which to feast; in *Ginger Snaps*, the men who cross Ginger's (and later, Brigitte's) path are often, quite literally, the pursued.

The appearance of a female werewolf, then, forces a stricter examination of masculinity within the context of the film. One need only look at Ginger and Brigitte at the start of *Ginger Snaps*, who have successfully de-sexualized themselves, and, in some ways, already adopted the masculine. Judith Halberstam writes that "[t]omboyism tends to be associated with a 'natural' desire for the greater freedoms and mobilities enjoyed by boys" (358), and this sentiment blends well with Ginger and Brigitte's desires to leave their hometown and otherwise break out of the monotony of the suburbs. In many ways, the female werewolf is not only metatextually subversive—rejecting decades of recycled tropes and plots—but is also a consistent reminder that masculinity is an artificial construct that can be adopted by either sex. The disruptive presence of the female werewolf, then, lays bare the fact that "the male spectator['s ...] hold on power is structural and provisional rather than personal" (Hutchings 92). This dawning realization—that masculinity is constructed well outside of one's agency—is the source of much of the "tragic" form of masculinity. Men not only go the usual route of being victimized, but, in many ways, they learn that their autonomy simply doesn't exist: they serve at the whims of the female werewolves, who bring forward a more dominant version of masculinity. Alternatively, with few notable exceptions, the women who *aren't* werewolves in these films are often those without any sort of agency; they exist to be hunted, either romantically or literally.

Yet, this chapter won't be solely about female wolves, for that would be incredibly limiting as a concept. To further uncover how masculinity is depicted in werewolf cinema, especially the concept of the "tragic" male, it becomes exceptionally important to understand how female characters are often depicted in werewolf cinema, ranging from the earliest portrayals in *The Wolf Man* through *The Howling* and the films of Paul Naschy, among others. Even though these films focus on the man turning into a wolf as the main thrust of their narrative, the roles of the female characters in these films reveal an equally concerning and often hegemonic viewpoint.

Cry of the Werewolf

As the first surviving film to feature a female werewolf, *Cry of the Werewolf* breaks little new ground in terms of gender. The film functions as a strange police procedural for much of its runtime, as a pair of nattering detectives argue with one another about a murder that apparently involved a wild animal. The murderer, of course, is a werewolf, with the human side represented by a Gypsy woman named Celeste. Celeste is the "princess" of her Gypsy "tribe," and, as such, is tasked with protecting the group from all outsiders. Dr. Moore, a researcher, ventures too close to finding out the Gypsy secrets, and Celeste, in wolf form, is forced to murder him. In the end, the film becomes an odd love triangle, between Dr. Morris's son, Bob, Celeste, and Bob's new fiancée, Elsa.

Celeste is, without a doubt, the antagonist of the film, but she yearns to be a "normal" woman, accepted and loved by the men outside of her society. She openly romances Bob, at one point, lying down beside him, and asking him if she was "easy on the eyes." A smitten Bob agrees, and Celeste suddenly understands what it feels like to be domesticated, the source of ardor for a young and successful man. In many ways, Celeste's jealousy—not her stated desire to protect the secrets of her tribe—fuels the climax of the plot. At one point, Celeste confronts Elsa, and, using *Dracula*-like hypnotic powers (complete with a light shining across her eyes), tells Elsa that

> You shall be my sister, it is in my power. [...] Do not fear that my sister, yours shall be a better fate. I shall teach you a new worship, a new religion. Your first sacrifice upon this altar will be the fate of the man you love. Since I am forbidden to love him, so shall you be! You will learn to live as I must live—apart, beyond the reach of men and mortals. And for that love which once shown in a man's eye, loathing shall be substituted. You shall be feared and hated.

Elsa immediately faints, but, as Bryan Senn notes, Celeste's voice is "tinged with sadness" before "harden[ing]" as she speaks (58). Celeste's curse, in many ways, is to simply be a woman who is independent, powerful, and thus, removed from societal conventions.

The subtext is so clear that *Cry of the Werewolf* seems to beg women to reassert their domestic roles and eschew any form of independence. Again, Bryan Senn puts it succinctly, noting that

> *Cry of the Werewolf* seems a backhanded reaction to the patriarchal society's wariness towards this new breed of female. As such, the film casts the woman in power—the

leader or her tribe—as a literal monster, one who literally sacrifices the notion of love and support to instead walk the path of brutality and evil, a perverted form who wields her power with a murderous fist [...] Here, female strength and independence equates to savagery. It's almost a reactionary plea to restore the status quo .... [57].

Celeste's wooing of Bob is real, even if a little clumsy, and her brief flirtation with the "status quo" seems to linger in her mind. By the time she hypnotizes Elsa, Celeste has been constantly reminded of her role by the rest of the Gypsies, in particular Bianca, who functions as her caretaker and lead chastiser. After Celeste, in wolf form, attacks and kills a fellow Gypsy who was in danger of "bringing the police down" on the tribe, Bianca consoles her. As Celeste weeps, Bianca pats her on the back and says, "Weep, child, weep. You cannot help the things that have been, or the things that must be. It is your destiny. You are a high priestess. The welfare of our tribe is in your keeping. It was ordained so by your mother, and she placed you in my care. You are the daughter of the werewolf." Celeste's immediate response—a dramatic and sudden whisper of "I am a werewolf"—indicates an embrace of her role, but this is only temporary, and her continued dalliance or flirtation with Bob under the guise of protecting the Gypsy tribe is self-serving. In Bob's often clumsy ardor, Celeste enjoys the domain of the domestic, or, at least the guise of it, but she is ultimately pulled back to her wolf form and her responsibilities.

In a final showdown, Elsa, Bob, and Celeste all stand facing one another, and, this time, it is Elsa's turn to make her decision. Celeste attempts to keep Elsa hypnotized, as their "sister" status has become quite literal—when Celeste is shot, Elsa feels pain in the same shoulder. "Kill him," Celeste commands Elsa, and Elsa's choice—a wild freedom promised by Celeste, or the supposedly domestic bliss provided by Bob—comes into stark contrast. Celeste and Bob exchange no real argument for Elsa: Celeste commands "do as I say," and Bob replies "Elsa, put that gun down," and for the next few minutes, the words of Celeste and Bob are variations on those themes. Thus, the choice is inherently Elsa's, and her ultimate response to the tension is to faint (again).

As a wolf, Celeste attacks Bob, the police arrive, and, as would become standard in many werewolf films, she dies in a hail of bullets. The ruckus causes Elsa to awaken, and the dialogue seems to be plucked from any number of pseudo-romance films of that era. "Are you all right, darling?" Bob asks, and Elsa, crying, throws herself into his arms as he comforts her. "Nothing can harm you now," he says, holding her. Aside from an odd comedy-slash-epilogue exchange of lines between the police officers, this is the finale of the film, and patriarchal order is restored. Elsa's brief flirtation with independence, provoked by the troubled and obviously misguided Celeste, is overcome, and Elsa reasserts her role as a wife, destined to dote on her husband.

To be clear, both of Elsa's options feature a distinct loss of agency, but Celeste's offers to Elsa, to live "beyond the reach of men and mortals," and to help "rebuild a temple" feature a distinctly independent streak. In fact, Bob's counteroffer, made earlier in the film, is put as "I'll give you two weeks to make up [your] mind [...] To come back to Washington with me as Mrs. Robert Morris." Bob's offer involves not only a distinct deadline, but also an assurance of a complete loss of Elsa's identity: her name and location wiped away under the guide of domestic bliss. Compared to Celeste's literal promises of wildness, *Cry of the Werewolf* does indeed function as a less-than-radical endorsement of Senn's "status quo," and Elsa's hysterical sobbing as the film ends only cements her future role as a wife. In the formula of *Cry of the Werewolf*, "wild" and independent women are destroyed by the officers of the law, while women embracing their domestic role are embraced and comforted for doing so.

Paul Naschy as Waldemar Daninsky

Although it may seem odd to include Paul Naschy's werewolf films in a chapter on the female wolf and masculinity, I think it is important to note that Naschy's oeuvre often places heightened emphasis on the role of the woman in the lore of the werewolf. In fact, Naschy's love for his conception of Waldemar Daninsky and his Wolfman led to the creation of over a dozen films, and a complete examination of all of them (and the roles of women in these films) would take up an entire volume. In all Naschy's werewolf films, many of which are lost or are nearly impossible to find in their originally envisioned form,[4] he plays Waldemar Daninsky, a Polish nobleman who is always, during the film, infected with the werewolf "curse." How he gets the curse often changes from film to film, and, confusingly, each film seems to "reboot" the Daninsky character. Yet, even though the films are star vehicles for Naschy, the narrative often relies on the machinations, often evil or sundry, of an assortment of female characters. This mixture of dangerous and seductive natures falls in line with most depictions of female vampires in the 1970s, a reflection of "the rise of the women's liberation movement, which also led to public fears about a more aggressive expression of female sexuality" (59). In many cases, the film's narrative relies on the female to both provide the curse and to cure Daninsky of the curse, and, in many cases, vampiric women are often responsible for Daninsky's curse. This trope provides, even in a Naschy star vehicle, a central focus on how females are depicted in these films. Mary Hartson claims that Spanish films during the era in which Naschy first started were symptomatic of the male being "forced to recognize himself in the traditionally feminized role of object for consumption" (126).

To combat this sudden seething capitalistic intent, where masculinity itself becomes commodified, Naschy's work often re-places the objectification and the subjugation firmly back on the females.

The method in which Daninsky can be freed from his curse almost always remains the same: he must be killed by a woman who is truly in love with him. Otherwise he can, as in the case of *Night of the Werewolf*, apparently be buried for hundreds of years and re-awakened to resume his previous life. Of course, Naschy, despite his prodigious talents as a writer, director, and actor, produces low-budget horror, and the focus on gore and nudity (as well as incongruous and anachronistic 1980s electronic music) can, at times, be overwhelming.

Yet, Naschy's films are all based on Daninsky's magnetic charms, and his overarching need to seduce a woman, at first, romantically, but his secondary motive is almost always that a woman that loves him will lead to his demise. This, of course, leads to nudity (always female only, it seems), and it means that the female character must always be the enabler of the curse as well as the destroyer of the male. The tragedy is that Daninsky must harvest love (or lust) so that he may be killed and freed from his curse. Otherwise, he remains immortal, and vulnerable to long stretches of the misery of being buried alive for hundreds of years. Yet, unlike Larry Talbot, who routinely rejects women after his initial curse, Daninsky actively pursues women, even if it—and it often does—puts them in direct danger. Daninsky's attempts to find "love" are deeply tied in to his desire to rid himself of his curse, and his pursuit of "love" (which often suddenly arrives in the form of a young woman who immediately becomes smitten with Daninsky) is self-serving. Daninsky's desire to die, then, is deeply hegemonic in its outlook, as he essentially manipulates women to his own self-serving ends. The tragedy, in many ways, moves from the carrier of the curse to the person who is expected to free him from the curse—after all, the character arc for many of the women in Naschy's films is to fall deeply in love with Daninsky and then murder him, which could be fairly called a bit of an emotional rollercoaster ride.

In *The Werewolf and the Yeti*, Daninsky is a scientist obsessed with finding evidence of a Yeti in Katmandu. He joins an expedition, and, along with his guide, gets lost upon leaving their camp. What happens next is a fever dream for Daninsky, and an odd hodgepodge of erotica, horror, and shootouts for the viewer's eyes to feast on. Daninsky, after wandering through the woods for a time, collapses, but sees a cave in the distance. Upon entering the cave, Daninsky meets two scantily clad women, who furtively speak about how he will make a good mate for them. Of course, nudity ensues, as the two women roll around naked on Daninsky's semi-conscious form.[5] When Daninsky awakes, with a vague memory of his *ménage à trois*, he finds the two women consuming human flesh. The two women, presumably vampires, have lost even more clothing, and spend the remaining portion of their screen time running around the caverns and wrestling with Daninsky wearing only very airy chiffon robes. Daninsky eventually stakes the two women,[6] killing them, but not before being bitten, and incongruously "cursed" with the werewolf.

The narrative of the film, then, is the corruption of Daninsky by vampiric women, a theme that Naschy will also explore in *Night of the Werewolf*. The two vampiric women are objectified from almost the first moment they appear on screen, through their deaths, as they lie semi-nude on the cavern floor at Daninsky's feet, seemingly begging for sex. Although they rescue Daninsky, they do so at the price of his unmolested humanity. He is, for much of the rest of the film, a werewolf, struggling between his human form and his feral form. That the male is victimized by female sexual aggression, leading him to a curse that brings upon him misery and torment, is a point not to be missed. Daninsky's films seem to lay the blame for all of his woes—and his eventual freedom—on the women in his life. They are the alpha and omega of Daninsky's existence, and their ability to hurt or injure him leads him to seek out death.

Yet, the fact that Daninsky becomes a werewolf is the very thing that turns him into a near-superhero. He rescues a young woman (who, at the start of the film, he leers at and comments on her attractiveness to her own father), Sylvia, as she is being sexually assaulted by a group of bandits (this occurs after she is nearly sexually assaulted by a drunken party member). Naschy viciously destroys the offenders with a series of quick slashes, before turning away from Sylvia. When Daninsky awakes, Sylvia clearly mistrusts him, but, in Daninsky's eyes, he has become a savior of sorts for her. Her love for him is suddenly based on the protective hegemonic masculinity that he works so hard to hide: the regal and educated "soft" masculine earns no interest from the woman; she prefers the dangerous and sometimes violent wolf. This leads to numerous and oddly juxtaposed romantic interludes.

What happens next relies on the subplot, which can, admittedly, meander. The rest of the expedition, to find Daninsky, set off through the wilderness, only to have their superstitious Sherpas—who speak frequently of "demons" within the woods—abandon them. Soon, they are attacked by bandits, and taken back to the leader's castle. There, the remaining expedition members are brutally tortured, which is just the situation for a new werewolf to flex his protective hegemonic muscle. However, Sylvia and Daninsky decide to wait for a few days at the home of a Tibetan monk. This allows for two things: Sylvia to be nude on camera, and for the monk to explain to Sylvia the rubric that dominates many of Naschy's werewolf films: now that she loves him, it is her responsibility to determine Daninsky's fate. The choices are either to stab him with a ceremonial dagger, or to mix her blood with rare flowers to "cure" him.

Daninsky manages to overcome the bandits, even after he and Sylvia are captured. An odd subplot emerges where semi-nude slave women overthrow the camp with the help of Sylvia's ceremonial dagger. The women kill Wandesa, the true leader of the bandits, who is purposefully weakening the chief, Sekkar Khan, to strengthen her grip on the bandits. Interestingly, Wandesa is aware of Daninsky's wolf form, and attempts to seduce him, in an awkwardly edited scene,[7] by showing him her breasts and by commanding him to work with him. When he refuses, she demonstrates how she "heals" Khan—by peeling the skin off the backs of nude women—and threatening to do the same to Sylvia. Daninsky is rescued by Sylvia during the slave woman uprising, and, after killing Sekkar Khan, he and Sylvia escape, the lone survivors of the original expedition. This entire sequence deeply sexualizes women, consistently exposing their bodies, both living and dead (the ultimate objects), to the camera (Hartson 131).

Not everything is happily ever after, however, as Daninsky is still "cursed," and the titular Yeti, which appeared in the first few minutes of the film, but not again until the final few minutes, attacks the werewolf form of Daninsky, who, after a few leaps through the air, dispatches the Yeti, but only after suffering mortal wounds himself. When he collapses, Sylvia notices the rare flowers, cuts her palm open, and saves Daninsky, returning him, permanently, to human form. Carefree and unburdened, apparently, by the mayhem that occurred around them for the previous several days, they walk down the mountain holding hands.

Women in *The Werewolf and the Yeti* are, first and foremost, objects, and it seems like almost every female in the film must appear nude at least once, either by being tortured or being seductive (Daninsky has sex with three different women during the film). Additionally, women are split into two groups: victims and potential mates, and evil and murderous. Sylvia is nearly sexually assaulted twice, saved by Daninsky in wolf form three times, and saved again by Daninsky in human form a few times more. Melody, the other female on the expedition, is captured and killed, her back flesh peeled off by Wandesa. And Wandesa, and the two mysterious cave-dwelling vampire women, are the sources of most of the film's travails. In fact, Wandesa is responsible for most of the non-werewolf-related deaths in the film.

In between these different women, who are lovers, victims, or antagonists, is Waldemar Daninsky, who is cursed, but despite being horrified by the curse, enjoys the powers and virility such a curse brings. Daninsky is no doubt conflicted by the curse, as it allows him not only the power of becoming a wolf, but also, apparently, in human form, the power to become more assertive, aggressive, and murderous. In *The Werewolf and the Yeti*, after the curse is transferred to Daninsky, he transforms, quite literally, from a mild-mannered scientist, obsessed with finding a yeti, to a man who can almost single-handedly destroy a local guerrilla group armed with automatic weapons. In many Naschy werewolf films, the "curse" of the wolf gives Daninsky's masculinity a decidedly "harder" edge, by turning him into one who is athletic and nearly unstoppable, as well as aggressive. Daninsky, while cursed, incorporates aspects of the wolf into his own humanity, and many of his actions resemble the werewolf's actions. For example, the werewolf saves Sylvia; Daninsky, later in the film, saves Sylvia. The werewolf kills numerous bandits; the same happens later with Daninsky.

Sylvia, of course, as the film's central female, is the object of Daninsky's desire and salvation. She does play a pivotal role in the overthrow of the camp, but she does so almost accidentally: she is captured still clutching the ceremonial dagger. When the slave women notice the dagger, they take it from Sylvia, over her objections, and launch an immediate rebellion. Sylvia manages to find Daninsky and free him, where she spends much of the time running alongside him or watching helplessly as he wrestles various thugs. But, Daninsky is beholden to Sylvia's decision: it is up to her to decide how Daninsky will proceed by the end of the film: he will stay a werewolf, become a human, or die.

In this way, Naschy's depiction of his female characters can be somewhat alarming, although, to his credit, they do repeatedly figure in as major characters when women were, in horror films in the United States during the same era, essentially all victims or potential victims. In this regard, Naschy's films follow the well-established precedent. Although men are occasionally victims of the werewolf, it happens in such a fleeting manner that the sequences can be easy to miss. Unlike the murders of the women, the male "victims' bodies are shown only briefly, never undressed, and the camera does not linger over these scenes but rapidly moves on to the next plot point" (Hartson 132).

Night of the Werewolf is, as well, often confounding in its treatment of women. The film begins in a somewhat unique manner, starting with a flashback where Elizabeth Bathory and Waldemar Daninsky, along with other assorted criminals, are on trial. They are sentenced to death, and Daninsky is forced to wear a steel mask that denotes him as a criminal. Because of Daninsky's curse, and because of Bathory's alluring supernatural powers, neither of them are *truly* dead, and, the film fast forwards to the present time, where a group of young women decide to find the final resting place of Bathory, ostensibly as a part of their college anthropology courses.

In a nod to *Frankenstein Meets the Wolf Man,* Daninsky is awakened in his tomb by a pair of treasure-seeking gravediggers, who he immediately dispatches in wolf form. Soon after, he rescues the trio of college women from a sexual assault led by bandits (apparently, a recurring theme in Naschy's wolf films), by hovering in the woods in human form and killing the bandits with a crossbow. His timidity, however, evaporates, when the women—Erika,

Karen, and Barbara[8]—appear at the ruins of his castle. He plays a forgiving and indulgent host, all the while hoping to woo Karen. In his past life, he had rescued a woman, Mircaya, from being burned at the stake, and she has prophesized Karen's arrival and love. Daninsky's interest is somewhat self-serving, however, as he can only die by the hand of the woman who loves him, and, thus, he needs a woman to love him in order to die. Mircaya prophesizes that Karen is the woman who can free him; meanwhile, Erika, who has deduced that Daninsky is in fact the werewolf of legend, sets about freeing Bathory from her coffin. Bathory, after biting Erika and enslaving her, decides to, like Wandesa in *The Werewolf and the Yeti*, enslave Daninsky as well. Both women realize that having a super strong werewolf as a servant and instrument of terror would serve their desires well. If the plot sounds a little convoluted, it is, and most of the events are designed to put Daninsky either with, or opposed to, a series of women.

This unusual set of events leads to odd set-pieces where a trio of young, female graduate students sit down to a formal dinner with their host, an undead werewolf in human form, and they do so in his dilapidated castle. Daninsky's ardor moves from woman to woman as he seeks to find, first and foremost, a woman who will fall in love with him. Ultimately, it is Karen who becomes smitten with the centuries-old man, and the two begin a love affair, all occurring rather lazily compared to the violent urgency of Erika's resurrection of Bathory. Erika, who resurrects Bathory by killing Barbara and soaking Bathory's tomb in her blood, is immediately bitten by Bathory, and turns into a vampire herself, leading to the climax of the film—werewolf versus vampires. For once, however, the werewolf gets the upper hand on the vampire, although the climactic battle essentially focuses on the heavily muscled and make-up laden Daninsky physically beating a series of women.

Daninsky's wolf, unlike other depictions in the Naschy werewolf saga, is far more untamed, and is decidedly not heroic—his toxic, feral nature makes him much harder to sympathize with. In one sequence, Daninsky turns into a wolf, kills a bandit, and then marches on to a town, where he murders a young woman who is out to fetch water. He tosses her prone body into the well before skittering away. Yet, despite this, Karen still loves Daninsky, all while acknowledging that, when the "time" comes, she would hopefully be "brave enough" to kill Daninsky while in wolf form. After Daninsky kills the innocent women, he arrives back at the castle, in human form and drenched in her blood, and Karen, upon seeing this, *hugs him*, and they later have sex. Karen's destiny, then, as a foil to Daninsky, quite literally requires her to be unyielding in her affection for him.

Of course, the ending is Daninsky's wolf making short order of the vampire women—the turned Mircaya, Erika, and Bathory, before facing off against Karen, who herself has been bitten and manipulated by the vampires.

Daninsky's wolf attacks Karen, biting her, before she manages to kill him. Daninsky turns back to human form after dying, and Karen, apparently mortally wounded by the wolf's bite, collapses in his arms, echoing the ending with Talbot and Ilonka's "dying embrace" ending in *House of Frankenstein*.

The idea first depicted in *The Werewolf and the Yeti* remains the same here: women are either destroyers, saviors, or sexual beings, and in some cases, manages to take on the role of all three in the short span of an hour and a half. Karen, for example, in *Night of the Werewolf*, is depicted in a swimsuit at the start of the film, spends much of her time as Daninsky's lover dressed in gauzy lingerie,[9] and is soon tasked with the responsibility of destroying Daninsky. However, she is bitten by the vampiric Bathory, and leads Daninsky into danger, before eventually freeing him from his curse. She sacrifices herself so that Daninsky can be freed from his suffering.

Suffice to say that Naschy's depictions of women in his available werewolf oeuvre are, even by the standards of low-budget 1970s and 1980s horror films, dramatically unrefined. For the most part, the women are victims, antagonists, sadists, or love interests (or some combination thereof), and nudity seems to be a requirement to earn a major role in Naschy's films. Like most of werewolf cinema, it is fair to say that Naschy's work was deeply influenced by other contemporary horror films of the era, which also focused primarily on gore and nudity, with women being the subject of both.

The Howling

The Howling is quite possibly the first real attempt at creating a more realistic female werewolf, but that attempt still manages to pigeonhole the individual women within the narrative. Although there are three major female characters, and the men generally take a backseat to their roles in the film, each of the women—Karen, Marsha, and Terry—fill traditional wolves as victims, objects, or lovers. In some cases, these women are defined by the roles they play in the lives of the men around them *even when the men are not on the screen.* In other words, *The Howling* would resoundingly fail the Bechdel Test, for their existence as characters is almost entirely predicated on the men who are a major part of their lives: Karen (Bill), Marsha (Bill and Eddie), and Terry (Chris). Karen White is, for the most part, propelled from event to event, often nervous and horrified, and her mental frailty is made apparent at the start of the film. After being attacked in an adult theater by Eddie Quist, she loses portions of her memory and becomes uninterested in a physical relationship with Bill. This necessitates a visit to a psychiatrist, Dr. Waggner, who recommends that Karen seek therapy at a colony of his—it is mostly unstated, but the therapy consists of a boost in confidence and vigor by being infected as a werewolf. During her stay, Karen becomes suspicious, and summons her co-workers, Terry and Chris, to help her investigate. Terry, a young female researcher, is quickly dispatched by the resurrected Eddie Quist in a scene that is deeply reminiscent of slasher films.

And, by the end of the film, Karen finally makes a decision that frees her—but, as with many male werewolves who try to resist the curse, it ends in her destruction. Her co-worker Chris shoots her dead with a silver bullet. Karen's final fate is, in many ways, a near-complete gender reversal of a Waldemar Daninsky story arc. Although Chris is in love with Terry, his affection for Karen is clear, and, thus, it falls to him to be the one to finally end Karen's curse.

On the other hand, Marsha Quist revels in her wolf curse as well as her human seductiveness. She infects Bill and forcefully pursues him, at one point meeting him in the woods and stripping naked.[10] There can be little doubt that Marsha is an object, although a powerful one—she is highly sexualized, and is almost predatory (both physically and sexually) toward her male victims. Marsha and Karen are polar opposites of the same curse, and each occupy, as a result, nearly stereotypical roles for women in werewolf cinema. Marsha functions, quite often, as the sexualized object; Karen, the chaste and meek woman, afflicted with mental illness from a traumatic event; Terry, the victim.

The Company of Wolves

"*The Company of Wolves*," James Gracey writes, "is a story of sexual awakening, transformation—both literal and figurative—and the empowerment of women" (Gracey 61). Or, and this question is relevant for *Ginger Snaps* as well, is it? As Gracey himself notes, there have been several critics concerned that the "empowerment of women" is so closely juxtaposed to a sexual awakening involving—and almost entirely dependent on—men. In this regard, the same concerns hold true for *The Company of Wolves* as they do for *Ginger Snaps*, because, while the narrative focuses on women, the idea that provides the impetus for the plot is a young woman's growing sexual desires for men. Are these films, then, feminist expressions that appreciate the movement into "adulthood" (which, apparently requires sex with a man, or, at the very least, the realization of their burgeoning heterosexuality), or do they tell the same traditional story of women who become "empowered" through sexual activity, using werewolf lore as a ham-fisted symbol?

The source material for *The Company of Wolves* is a short story of the same name by Angela Carter. There can be little doubt that the short story— and Angela Carter worked closely with director Neil Jordan on the film adaptation—is the direct inspiration for many of the issues of sexuality, masculinity, and gender in the film. In fact, reading "The Company of Wolves" reveals a preoccupation with these themes, which are often more intense and graphic than in the film. In the film, for example, when Granny dies, much of the action takes place offscreen. There is little doubt that the werewolf's attack on Granny in the short story is deeply sexualized:

> He strips off his shirt. His skin is the colour and texture of vellum. A crisp stripe of hair runs down his belly, his nipples are ripe and dark as poison fruit but he's so thin you could count the ribs under his skin if only he gave you the time. He strips off his trousers and she can see how hairy his legs are. His genitals, huge. Ah! huge [149].

Later, after "he had finished with her," the wolf "licked his chops and quickly dressed himself again" (149) before disposing of Granny's remains. There can be little doubt that the source material, like *The Company of Wolves*, focuses almost entirely on the often tremulous relationship between feminine and masculine desire.

The Company of Wolves is most likely the most critically acclaimed and appreciated modern werewolf film in this book, having won multiple awards for special effects, direction, and design. And, like the original parable of "The Little Red Riding Hood," *The Company of Wolves* functions as a story designed to warn young women of men, many of whom "lurk in every guise," and whose words "hides sharpest tooth." Rosaleen, the young woman at the center of the film, dreams of a fairytale land that is haunted by folklore of werewolves. Rosaleen learns this folklore through various stories that she hears (and tells) as the main narrative progresses, and all the stories, in some way, are dire warnings against certain types of men that Granny describes as "hairy on the inside," beings who will "drag you with them to Hell!" Although this is clearly a reference to the werewolf curse, it is also a nod toward the duplicitous nature of many of the male characters that populate the stories Rosaleen and the Grandmother tell during the narrative: each of the men had assumed their hegemonic masculinity, usually at the expense of the woman.

These warnings from Granny tend to negate the idea of the film's celebration of "empowerment," as they paint men in a highly negative light. Yet, as Gracey notes, Rosaleen's mother "warns" her daughter "not to pay too much attention to the old woman, again enabling Rosaleen to see things from a different perspective" (68). Rosaleen's mother is the opposite pole of Granny, and, at one point, after Rosaleen sees her mother and father having sex (they share, in Rosaleen's dreams, a one-room house), Rosaleen asks "Does he hurt you?" Her mother's response is "not at all," before adding, "if there's a beast in men, it meets its match in women, too." The film's narrative continues to bounce between these two viewpoints until Rosaleen finally makes her decision regarding which point to adopt.

Granny spends much of her time complaining about the wiles of men, in direct contrast to Rosaleen's mother, who simply acknowledges the joy of sex and companionship with men. In Granny's first story, she tells the tale of a young woman who meets a travelling man, falls in love with him, and gets married. Granny notes that his eyebrows meet in the middle, a sure sign of someone to distrust. When the wedding night arrives, the traveler sees the full moon, steps outside, and disappears. After several years, the young woman has moved on, marrying another man, having multiple children, and seemingly overwhelmed by the demands of her domesticity. Soon, however, her first husband returns, demanding soup, and, upon realizing that she has had children, calls her a "whore" and "adulteress" before peeling back his skin to reveal his wolf form. Presumably, his anger would have driven him to kill the woman and her children, but they are saved by her current husband, who arrives and beheads the wolf. The husband, then enraged by his wife's astonishment at the now-severed head turning from wolf to human, slaps her harshly. In this respect, the toxicity doesn't just emanate from an outsider or a curse; it comes entirely from the men. Their "hairy on the inside" nature is Granny's way of warning Rosaleen of toxic or hegemonic masculinity.

Rosaleen's innocent reaction to the end of the story—in which the husband strikes the wife in anger—is telling. "I'd never let a man strike me," she says, but Granny argues that toxicity is rampant in men, saying that many of them are "nice as pie until they've had their way with you," adding "once the bloom is gone, the beast comes out." In other words, in Granny's formulation, beast or not, curse or not, men have the capacity—and often use that capacity—to romance young women, and then, after winning their hand or their bed, drops the veneer or domesticity or likability. The hair on the inside is revealed, and it is a scourge in the woman's life.

As the storytellers change in *The Company of Wolves*, so do the depictions of werewolves and men. Granny's stories continue to feature males and wolves designed to highlight toxic masculinity; Rosaleen's stories, however, feature women in "positions of power and experience" (Gracey 69), indicating that Rosaleen is far more sympathetic to her mother's view toward men than Granny's fire-and-brimstone perspective. In fact, Rosaleen's stories tend to focus on women earning their independence. In her first story, she tells her mother of a young woman who was taken advantage of and impregnated by a wealthy male, who promptly abandoned her. During his wedding to a different woman, the young woman appears and curses them all to become wolves, and, during an elongated and parody-driven scene, the wedding party turns into wolves, so that they can "come to sing to her and the baby at night." When Rosaleen's mother shares her concern about the ending of the story, Rosaleen foreshadows her own embrace of the wolf (and what it represents to *her*, at least), explaining that "[t]he pleasure would come from knowing the power that she had." In Rosaleen's perspective, the woman who controls the wolf controls the man within. The wolf is less a study in the power of men, and more of a study in the power of women, for only a woman with "power" can tame the cursed male. Thus, Rosaleen rejects Granny's stories not because they feature strong and toxic males, but because they *lack* strong women who are capable of capturing and maintaining a stasis in the relationship.

In other words, Rosaleen re-centers the female in folklore by providing them with agency. Yes, they may be traumatized by the males in their lives, but ultimately, they are not victims of any form of toxic masculinity; they simply refuse to be. Instead, they often earn their revenge or re-place themselves into their own narrative. A far cry from the young mother in Granny's initial story, who is torn between two toxic males, suffering multiple beatings and accusations while also pining for her love, the women in Rosaleen's stories simply move on with their lives, focusing on their own power and deriving their identity from a mixture of individualism and a simple embrace of their agency. Symbolically, then, Rosaleen's story is, in many ways, already told well before the ending of the film: an astute viewer can see Rosaleen's progression from the Granny-instilled fear toward a new sense of independence.

This is not to say, however, that *The Company of Wolves* is a film based solely on a young woman gaining agency and rejecting toxic masculinity. Indeed, the final scenes of the film cast much of this progression Rosaleen experiences into doubt. She is obviously smitten with the "Big Bad Wolf," and is rather unperturbed to find that her Granny has been eaten. She initially grabs a knife and then a gun to defend herself from the Huntsman (before he changes into a wolf), and tells him "it wouldn't do much good to me to be afraid, would it?" Increasingly worried by the Huntman's advances and his sudden and gory transformation into a wolf, she shoots him in the shoulder. This action, however, only makes Rosaleen suddenly sympathetic to the creature that had just killed her grandmother and symbolically tossed her red hood into the fireplace, literally defrocking her.

She tells her final story, of a young woman who creeps out of the underworld, to placate the wolf. This story is the final realization of Rosaleen, or at least who she believes herself to be within her own dream world. The young woman is also a wolf and is severely injured. Upset, she stumbles upon an elderly priest who fixes her arm, and she eventually makes her way back to the underworld. "And that's all I'll tell you, because that's all I know," she says to finish the story, and, in many ways, her parable is complete: for the first time, there is no immediate moral to the story other than the elderly priest's statement "what do I care whose work you are?" when he equivocates if the young bestial woman is Godly or demonic. The dualism is lost for Rosaleen, and she can see the nuance through the pity she's developed for the now lupine Huntsman. She, too, with the villagers approaching, becomes a wolf (although, to the consternation of many critics, the transformation does not occur onscreen), and runs into the woods with her new mate.

As such, Rosaleen's final sequence—both her storytelling and her cradling of the wounded Huntsman—is not necessarily a marker of a newfound independence. In this regard, Rosaleen embraces her mother's mantra entirely: that if men are beasts, women can be too, and its little surprise that Rosaleen's mother saves her young daughter's life by deflecting a shot intended for her wolf form. Rosaleen, like Kelly Ann in *Wild Country*, finds meaning in domesticity, a meaning that she had been unable to locate between radically opposing poles of masculinity as presented to her by others.

If the movie ends there, critics would be only slightly confounded, but one more sequence plays out: Rosaleen awakens from her dream world and finds herself surrounded by wolves. As a wolf crashes through her window, symbolically tearing her bedroom apart, Rosaleen seems to revert to Granny's philosophy, and, indeed, as she screams, Rosaleen's voiceover recites a very Granny-sounding warning:

> Little girls, this seems to say:
> Never stop upon your way;
> Never trust a stranger friend
> No one knows how it will end.
> As you're pretty, so be wise
> Wolves may lurk in every guise
> Now, as then, 'tis simple truth:
> Sweetest tongue hides sharpest tooth.

What to make of this sudden twist ending, which itself followed a twist ending? It may be simplest to say that in the supposed "real world" in which Rosaleen wakes (stalking packs of wolves outside of suburban bedrooms notwithstanding), toxic masculinity still reigns supreme, often far away from rehabilitation through sympathy or love.

As in *Ginger Snaps*, the further one considers the intricate layers of masculinity and femininity and the lore of the wolf at the core of werewolf cinema, there is little that is easy to interpret, and aspects of gender seem to fold in among themselves. Rosaleen's sudden shift from embracing a wolf so much so that she becomes a wolf is all washed away by her apparent and immediate fears of wolves outside her door. *The Company of Wolves* is a Möbius strip of gender and gendered identities, and it still confounds critics who approach it.

Dog Soldiers

Dog Soldiers features only one woman in an all-male ensemble: the mysterious and soon-to-be-revealed nefarious Megan. Her plan, apparently, was to escape the area of her werewolf family and to join society at large. To do so, she stays "undercover" as a human for as long as she can, so that the men can "rescue" her. Like many werewolf films that feature female wolves, the idea of a female werewolf is closely tied to sexuality and fertility. She begins her transformation by remarking that it is "that time of the month," clearly tying together the monthly cycles of menstruation and full moons. She also tells Cooper that he "may think all women are bitches ... but I'm the real thing." In these few moments of the revelation of Megan becoming a werewolf nicely summarizes much of the framework for films such as *Trick 'r Treat* and *Ginger Snaps*.

In Megan lies an often-caustic combination of seductiveness, fertility, and aggression, a combination which often puts the surrounding males in some degree of dire straits. As the youngest member of a family of werewolves—all of whom are the ones stalking the soldiers—Megan is quite content to calmly watch the events play out, confident, in the end, of her family's victory. Indeed, the role of the male non-werewolf characters in films where the female plays a werewolf is one where they spend most of their time nonplussed by their surroundings. The unit in *Dog Soldiers*, for example, refuses to acknowledge the presence of a pack of werewolves until deep into the film's runtime, and, even then, it truly takes one of them—the evil secret services officer Captain Ryan—transforming in front of them to fully convince them. Up until that point, Megan, who has yet to reveal her own pending transformation, has been routinely dismissed by many of the soldiers for her discussions about werewolves. In fact, the irony of her statements seems lost on the soldiers: at one point, she directly compares the small unit of military men to the wolves themselves, pointing out the "two alpha males" cooperating in slowly wearing down their defenses, a clear nod to the effective power sharing between Private Cooper and Sergeant Wells. In *Dog Soldiers*, however, Megan is quickly "put down" by Sergeant Wells, who shoots her as she begins her transformation. In this action is a patriarchal rejection of Megan's aggressiveness and sexuality. Megan is not simply a werewolf, but she represents a disruption in the dominance of the males around her. She is routinely ignored, and, when she is revealed to be more powerful than them, both intellectually—as her dupe lasts much of the film—and physically, she is put down quickly and brutally. Megan's death restores, somewhat, the dominance of the remaining men, especially Cooper, who survives until the end of the film, an alpha male that even manages to have a subservient dog follow him into the sunrise.

Cursed

It is inherently difficult to understand or to write about the Wes Craven film *Cursed*, as the movie lingered in production hell and enjoyed multiple reshoots and rewrites, which muddies much of the plot of the film. The aspects of the men in *Cursed* have been mentioned elsewhere in this volume, however, two women in the film—Ellie and Joanie—are werewolves. Each female, though, seems to have wildly different perspectives on their "curse," as Ellie works to resist her transformation, where Joanie embraces it. This matches their personalities, and, really, their character arcs, as Ellie is the "good," sympathetic female in the film, and Joanie is the sniping, petty, and "bad" female in the film.

One of the main plot holes in the film is that both Ellie and Joanie were infected by the same man: Jake, the self-professed "alpha male" of the film. Joanie was presumably "cursed" before the start of the film, and has been a werewolf for much longer, yet, her experience does not seem to match Ellie's. In Ellie's case, in the days after being bitten and infected by the werewolf, she suddenly gains super sharp reflexes, a heightened sense of smell (especially of blood), and, a heightened sex appeal. In an era before sexual harassment became more vigorously prosecuted in Hollywood, Ellie's entry into her production office is accompanied by men tilting their heads around corners, referring to her newfound "saucy" nature, and discussing how "hot" she has become.[11] Indeed, at a party, Scott Baio, playing himself, tells Ellie that she has an "aura" of sexual attractiveness that is almost irresistible.

One of the climactic battles of *Cursed* is the showdown between Joanie—who turns into a werewolf—and Ellie, who remains in human form. Ellie (and her younger brother, who is mostly ineffectual in the battle) are assaulted by Joanie, and their rivalry over Jake is the primary source for Joanie's ire. Thus, the human but superpowered Ellie faces off against Joanie as a wolf. In many ways, Joanie's embrace of her wolf powers is a direct result of her jealousy for Ellie, who consistently, since her curse, attracts men and is generally more successful. Joanie, thus, embraces the corrupting influence of the curse, whereas the heroic Ellie resists the curse (and most of its sexual enhancements) as much as she can. In one of the more memorable moments in the film, Ellie goads the wolf Joanie into coming out of hiding by mocking her physical appearance: "Yeah, she's like, what? Five foot seven? She's got a bony ass, and fat thighs and bad skin!" Joanie does indeed appear, and in wolf form, smashes a window and gives the gathered crowd—and specifically Ellie—the middle finger, an image which has spawned numerous memes. Ellie, however, knows that Joanie's human inadequacies are what has caused her to embrace the wolf, as, if she can't get noticed or loved as a human, the werewolf aspect of her character will garner the attention she craves.

In this regard, the werewolf mythology of the 1980s onward—where becoming a werewolf is less of a tragic curse and more of a personal boon—continues forward. Although Ellie ultimately rejects her curse, Joanie revels in the benefits she receives (Ellie does, too, to a certain extent, but decides to retain her humanity): sexuality, strength, power, and all of it translates directly into her human form as well. In this regard, Joanie attempts to become the alpha in her own way, taunting and then attacking the obviously more popular and capable Ellie. In fact, it is revealed that Jake is not the obvious murderer of the numerous female victims mentioned in *Cursed*: it is Joanie, who uses her wolf form to literally eliminate the competition and try to continue to win Jake's ardor. Joanie's death, which stems from a hail of bullets from the police, a return to the endings of films like *The Undying Monster* and *I Was a Teenage Werewolf*, leaves Ellie in a final battle against Jake.

The finale of *Cursed* lays bare the film's hodgepodge origins. Ellie and her brother Jimmy eventually overcome Jake, whose character motivation essentially turns to (and this is paraphrasing a much longer diatribe): "if you won't join me as a werewolf bride, I guess I'll have to kill you." The wolf-in-sheep's-clothing metaphor, however, comes full circle, as Jake's hidden toxic agenda comes to the forefront. Jake, who, as a young man in Hollywood, has enjoyed his multiple sexual dalliances, many of which stem from, at the very least, a hegemonic viewpoint, and Ellie's resistance to Jake's invitation to be by his side as a wolf couple turns him toxic, with his violent attack only narrowly being averted by a silver spatula, placed directly into his heart.

In the end, *Cursed* is filled with many of the same plot beats and elements of the later werewolf cinema era. Unlike the tragic male, the characters in *Cursed*, male and female alike, revel in or enjoy (even temporarily), their newfound powers. Joanie displays a certain toxic femininity in trying to eliminate her rivals, and Jake, her former lover, simply assumes his dominance over Ellie, and when she and Jimmy refuse his hegemonic viewpoint, he becomes increasingly violent. Ellie and Jimmy's victory over Jake not only frees them of the curse but reinstitutes a world where Ellie functions with some degree of agency. In this regard Ellie's story arc moves her toward a rejection of everything that subverted her own independence. Although she no doubt enjoyed the newfound sexuality and powers she received as benefits of her curse, she ultimately rejected those same characteristics and remained, in the end, fully human. Unlike Joanie, then, Ellie turns away from the wolf and embraces her "normal" life.

The *Ginger Snaps* Trilogy

Ginger Snaps, of course, has been long viewed as a redefinition of the werewolf genre, and rightfully so, as it uses the werewolf "curse" and a juxtaposition with the female "curse" (as Brigitte refers to it) of menstruation and an entry into feminine sexuality. The arrival of Ginger's curse creates a nearly irrevocable split between the two tightly knit sisters. Ginger, who derided the boys "checking" her early in the film, soon descends into what Brigitte describes as "the mindless breeders machine" of high school, a "hormonal toilet" of a gender defining preoccupation with sex and sexual activity. In this way, both Brigitte and Ginger have rejected their femininity, and they keep the concepts of femininity and masculinity at bay by wearing baggy clothing and generally staying away from everyone else. They are "[c]lad in dark, oversized sweaters, baggy, hooded sweatshirts, voluminous shorts overtop dark tights," in direct contrast to the other women in the film, who wear "light-colored athletic clothing" (Miller 293). Brigitte and Ginger are also often visibly sickened by their mother's attempts to "normalize" them. Pamela, their mother, is the center of an overarching societal "desire to see them enter into the normalizing, reproductive order valued by their suburban community" (Miller 291). In other words, both Brigitte and Ginger are spiritually adrift in a culture that prizes conformist feminist roles: sex-hungry teenaged girls, or deeply repressed suburban housewives. Miller also notes that the *Ginger Snaps* franchise repeatedly points toward violence, and, as such "suggest that girls are no less likely than men to harbor violent tendencies or a desire to lash out at an unjust world" (300). This is no doubt true, but, when *Ginger Snaps* is placed within the contextual canon of the werewolf film genre, it becomes clear that *Ginger Snaps* is subverting gender roles by flipping them, rather than simply saying "girls" can be violent, too. Throughout the entire franchise, but especially in the first film, the stereotypical "masculine" werewolf question simply gets flipped to incorporate a young woman who must deal with the sudden arrival of a separate masculinized identity. Very rare are the werewolf films that feature a "feminine" or "female" wolf (*Wild Country* may by the exception; that is discussed below). The gender confusion that results because of the gender swapping no doubt leads to "a phallic female subject" (Miller 300).

In fact, the two sisters at the start of the trilogy have made a pact to circumvent their entry into the gendered world, "Out by sixteen or dead in this scene but together forever," they repeat several times throughout the course of the film. They anticipate and dread the "official" arrival of their sexual maturity and work hard to reject any notions of changing into a more conformist stance, as their mother begs them to do. Indeed, their obsession with death manifests itself in suicide ideation, much like Larry Talbot, and they both desire to kill themselves before having to deal with the ponderous issues of gender and sexuality. Their desire is so profound that much of the initial introduction of Brigitte and Ginger in *Ginger Snaps* features the pair staging complex suicide scenes and presenting them to the class as a class project. Both Brigitte and Ginger take some delight in shocking people with their non-conformist perspectives and suicidal thoughts, and their complete distaste for traditional gender definitions provides the philosophical undergirding for the film. Throughout the course of *Ginger Snaps*, however, the decision to deal with gender and gendered perspectives is forced onto them, dramatically changing their perspectives along the way.

As Ginger and Brigitte walk through a park late at night to play a prank on Tina, a female rival, Ginger's "curse" arrives doubly. First, menstrual blood flows down her leg, which disgusts Brigitte. Ginger, humiliated at this sudden arrival and her now forced participation in the world around her, and all its trappings of gender and identity, laments "kill yourself to be different and your own body screws you" before telling Brigitte to "shoot" her if she starts "simping around tampon dispensers and moaning about PMS."

The arrival of Ginger's menstruation is almost immediately coupled with the arrival of her more metaphorical curse, as a werewolf suddenly and brutally attacks her. It is interesting to note, here, that Brigitte, unlike many male protagonists, such as David in *An American Werewolf in London*, immediately jumps into the fray to help her sister. After a few beats, she finds the wolf mauling her sister and begins hitting it with her camera, eventually separating her and Ginger from the wolf long enough to escape. Even so, the attack is enough to infect Ginger, and her slow transformation into what her mother would call "womanhood" is matched by her slow transformation into a wolf.

As both transformations occur, the narrative shifts to Brigitte, who is openly concerned that Ginger's changes mean she is turning into something more than "just being female," and indeed, Ginger's werewolf curse seems to turn her into a more masculinized form. Her newfound sexuality, symbolized in a scene where Ginger, in slow motion, arrives at school in much slinkier clothing as people turn their heads as she lets a slight smile play across her face, is essentially a trap. She is a predator, and this requires her to adopt the masculine, to become a part of the long cinematic tradition of werewolves exhibiting an "uncontrollable youthful teenage sex drive" (Bernhardt-House 170). When Jason, the young man she rejected earlier in the film, tries to have sex with her in the backseat of his car, Ginger takes the initiative by pushing him down and clambering on top of him. Jason is upset by this and repeatedly asks "who's the guy here?" Later, Ginger re-adopts the feminine role by realizing that, to Jason, she is mostly like "just a lay" to him, and that any emotional or physical attachment she felt to him was most likely entirely one-sided.

The next time Jason appears on screen, he is abashed and carries multiple scars from his sexual liaison with Ginger. In fact, when he approaches his male friends, one of them notices a spot of red on the crotch of his pants, and asks "did you get your rag, too?" In this moment, there is a radical retooling of the werewolf mythos, as Ginger not only infects others through sex, but doing so completely feminizes her male partners. Later, as Jason goes to clean up and to urinate, he panics to see that his urine slowly turns to a massive fountain of blood (akin to the "geyser" Ginger experiences in the women's restroom as a horrified Brigitte watches). Jason's "curse" is to lose his masculinity through what should have been, from his perspective at least, the most masculinity-affirming action of all: pursuing and succeeding in deflowering the attractive virginal girl. Jason is eventually "cured" of his curse by Brigitte, who finds an increasingly lupine Jason accosting a young child. After he receives an injection of an herb called monkshood (also known as wolfsbane), he runs away from Brigitte, never to be seen again. Yet, Ginger is clearly masculinized by her werewolf curse, becoming not only a sexual aggressor, but a physical one as well. She physically assaults Tina during field hockey, pinning her down and repeatedly punching her in the face, and accidentally murdering Tina while physically beating her when Tina arrives at her house for retribution.

As Ginger's body changes, she vacillates between a form of self-loathing and a reluctant enjoyment of her new body. Her humanity and her sexuality become a point of pride, so much so that she frequently accuses Brigitte of jealousy whenever Brigitte attempts to cure her. But Ginger also shaves her body, and attempts to cut off her slowly growing tail. At one point, when Ginger is shaving, a process that requires an ever more copious amount of chemicals and razors, her mother walks in, and Ginger demands she leave, explaining that she is "fat," which is, of course, untrue, but aligns with her mother's own visions of teenage women's views of their own bodies. Mother attempts to reassure her daughter, telling her all the models she sees "are on speed" before leaving. Ginger's true body image issues, however, are ones she simply cannot explain, so she adopts somewhat more realistic body issues to placate her mother.

Of course, most of the contemporary criticism revolves around Ginger, but Brigitte herself is a rich character for gender study. Brigitte is younger than Ginger by only one year, but both girls are, according to their mother, "three years late" for their period, almost as if they have been willing away their sexual maturation through sheer force of will. As Brigitte works to find a cure for Ginger, she teams up with local horticulturist and drug dealer Sam, a young man who supplies marijuana to the high schoolers. To get Sam to help her, however, Brigitte lies and tells Sam that *she* is the one with the curse, and that it is a secret from Ginger. The motivation for her lie is clear: she wants to interact with Sam without her older sister's heavily sexualized interference, and the pair work together on several theories (silver, herbal remedies) to cure the "infection" of the werewolf curse.

Interestingly, when Ginger pieces together Brigitte's involvement with Sam, she literally forces her way into Sam's bedroom and chastises them both. Ginger calls Sam a "wank job" and, later, a "pervert," yelling at him that Brigitte is "only 15." When Brigitte asks Ginger to leave her and Sam alone so they can work on a cure, Ginger tells her younger sister that if "he rapes you, don't come crying," before leaving. The specter of sexual activity hangs thickly in the air after Ginger leaves, and, to defuse the sudden tension, Sam tells Brigitte "I do not think of you that way." Brigitte's brief physical reaction to that statement, however, indicates that she was aware, at least, of Sam as a sexual creature and had come to appreciate their burgeoning friendship. By not thinking of Brigitte "that way," he has essentially depowered Brigitte's attempts at fostering a genuine relationship between the pair. This moment reveals that, even if Brigitte is not jealous of Ginger's sexuality, she is, at least, aware of her sister's maturation, and desires to follow her into that world they both so readily dismissed before the arrival of the "curse."

However, Brigitte has a limit to her own desires for transformation, and when Ginger invites her to join Ginger as a werewolf through a swapping of blood, Brigitte refuses. Ginger goads her, telling her "You'll love it. Should come for the ride. A little scratch. Swap some juice. We'll be our own pack, like before." Brigitte replies that she would rather be dead, and, here the duality of Ginger's curse returns to the narrative. Ginger is referring to her werewolf transformation, but Brigitte understands the offer (especially with the sexually laden overtones of "ride" and swapping "juice") as a descent into sexuality—immediately before her invitation, Ginger likens the process of killing and eviscerating prey to "touching yourself." Brigitte, realizing her own burgeoning femininity, and perhaps recalling Sam's summary rejection of her, re-embraces her desire to avoid the "toxic" environment of sexuality and "hormones," and, in many ways, chooses to stay gender neutral.

Ginger, arriving at a Halloween party at Sam's greenhouse, appears in her final human state, with a lupine appearance which everyone drunkenly dismisses as a costume. She attempts to seduce Sam, trying to drive a wedge between Brigitte and Sam's friendship again, but Sam rejects Ginger, roughly throwing her to the ground. This is as violent as Sam gets during the entire film; in this case, Ginger's sexual aggression feminizes Sam, and he has little choice but to reconstitute his agency, and even his dominance. Ginger's faith in her own animal sexuality is shaken, and she leaves the party to go home, where she completes her transformation into a full wolf.

The final sequence of events, which features Sam and Brigitte entering the sisters' home and trying to cure the fully wolven Ginger, finishes the gendered equation. Brigitte is infected by Ginger—she agrees to swap fluid with her only, as she explains to Sam, to lure Ginger to the house so she can cure her, and Sam insists that he "protect" Brigitte by trying to cure Ginger on his own. The plan backfires horribly, and Sam is brutally injured, forcing Brigitte to face off against a more primal version of her sister. Eventually Brigitte finds Sam, and Ginger, as wolf, kills him in front of her. In this way, Ginger has finally, from her perspective, "protected" Brigitte from Sam, and Brigitte's burgeoning curse puts her ever closer to embracing a highly sexualized and masculinized view of the world around her.

Ultimately, however, Brigitte kills Ginger, but, we can assume, accidentally, as Brigitte mourns Ginger's death. The final scene of the film is Brigitte feeling Ginger's—in wolf form—breath slowly coming to a halt. Ginger's demise at the hands of her sister is due solely to the corrupting influence of her curse. Ginger's increased sexuality and her slow ascent (or, from Brigitte and Ginger's viewpoint, descent) into full "womanhood" closely matches Ginger's bodily transformations from tomboy-like physical appearance, shorn of the same sexuality many of her female classmates flaunt, to a nearly dominatrix style of dress and appearance as she turns into a wolf. Ginger moves from merely protecting Brigitte from the same fate, to murdering her potential romantic interest, to simply realizing that Brigitte will eventually change, and trying to murder her to keep her pure and unattached.

Ginger Snaps 2 focuses on Brigitte, who is infected with the werewolf curse because of her final battle with her sister. The sequel tinkers with a few of the world-building rules in *Ginger Snaps*: most importantly the injection of monkshood turns out to only delay the onset of the cure rather than provide a direct cure. Thus, Brigitte is on her own now, and we are re-introduced to her as she, alone, searches out a library for any assistance in her curse, including a book on bloodletting. If a significant amount of time has passed since *Ginger Snaps*, Brigitte is now "cursed" with both the werewolf and sexual maturity. The film wastes no time in establishing that Brigitte, who was quite successful fading into the wallpaper for much of *Ginger Snaps*, is now an object of desire in *Ginger Snaps 2*: the male librarian flirts openly with her, which disgusts her so much that she simply leaves him (and the books she wanted to check out) at the desk.

Her disgust, however, also stems from something lurking in the shadows: another werewolf who wants, as Brigitte will claim later in the film, to "mate with" her. Although the film does not explicitly state it, one could assume that the male wolf is Jason from *Ginger Snaps*: he, after all, receives only one dose of monkshood, and then promptly runs away and does not appear in the film afterwards. In this regard, the duality of the "curse" appears again: the werewolf curse and the curse of sexuality. These curses eventually transform into a base under siege-style story, with Brigitte being discovered unconscious and shipped to the ironically named Happier Times rehabilitation facility, where a group of women who are in rehabilitation from drug use mingle with the patients with severe trauma.

Brigitte is trapped, and without her regular monkshood injections, begins to confront both her werewolf curse as well as her sexual maturity. At one point, as a group of girls lie on the floor in a relaxation exercise, Brigitte begins to imagine them all furiously masturbating as the relaxation coach cajoles them on. The pseudo-fantasy shocks and disgusts Brigitte, and she screams out, disrupting the class.

While in the rehabilitation center, Brigitte is pursued by two suitors: the wolf that prowls the grounds at night, and Tyler, the head nurse. Brigitte soon discovers that Tyler trades quick fixes of drugs to the other women in the center in exchange for sexual favors. Tyler's expectations of Brigitte are no different, and he asks to inject Brigitte where "no one else will see," before demanding that she "pull down [her] pants." Brigitte, disgusted, rejects Tyler's offer. However, as her curse continues uninterrupted without her regular injections of monkshood, she eventually relents. As Tyler begins the injection, he tells her that "there's this vein down here that is very private" and then asks, "do you shave?" His question reveals that Brigitte's path is much the same as Ginger's in *Ginger Snaps*. Bereft of a cure, Brigitte not only has to acknowledge sexuality, but must embrace it as well. This embrace, of course, is partially symbolized by the growth of, and rejection of, the signs of maturity: pubic hair, for example. Brigitte's shaving of her body is dualistic in nature: a rejection of the same curses that Ginger attempted to reject.

Tyler makes no additional headway with Brigitte, and she eventually hatches a plan to escape the rehabilitation center, snatching Tyler's cache of drugs along the way. Along with the thirteen-year-old girl nicknamed Ghost, the two escape, and take shelter at the home of Ghost's grandmother. Yet, the male werewolf still pursues Brigitte, and she continues to resist her own transformation, as, true to form, she does not want to mature sexually. Brigitte, as in the first film, remains repulsed by sex and sexual activity, and is unwilling to debase herself to get her monkshood from Tyler. No small part of Brigitte's transformation—besides the fact that it is apparently complete and irreversible—is that she is being pursued by a male werewolf, and there is a definite prospect of Brigitte's wolf form being sex-driven, and, eventually, pregnant, consigned to the role of motherhood that so disgusted her in the first film.

Yet, the true villain of the story turns out to be Ghost, who continually manipulates Brigitte and the rest of the female patients. Ghost knows, and is willing to understand, that Brigitte is attempting to delay or circumvent her eventual transformation into a wolf. In Ghost's mind, true power resides with being able to control any situation and capturing Brigitte and allowing her transformation to occur unencumbered means that Ghost will have an aggressive and deadly werewolf of her own.

Much can be said about how *Ginger Snaps: Unleashed* approaches mental instability as a key trait of many of the female characters. The women who are in treatment are no doubt stuck in a patriarchal system, as exemplified not by the psychiatrists—who appear only briefly in the film—but by the commanding, demanding, and daily presence of Tyler. Tyler's toxic masculinity is such that he expects and then essentially forces compliance in all aspects of his interactions with his female patients, and he does so completely unmoored from what most would consider to be civilized behavior. Tyler doesn't simply expect obedience; he demands it.

It is important to remember that Brigitte's mental "illness" is based on her own reality—she is slowly turning into a werewolf and she is being pursued by a werewolf. In fact, the only manifestation of what many viewers would consider mental illness is the regular appearance of the now-deceased Ginger, who appears just long enough to tease Brigitte before disappearing again. Although this is somewhat of a homage to *An American Werewolf in London*, where the person affected by the curse can "see" the dead, it does exemplify Brigitte's wavering in her sanity ("I'm going crazy," David says when he sees Jack's corpse walking and talking in *An American Werewolf in London*). Yet, for Brigitte, much of her behavior is the same as in *Ginger Snaps*, and much of her "illness" stems from her unwillingness to embrace her role in the patriarchal powers of society—she still refuses a mate, is somewhat disgusted by sex, and prefers to be isolated from the rest of the world.

As for Ghost, however, her mental instability rings true. She is coldly manipulative, often tricking others into doing her bidding for her, and these actions result in several deaths. Even Brigitte, who is one of the most intelligent characters in horror cinema, is duped by Ghost and is left responsible for a murder. Yet, Ghost can sense that Brigitte is a werewolf, and, what's more, she is being pursued by a werewolf. Much of Ghost's concern is false; she is simply manipulating Brigitte, slowly coaxing her into trusting Ghost, and, what's more, slowly facilitating Brigitte's descent into becoming a werewolf. Thus, in the end of the film, just as in *Ginger Snaps*, the sister is defeated and, despite their best efforts, are defeated *by becoming a werewolf*, either wittingly or unwittingly. If the werewolf form or the "curse" represents sexuality, it can be assumed, then, that both Ginger and Brigitte are not victorious in their efforts. In Brigitte's case she is not killed and freed from her curse, as Larry Talbot so desired, but is captured and enslaved. Brigitte's fate is far worse, then, than the fate of many characters in werewolf cinema who fear the wolf. Brigitte's fears—of not only becoming a werewolf, but of staying as a werewolf—become a harsh reality. And, what's more, Brigitte is enslaved by a young girl with fantasies of murdering her "enemies," as the film ends with the ominous ring of the doorbell.

Ginger Snaps Back is the third film in the series and moves even further away from the nuance found in *Ginger Snaps*. In this case, the story of Ginger and Brigitte is re-placed in colonial Canada, where the two young women are found alone in the forest, their parents both killed. They are eventually led to Fort Bailey by the young Native scout known only as Hunter. Once inside the fort, the basic plot of *Ginger Snaps* is re-enacted, with Ginger becoming infected and Brigitte desperately trying to keep her from changing.

And, as in *Ginger Snaps*, as Ginger's wolf curse grows, so, too, does her lust. At one point in time, she dreams of passing Hunter in the hallway, only to begin kissing him. When Ginger awakes, her relatively fresh wolf bite has covered the bed in what could only be interpreted as the sudden arrival of her period as well. Ginger is horrified by the sudden blood loss, and the two sisters attempt to leave the fort, but are stymied by the all-masculine presence within the fort: a fire-and-brimstone Reverend, a Captain with a secret, and several scouts and guards, more than a few with designs on Ginger and Brigitte. And, outside the fort is a roving pack of werewolves, who have been picking off the fort's survivors one by one over the past months.

Thus, *Ginger Snaps*, reinterpreted in a different time period, reveals a uniquely modern take on the role of women in society; in fact, *Ginger Snaps Back* follows the same ideas and tropes as *Ginger Snaps*, and, although the setting and even era have changed, little has changed in terms of the overall content. Ginger is still sexualized and dangerous and viewed as a threat by the men. Brigitte is still overwhelmingly protective of her sister and reacts in horror to Ginger's slow transformations. The difference, however, resides in a slightly more problematic ending. The fort that Ginger and Brigitte join at the start of the film slowly turns from a sanctuary to a prison, with a patriarchal structure in place, embodied in the guise of the numerous men who consistently fight one another and argue. In fact, Ginger is viewed as the catalyst for the slow dissolution of the relationships within the fort. The fact that neither Ginger nor Brigitte, in the words of the Reverend Gilbert, are not "good Christian women," and that their presence has exacerbated "the devil's grip" that holds the fort in its sway. The very presence of both women sparks a series of murders and beatings amongst the men as they attempt to get close to either woman, either to romance them or to murder them.

Eventually—and this is where the film's theme deviates the most from the prior two films—Ginger and Brigitte must leave the fort. This time, Ginger, herself cursed, allows the other werewolves to storm the fort, killing the men inside. As Ginger and Brigitte huddle together in the forest, snow packed around them, Ginger realizes that, because of her curse, she no longer feels cold. Brigitte, however, is still fully human, and is dying from the cold. Ginger and Brigitte cut their hands open and mix their blood, which means that Brigitte, so unlike the previous two iterations of *Ginger Snaps*, willingly embraces the wolf "curse."

This is most likely because *Ginger Snaps Back*, as a prequel, doesn't necessarily have to follow the same logic as *Ginger Snaps*; yet Brigitte's rather willing desire to become a wolf to save her own life means a near-complete rejection of the major themes of female sexuality coalescing with the werewolf "curse" that was so prominent in the rest of the franchise.

Trick 'r Treat

The horror anthology *Trick 'r Treat* mines much of the same thematic material as *Ginger Snaps*. At the start of the film—which focuses on several characters and is told out of chronological order for the most part—we are introduced to a set of young women who are purchasing Halloween costumes. The dialogue is short and snappy and sets up the double conceit of sexuality and violence. Maria, in response to the other women mocking her sexual misadventures the year before, in which she accidentally seduced a woman instead of a man, replies: "So what? She had a nice ass. It all tastes the same to me anyway." Clearly, the women's search for "fresh meat" for this Halloween—coupled with their remembrances of Halloweens past—provoke the ire of another, older woman, who chastises them to remember the presence of children in the store. In this instance, the woman thinks that they are talking about sex, but they are discussing feasting on their prey. The seduction comes first, but what follows isn't sex, but rather death. And, if there's any hint that the conversation is solely about sex, it quickly evaporates when Anna Paquin's character, Laurie, comes out of her changing stall dressed as Little Red Riding Hood.[12]

The narrative focuses primarily on Laurie, who is repeatedly reminded that she is a "virgin at 22." The virginity, however, stems not only from presumed sexual activity, but also from her inability to locate a male victim and consume his flesh. Laurie is dressed far more conservatively and is far more socially shy than the other women, who have no compunction in finding men to meet them for a "party" in the woods. Eventually, unable to find a male to bring to the party, she wanders into the woods to be accosted by Steven Wilkins, from an earlier segment of the film. Wilkins is masquerading as a vampire and is clearly dangerous, having murdered a few people during the film to this point. The other women have already found a "nice" man for Laurie, who is overweight and passed out, but she instead gets the upper hand on Wilkins and drops him, literally, into the party. Again, the tie between sexuality and violence becomes clear, as Danielle asks Laurie what happened. A very calm Laurie says that she "played hard to get," and as Wilkins comes to, he sees the women turning into werewolves and consuming the other partygoers. As Laurie metamorphoses, she tells Wilkins "It's my first time, so bear with me."

In many ways, what fuels this narrative is the inversion of gender narratives that have dominated many werewolf films. In many films from *The Wolf Man* onward, the strong, sexually aggressive males pursue the often-meek females. In *Trick 'r Treat*, however, the women are the ones who take on the masculine role as predators, and the men—some of whom are established as murderers themselves—become the unwitting victims. The film enhances the "sexiness" of the women by putting them in fairy tale-style costumes, but in "sexy" versions of those costumes. The women being able to find willing men to join them for a party, then, shows their usage of their own sexuality to dupe their victims, who are led to slaughter. Laurie's meekness, symbolized by her comparatively chaste Red Riding Hood ensemble, soon goes away during the orgy of violence, and, just as in *The Company of Wolves*, the young woman finds a certain joy and freedom in becoming a werewolf and feasting on her victims.

An American Werewolf in Paris

Among some of the least flattering and rather unnuanced portrayals of women and female werewolves occurs in *An American Werewolf in Paris*. This film follows many of the same basic plot points of *An American Werewolf in London*—ghosts of friends that are harbingers of doom, klutzy and goofy American becomes a wolf and wins the girl—but that's where the resemblance essentially ends. *An American Werewolf in Paris* follows three distinctly less likable American males than David and Jack. Unlike *An American Werewolf in London*, in which David and Jack are simply traversing the British countryside, Chris, Brad, and Andy are all on a journey of "scores" through Europe. Their "scores" are for performing ridiculous stunts or for bedding attractive women. As they ride in a train to Paris, Chris and Brad loudly chastise Andy for not earning any "sex points" on the trip so far, and ask him when he last had sex, insinuating that Andy's differentiation between "sex" and "love" makes him less manly—or at least less masculine—than they are. Their teasing gets under Andy's skin, who decides to perform a stunt that would earn him numerous points: breaking into the Eiffel Tower and bungee jumping off the top.

This is where Andy meets and immediately falls in love with Serafine, a Parisian woman who is about to commit suicide by leaping off the Eiffel Tower. Serafine is a werewolf, of course, and she performs an oddly matriarchal role at the start, at least from her perspective. Andy and his friends, of course, initially view Serafine as a conquest, and, as such, Andy tries to score "points" with her before she ultimately rejects him. Later, when the two of them are reunited, Andy has been bitten by a werewolf. As he panics, Serafine tears off her shirt and places his hands on her bare breasts. Serafine does this, presumably, to calm Andy, not for sexual gratification. Naturally, Andy feels that Serafine is trying to have sex with him. *An American Werewolf in Paris* plays with this tension throughout the film: Serafine is assuming the role of Andy's mother, in many ways, by protecting him and guiding him through multiple new experiences, while Andy views Serafine as a romantic partner. This conflict leads a hypermasculinized Andy to seek out his sexual fantasies elsewhere, stumbling across an American tourist named Amy. They soon have sex on Jim Morrison's grave, and Andy transforms into a wolf as he climaxes, devouring Amy as she screams.

All of this makes the ending of the film very bizarre, as Serafine moves from mother to lover (a possible homage to Alex's role in *An American Werewolf in London*), a transformation that powers the narrative almost as much as Andy's transformation into a werewolf. Serafine, the experienced hand at being a werewolf, guides Andy to maturity as a wolf, and, finally, provides guidance to returning to human form after breaking his curse. At one point, the roles invert, as Serafine, held captive along with Andy by a police officer, loses her cool and begins berating the officer, only to have Andy calm her down. Soon after, Serafine's transition from mother to subservient female lover becomes complete, as she gives Andy a knife, and the power to kill her. "Cut out my fucking heart," she screams at him, baring her chest, "go on, do it!" Andy refuses to do so, and Serafine begins to weep about, not *her* curse, but about *his* curse. Now completely subservient, the Serafine who shot at enemy werewolves and guided Andy through his initial steps in his curse, has transformed into the Serafine who watches in awe as Andy hatches plans and calmly disarms people.

And Serafine's transformation to a wolf ironically completes her transformation to victim. Trapped in a tunnel with Claude, an evil werewolf, and Andy, she transforms into a wolf to even the odds, at which point, Andy shoots her. This changes her back into human form, and Serafine again begs Andy to kill her, which he refuses. In this moment, Serafine has fully embraced her subservient role, needing to be rescued by Andy, whose actions actually effectuated the rescue. In other words, Andy, who seeks a lover, not a mother, shoots Serafine in aggressive werewolf form, and she, quite literally, transforms twice: from wolf to woman, and from independent woman to full and complete subservience.

The next time Serafine appears, she is bungee jumping off the Statue of Liberty with Andy as a part of their wedding ceremony. This bookended conclusion highlights the change in Serafine. She has moved from an independent woman who, although she attempts suicide, quickly rejects Andy's attempts at "rescuing" or "saving" her throughout the film. Her first jump is, for her, one toward freedom. Her second job is the figurative plunge into matrimony. Her role, and her transformation, into a woman who functions completely as the object of Andy's desire, becomes fulfilled. Perhaps no werewolf film fulfills the roles of enemy, mother, lover, and object as completely as *An American Werewolf in Paris*, and the transformation from one role to the next occurs entirely within one character: Serafine.

Wild Country

The mostly forgotten *Wild Country*, although certainly forgotten for a reason, does have nuance in how it depicts masculinity and women in its narrative. The film opens with young teen Kelly Ann giving birth. A little while after the child is born, Father Steve appears at the door, telling Kelly Ann that her giving the child up for adoption was the best thing she could have done. This sets up the framework for the second part of the film, as, for a moment, Kelly Ann's postpartum depression and desire to regain her child play out.

Before this narrative comes to fruition, however, the basic setup for the film reminds one of the opening moments of *An American Werewolf in London*, where victims are pursued over rugged terrain, only played out over much of the film. Father Steve drops off a small group of teenage ne'er-do-wells, and tasks them to hike to a destination as part of a group adventure. The group consists of Kelly Ann, Louise, and the brothers David and Mark. As these things go, a young man named Lee, ostensibly at the invitation of David, joins the hike. Lee is the father of Kelly Ann's child.

A clear pecking order is established among the males of the group, and the film's narrative briefly focuses on the interplay between them. Lee is the oldest of the group, sexually active, and drinks beer. He also carries, and cue Freudian interpretations here, a switchblade. David, Mark's older brother, wants to be like Lee, and he often joins Lee is victimizing Mark in a variety of ways, all designed to make him feel inadequate. Thus, the teenaged pack is in place: Lee is the alpha male of the group, David his close companion, and Mark the much-maligned "weak" male. They even nickname Mark their "mascot," which leads him to tears, pushing him further away from their toxic masculinity.

Of course, night falls, and the wolves soon appear, but not before a memorable jump scare featuring a sheep, which may be a cinematic first. Of course, the wolves are not discriminatory in their attacks, and quickly (and ironically) kill a shepherd who was spying on the group. David, in his desire to be more like Lee, kicks Mark out of his tent and invites Louise over, while Kelly Ann and Lee giggle. Mark, who initially joined in mocking Louise's weight, seems to be quite delighted by the prospect of exhibiting his masculinity to David and Lee. Kelly Ann soon hears a baby crying in a nearby castle, and she and Lee investigate, finding a male infant among multiple human remains. Kelly Ann begins to breastfeed the hungry child and complains that the infant must have a tooth coming through.

After Mark is captured and torn apart by the wolves, the group tries to continue toward some safety, but are pinned by the wolves, and Louise is soon dead as well. David, only slightly nonplussed by the brutal deaths of his younger brother and apparent new girlfriend, retreats with Lee and Kelly

Ann back to the abandoned castle, where the wolves have kept a storeroom of human remains. Thus, the trio hatch a plan to kill the wolf, and are successful, bashing it in the head with an absurdly large rock and then stabbing it with sharpened sticks. It is here, however, that the film reveals that they are not being pursued by one wolf, but two.

Despite its remarkably obvious low budget, *Wild Country* succeeds in having a rather sudden tonal shift, moving from a man vs. wolf narrative to a narrative that focuses entirely on the female. In this case, Lee meets his demise somewhat heroically, confessing that he would not have been a good father to their child before sacrificing himself to the wolves so that Kelly Ann could escape and seek out Father Steve's help.

Ironically, Father Steve is the most toxic male in the film; bereft of anything other than the cloak of moral superiority, Father Steve lied to Kelly Ann and Lee so that their baby would be put up for adoption. Additionally, Father Steve becomes quite smitten with the local innkeeper and is quite happy to have sex with her while the teens make their way toward the inn. When Kelly Ann arrives, Father Steve dismisses her werewolf story as fantasy, accusing her of stealing the baby from another couple. Father Steve's duplicity can only carry him so far, however, as the wolf has followed Kelly Ann to the inn, where it quickly dispatches the innkeeper, and builds to the film's final—and somewhat puzzling—reveal. Father Steve dashes up the steps—having locked the door on the innkeeper so she could not escape the enraged wolf, which is itself an action borne from his concern that the innkeeper won't keep their tryst a secret—and opens the door to see that Kelly Ann, too, has become a werewolf, with a tiny wolf suckling at her teat. It can only be assumed that Kelly Ann's act of breastfeeding the child allowed the "curse" to be transmitted.

But, in *Wild Country*, becoming a werewolf doesn't seem to be a curse at all. In a bizarre tonal shift, the credits begin to roll over a bucolic scene of two werewolves and one tiny werewolf playing together in a pasture. To make the scene even more bizarre, as they frolic, the Sam the Sham song "Li'l Red Riding Hood" plays. Despite the brutal deaths of Louise, Mark, David, and Lee, and the forced adoption of her own child, Kelly Ann apparently finds a sort of freeing happiness in becoming a wolf, murdering Father Steve (presumably, at least, for the camera zooms in on Peter Capaldi's screaming face before cutting away) and joining her own new and unfamiliar pack. Considering that the baby was, at first, human, this means, too, that the wolves were following and tracking Kelly Ann not because they want to kill her—although that could be a side benefit—but because they want their baby to be returned to them.

This opens a series of intriguing possibilities in the narrative. After all, both wolves worked together to isolate Louise so that they could lure Lee and

David to her, leaving Kelly Ann alone, unprotected, with the infant. In this regard, then, the wolves were quite intent on recapturing their child. But something changes, as one of the wolves is killed, the other wolf gains vengeance, and then merely accepts the wolf Kelly as a part of the family.

No small part of this confusion stems from a lack of detail to the wolves themselves in the script. This is a movie that is, ostensibly, focused on Kelly Ann and her plight,[13] and thus, there is precious little backstory given to the wolves. For almost any other film that features even a partial man vs. wolf theme, this is unusual: *Dog Soldiers* revealed the "human" side of the wolves, for example. But the wolves that are set as antagonists for the teens in *Wild Country* may be simply oversized and bizarre ... wolves, completely without the "were" part.

This creates numerous problems in interpreting *Wild Country* with any success, and its little surprise that the film, in all of werewolf cinema, is rarely mentioned. Peter Hutchings notes that the strangeness in *Wild Country* stems from Kelly Ann's near-total shift into a loss of gender identity (171). The viewer only sees Kelly Ann for a few seconds, and, save for the small wolf feeding, she is indistinguishable from the other male wolves. In other words, the film wants the viewer to feel that Kelly Ann has somehow gained her freedom, but in so doing, she has lost, entirely, her feminine identity. She becomes, quite simply, just another member of a pack.

This ending, quite naturally, spoils the entire film's attempt to turn Kelly Ann into an independent female character, who is defined by her ability to survive as well as her own mental fortitude. Of course, a criticism could be made that *Wild Country* focuses on the relative anonymity of motherhood, and the overwhelming pressure on women to conform to maternal instincts in Western society. Yet, if this were the case, then one would suspect that Kelly Ann would not be cast as a sympathetic character who is literally tricked by the antagonist Father Steve into giving up her child. Additionally, Kelly Ann wouldn't seek the forgiveness or explanation of Lee, and she certainly wouldn't be so quick to pursue a crying babe in the wilderness.

In this regard, Kelly Ann's ending, and her eventual descent into a werewolf is at once liberating and entrapping, for her "curse" reunites her with an infant and gives her an instant family. However, Kelly Ann is forever stuck with those same benefits, and her anonymity granted by a purely matriarchal role is assured. In some ways, Kelly Ann's turn into a werewolf essentially erases her from existence. Her boyfriend, her friends, her pastor, are all dead, and the only person who exists at the end of the film that has any sort of relationship with her is her mother, who makes a brief appearance at Kelly Ann's bedside at the start of the film. And, it is safe to say, that relationship is most likely strained, as she encourages Kelly Ann not to "make the same mistakes," before Kelly Ann interrupts, "like you?" The statement—with its insinuation that Kelly Ann knows that she, too, is a "mistake"—essentially erases the mother from the film. She never appears again.

Although *Wild Country* was essentially ignored by critics, with only the relative heavyweight actor Peter Capaldi stirring vague interest in the work, the film does take a relatively *Ginger Snaps*–like approach to gender. Kelly Ann's pregnancy and the loss of her child forces her to seek out her matriarchal role—whether she likes it or not—among the wolves, and her eventual transformation into a wolf is leaden with deepening questions regarding gender, all hidden in the cloak of a near-typical "base under siege" and revenge-driven narrative. For all its flaws, and especially in the consistent exposure of its incredibly low budget, *Wild Country* does try something new. Like the werewolves in the film, which never quite manage to look like the traditional werewolf, *Wild Country* is a film that also seems, also perhaps due to budget constraints, to never quite manage to pursue the traditional gender-normative narrative of the traditional werewolf film.

Although *Ginger Snaps* and *The Company of Wolves* are no doubt some of the first werewolf films that will spring to mind when one mentions female werewolves, the genre has generally struggled to maintain rounded and positive depictions of femininity over the years. Indeed, many of the women are pigeonholed into the same sort of roles as the slasher film. Even films such as *Ginger Snaps* or *Wild Country* that attempt to explore new roles for female werewolves—and female characters in werewolf cinema—are often burdened by the decades of gender definitions that dominate werewolf lore, and, as a result, these individual female werewolves and their genders are problematized by the presence of the wolf itself. In many ways, a "liberated" female character such as Ginger may only be as feminine as the genre of werewolf folklore and cinema allows, and the formation of Ginger's gender identity, among many other female werewolves, becomes almost entirely dependent on the genre's prior gender explorations. In other words, werewolves are so imbued with the interrogation of masculinity that the very presence of a female werewolf problematizes both genres, and as a result, these films often raise more questions than they try to answer.

Conclusion

There are far more werewolf films than appear in this volume, but the overall trend generally holds when one examines how masculinity is portrayed over the decades since Dr. Wilfred Glendon first turned into a wolf. In the end, the earliest werewolf films embraced the "tragic" aspects of the afflicted male; in fact, the male affected by his new "curse" was often the source of sympathy for viewers, and his opposite, the wolf itself, was the horrible opposite pole, to be loathed by viewers. Even though the man and the wolf, primarily because of limitations on special effects, often resembled one another, their actions were extreme. Men like Larry Talbot and Glendon clearly struggled with and disliked their alter egos, going to often suicidal extremes to reject their curse.

As the decades passed, however, the lines blurred. Tony Rivers struggled with his curse, but his actions as a human were also violent—a juvenile delinquent who struck out violently in almost every direction for no reason. For Rivers, his wolf wasn't a form opposite of his own masculinity—it was a significant expansion, highlighting all the violence and toxicity that he had mostly repressed. And, although films like *The Werewolf* still attempted to get viewers to sympathize with the man and hate the wolf, *I Was a Teenage Werewolf* heralded a new perspective on the man, the wolf, and their collective relationship to masculinity.

Thus, the 1980s. The werewolf film enjoyed a popularity not seen since four decades prior, and multiple productions began to tinker with the tried-and-true formulas of their ancestors. In many ways, films such as *Teen Wolf* and *The Howling* modified the tragic aspects of the curse; shame, resistance, and hatred of one's wolf form began to fall by the wayside. Scott Howard (as well as his father) not only embrace the new aspects of masculinity that their wolf forms bring—they revel in it, as do those completely unshaken characters who simply accept that their best friend in high school can, indeed, turn into a wolf.

Alternatively, male characters such as Bill in *The Howling* shows a man completely changed by his wolf form. Bill doesn't actively resist his curse; his human side embraces the violence and toxicity of the wolf, and his actions are a seismic change in his masculinity. His caring, almost maternal nature toward Karen is replaced by his less-than-clandestine affair with another woman and his physical attacks on Karen. Bill is one of the dividing lines in werewolf cinema: he is one of the final male characters to undergo not a wolf transformation but a distinctly masculine one: from soft to toxic, from sympathetic to unlikable. From *The Howling* forward, men like Bill become a rarity; instead, men will embrace their newfound (to borrow from Montague Summers) "abnormality," sometimes to their detriment, but often to their advantage.

And, of course, *An American Werewolf in London*, which has been, and remains, the standard for American werewolf films. In many ways, although the spectacular special effects are one of the primary draws for the film, the experience of David Kessler harks back to the experiences of Larry Talbot. Kessler is afflicted with a curse he can't understand, and legitimately fears, and his friends and lovers are unable to help him. The new and more advanced special effects, however, allowed the symbolism of the massive split between wolf and man to come into greater focus. Whereas Lon Chaney, Sr., plays Larry Talbot, and then a Wolf Man that still resembles Larry Talbot, or at least a human male, the special effects had progressed far enough by the 1980s that the wolf could, quite literally, be a body apart from the human actor.

The resulting era of werewolf films are a unique hodgepodge of attempts at subverting the previous narratives, and their resultant expectations and interrogations of masculinity. *Wolf* gleefully embraces the supposedly positive aspects of becoming a "hard" (or, one could argue, "toxic") male. Films such as *Dog Soldiers* and *Late Phases* focused on the wolves as an external threat, mostly unknown to their human combatants. *Ginger Snaps* attempted to portray and symbolize the male "curse" as a uniquely feminine experience. And films like *Wer* and *Howl* depicted males who slowly doffed their soft masculinity and delighted in the power that their "curse" brought to them. Shame and stigma no more for these characters.

At the center of many werewolf films, however, remains gender identity, especially in regard to masculinity. In many respects, the werewolf film never quite carved out its own niche in the same way that, say, the Dracula (or more generically, vampires), or Frankenstein-style monsters did. Instead, the werewolf film, especially the representative works covered in this book, often borrowed liberally from the themes and tropes of their time period; this is never so readily apparent as the 1980s forward, where werewolf cinema became an unusual amalgam of the classic tragic male in the vein of Larry Talbot, the musclebound, uber-masculine revenge fantasy, or the generic spin on the horror slasher film, replete with copious amounts of gore.

Conclusion 155

The various forms of masculinity, however, are all the uniting factors across much of werewolf cinema. Whether they be the tragic male who throws himself off a cliff, or die in a hail of bullets, or gleefully murder their enemy, or the young woman who suddenly finds herself the dominant player in her social world, the scope and focus of the masculine remains the dominant theme.

Beyond the conversation about masculinity that dominates this volume are additional areas of exploration. The end notes mention werewolf cinema's preoccupation with heteronormativity; although these notes were not enough to cast into their own chapter and discussion, they do reveal a critical pathway to deeper investigations. In many cases, the werewolf film has refused to portray homosexuality openly, relying instead on stereotypes or Freudian insinuations. Additionally, with few exceptions, werewolf cinema has stayed within the standard horror trope of nearly all-white casts and characters. This could be easily dismissed as a vestige of the horror film itself, other franchises featuring vampires and even Frankenstein's monster have fielded multicultural casts. Clearly this topic, too, is one that could be ripe for critical exploration.

And yet, werewolf films remain, outside of brief spates of popularity, relegated to the critical backwaters of film study. A quick glance through almost any academic search engine will reveal even highly regarded films such as *An American Werewolf in London* or *The Howling* receiving scant critical attention. Much of this may be the very generic style of creature: there can be thousands of interpretations and "looks" for vampires and zombies, for example, but in the end, the cursed figure in werewolf cinema only has one direction to go—wolf. As Curtis Siodmak wrote, "The Wolf Man knows that he is going to kill when the moon is full. A thousand writers can write a thousand screenplays around those ideas, but the original idea cannot be replaced. The wheel would fall apart without its pivot" (270). Although the wolves often look different, and the human motivations may change, and many later films focus almost exclusively on special effects and the initial transformation scene, the character still turns into what is, identifiably, a wolf. This creature—an animal—makes it extraordinarily difficult to attach human ideas and emotions onto it without lapsing into parody (as in *Wolf Cop*). Other than a faint glimmer of recognition in the eyes, a pause before killing, the werewolf is a feral creature, unable to receive human emotions and motivations.

After the massive leap in narrative style and focus that occurred with films such as *The Howling* (which brought keen horror sensibilities back), *An American Werewolf in London* (the standard bearer for special effects and pacing), and *Ginger Snaps* (gender bending), there has been precious little creativity in the genre; in fact, those films that seem to take a fresh perspective on werewolves are the films based in parody: *What We Do in the Shadows* and *Wolf Cop*, for example. Almost every werewolf film since, including *Howl*, *Wolves*, and *Wer*, among others, bring forward the same notion that masculinity must somehow be aggressive at best, utterly violent at worst. Soft males become hardened or toxic by their curses, and they embrace and relish their newfound hardened edge. Instead of Larry Talbot literally trying to run away from his coming transformation, many male characters now rush headlong toward their newfound powers, incorporating the more vicious or assertive aspects of the wolf into their own human characters.

In this way, then, werewolf cinema has somewhat stagnated again. After the initial universe-building exercise of Universal's *The Wolfman*, a hodgepodge of bizarre and unusual werewolf films—most of them constrained heavily by budget—drew the genre downwards in the estimation of critics and fans. Yet, even the relatively dry spell of almost fifty years featured numerous films that are ripe for critical interrogation of gender issues. The domestic portraiture of *The Werewolf*, the directly contrasting toxic masculinity issues of *I Was a Teenage Werewolf*, the excoriation of independent (and violent) women in *Cry of the Werewolf*—all, for their relative lack of plot, special effects, and characterization, focused on gender as a central theme.

The current trajectory of werewolf cinema, however, has moved far away from interrogation of masculinity and femininity, and onward to a near-wholesale embrace of hegemonic and toxic masculinity, for better or for worse. The often-nuanced portraits of a cursed male (or female) have been replaced by a more simplistic take, no doubt influenced by the success of action films over the intervening decades. Slow burn films that focus on characterization and gender, such as *Late Phases*, are a rarity, as more action-oriented shooters such as *Dog Soldiers* or films that endorse violence and basic horror tropes, such as *Wer*, take their place.

Interestingly, the past few decades have seen women playing the role of the werewolf more frequently. After *Cry of the Werewolf*, female werewolves largely disappeared from the screen until *The Howling*, when they were either sexual predators (Marsha) or sexually repressed (Karen); their existence, however, was only to propel the plot surrounding the men forward. Although Karen is ostensibly the main character of *The Howling*, she often exhibits little to no agency, bandied about by forces against her will. Ironically, her final decision—to reveal to the world the reality of the werewolf—leads to her complete destruction. The moment she takes autonomy is followed by the moments when she is erased from the world.

Ginger Snaps and *The Company of Wolves* would truly be the first films to attempt to take a uniquely feminist perspective on the male-dominated lore of the werewolf. Both films associate a young woman's coming of age with the "curse," *Ginger Snaps* doing so more literally. Yet, the tremendous associations of the werewolf with hegemonic or toxic masculinity confuse these attempts—in seeking to establish a uniquely feminine experience, Ginger and Rosaleen become or otherwise embrace violent predators. Ginger's attempt to resist her "curse," through such actions as piercing herself with a silver bellybutton ring, only seem to accelerate her discomfort, and by the end of *Ginger Snaps* her previous identity as a young woman resisting her stereotypical gender definitions has shifted to a nameless beast, lying dead on the floor. In the case of Rosaleen, she actively rejects her Granny's admonitions regarding the presence of men, and instead embraces her Granny's murderer, willingly turning into a wolf herself (although the framing of the narrative will throw this into doubt). Thus, although gender and femininity were central to the core of both films and were ultimately successful attempts at reinventing a new narrative, the question of the masculine appears frequently in both films.

In the end, there are, without a doubt, independent filmmakers and actors who are willing to investigate new angles on the werewolf legend, but they are often drowned out by low budgets and a near-literal sea of schlock. In many ways, werewolves continue to remain a bit player in a larger universe of monsters; never quite frightening enough to be anything more than a basic slasher film, never quite nuanced enough to avoid treading old ground while embracing prevailing trends. Even in films with more than one monster, the werewolf has been relegated to playing support behind vampires.

Yet, the history of the werewolf film—as spotty as it may be in some places regarding overall quality—remains ripe for critical examination. As gender definitions and ideas regarding masculinity shifted over the decades, so, too, did the very definition of the "curse," and its ramifications for those afflicted with turning into a wolf. This volume is hopefully one of the first of many to explore how werewolf cinema has routinely returned to gender and masculinity as central themes throughout their collective history, and perhaps join the critical attention that other franchises, such as those featuring vampires or Frankenstein's monster, have already received.

Filmography

Werewolf of London (1935)
The Wolf Man (1941)
The Undying Monster (1942)
Frankenstein Meets the Wolf Man (1943)
Cry of the Werewolf (1944)
House of Frankenstein (1944)
House of Dracula (1945)
The Werewolf (1956)
I Was a Teenage Werewolf (1957)
The Curse of the Werewolf (1961)
The Boy Who Cried Werewolf (1973)
The Beast Must Die (1974)
The Werewolf and the Yeti (1975)
An American Werewolf in London (1981)
The Howling (1981)
Night of the Werewolf (1981)
Wolfen (1981)
The Company of Wolves (1984)
Silver Bullet (1985)
Teen Wolf (1985)
Teen Wolf Too (1987)

Wolf (1994)
Bad Moon (1996)
An American Werewolf in Paris (1997)
Ginger Snaps (2000)
Dog Soldiers (2002)
Underworld (2003)
Ginger Snaps 2: Unleashed (2004)
Ginger Snaps Back (2004)
Cursed (2005)
Wild Country (2005)
Trick 'r Treat (2007)
Underworld: Rise of the Lycans (2009)
The Wolfman (2010)
The Grey (2011)
Wer (2013)
Late Phases (2014)
Wolves (2014)
What We Do in the Shadows (2014)
Wolf Cop (2014)
Howl (2015)
Another Wolf Cop (2017)

Chapter Notes

Preface

1. For that, one should look for Bryan Senn's brilliant *The Werewolf Filmography*, which covers over three hundred werewolf films, coupled with write-ups for each one.

Introduction

1. In werewolf cinema, the two sets of characters—Jekyll and Hyde, and man and werewolf—only appear together once, in the Paul Naschy vehicle (featuring, of course, the long-suffering character Waldemar Daninsky) *Dr. Jekyll and the Werewolf*.
2. Paul Naschy's first career was as a professional bodyguard.
3. Ironically, for all of the pain of the transformation, Daninsky turns into a creature that isn't too far off from the classic look of the original special effects of *The Wolf Man*. Compared to the massive transformations that come in other films, and the animalistic results afterwards, the transformations of Daninsky are often startlingly long, anticlimactic, and just a little (unintentionally) comedic.
4. Some of the more critically acclaimed (or at least critically acknowledged) slasher films are also the same ones that worked hard to interrogate conventional, at least for the slasher film genre, gender roles. *Sleepaway Camp* (1983) and *A Nightmare on Elm Street 2: Freddy's Revenge* (1985) are two examples of slasher films that worked to defy traditional gender definitions in their main characters.

The Racial Dynamics of Werewolf Cinema

1. This idea—that the sexually active woman who exposes herself during the film is the one most likely to be killed—was parodied in *Cabin in the Woods*. However, the *Friday the 13th* franchise self-parodied this concept a full decade earlier in *Jason X*, when a futuristic Jason is automatically attracted to a pair of holographic and semi-nude women who squeal "We love pre-marital sex!"
2. Some of the earliest werewolf films juxtapose science and folklore or religion. Larry Talbot peers through a telescope in *The Wolf Man*; Wilfred Glendon is a botanist conducting experiments. And numerous scientists, mad or soon-to-be mad, appear in the ongoing Larry Talbot saga that spans multiple films.
3. Reagan's masculinity during his presidency was often dramatically heightened by his most ardent adorers. A poster with the caption RONBO was quite popular in the mid–80s and featured a smiling Reagan's face cropped over John Rambo's face. The poster, a clear mimic of the *Rambo II* film poster, was clearly designed to re-cast Reagan as a militaristic, muscle-bound patriot. There would be, among growing popular concerns about his age and mental stamina, no questions allowed about his masculinity.
4. It seems that one of the prerequisites for a werewolf film in the 1980s and 1990s is the early establishment of heteronormativity on the part of the male character—something that is almost always established almost immediately after the opening credits. Bill in

The Howling is in a relationship with Karen. David and his friend Jack talk about Debbie Kline, a woman who is a "mediocre person with a good body." Scott Howard openly pines for Pamela and is unaware of the crush Boof has on him. Andy McDermott and his friends talk about scoring points for sexual conquests. The early establishment of hetereonormativity in modern werewolf films avoids any questions regarding homosexuality; this may be due, in part, to critical interpretations of classic werewolf films such as *Werewolf of London* or *The Wolf Man*, where repressed homosexuality is assumed to be a consistent theme in those works. The stable but repressed romantic relationship between man and woman has been, over time, replaced by numerous male characters who court, or have courted, numerous women.

The Saga of Larry Talbot

1. Talbot's repressed sexual urges, of course, could also represent his struggle with latent homosexuality. In an oft-repeated theme in horror cinema, "[t]he multi-layered excesses of the horror form mask gay shame, 'covering up' gay men's anxieties about their own problematic masculinities" (Elliott-Smith 197). Of course, the symbolism of the wolf hiding "in plain sight" has been ripe for queer theory studies of the werewolf, and Larry Talbot's often confused actions and masculinity provides ample substance.

2. Talbot's diagnosis of himself, for that time period, was spot on, as "the werewolf is a literal instantiation of the 'lunatic'—a word reflecting he traditional belief that temporary insanity might be caused by phases of the moon" (Covey 1390). Mannering will never use this diagnosis for Talbot; at one point Talbot asks if Mannering's solution is "to put [him] in a lunatic asylum." Mannering replies "you know that's where you belong." Mannering, then, only agrees with Talbot, subtly, that he is a werewolf, and only after gathering sufficient evidence.

3. Curtis Siodmak wrote about Lon Chaney, Jr., in *Frankenstein Meets the Wolf Man*, noting that Chaney was "a tragic character who couldn't adjust himself to life [...] Lon played himself, which made his part frighteningly believable" (270). More than a few critics and contemporaries have insinuated that one possibility for Chaney's inability to "adjust himself to life" was due, in part, to the possibility that Chaney was a "latent homosexual" (Smith 41). In a letter, Siodmak would later assert that he never wrote love scenes for Chaney, because "he could not adjust to a sexual preference he was unable to accept" (Mank 100).

4. This sequence—a woman who loves the man afflicted with the curse and who must ultimately be the one to bear the burden of killing him—may have inspired Paul Naschy's Waldemar Daninsky series, in which Daninsky can only die if a woman who truly loves him is the one to kill him.

5. In an odd moment in *House of Dracula*, Dr. Edelmann refers to Frankenstein's monster as "the undying monster," which may be a nod to *The Undying Monster*, a werewolf film from three years prior.

6. Dr. Edelmann's theory—and his eventual successful cure—means that John Talbot was right in *The Wolf Man*: much of his son's troubles were indeed "only in [his] own mind."

7. Another possible reading would more closely mimic the queer readings of *Werewolf of London*. Talbot spends much of the series, after his initial rejected advances toward Gwen, ignoring or pushing away the women who approach him. Instead, Talbot seeks out, in every film, the man who can assist him—Dr. Mannering, Dr. Neimann, Dr. Edelmann, and his affection for the men as they try to cure him is strong. However, in their inevitable betrayal into becoming a "mad" scientist, Talbot has to reject them, too, either by destroying their proxy (often the Frankenstein monster), or by killing them himself. In the end, the wolf man that inhabits Talbot could be read as his latent homosexuality, an invisible curse that he attempts to keep repressed, even if it means his own death. It is only when he is "cured" by Dr. Edelmann's treatment, which smacks of phrenology, the study of the shape of one's skull. Victorian phrenologists felt that "adhesiveness" was a quality that could lead to homosexual behavior; "[m]ost of the descriptions of extremely strong same-sex passion appear in the literature as abuses of adhesiveness" (Lynch 91).

8. For clarity, the Lon Chaney film will be referred to as *The Wolf Man*, and the more

modern del Toro film will be referred to as *The Wolfman*.

9. For a film based on a classic work, the updated *The Wolfman* spends quite a bit of time hearkening back not to *The Wolf Man*, but to *An American Werewolf in London*, which appeared forty years after the source material. As Bryan Senn points out, the film provides some distinct homages to *An American Werewolf in London*, including "when Talbot's lycanthrope rampages through a crowded London street in a nineteenth-century version of the Piccadilly Circus rampage" in *An American Werewolf in London* as well as the "moment of recognition" in the wolf's eyes when confronted with the love for the woman—before attacking her and being killed (264).

10. The tomb itself resembles, in some ways, the central tomb "in the cellar" of the Hammond mansion in *The Undying Monster*.

The Pre–1960s Werewolf

1. Of course, "wolf" is now a somewhat antiquated term for a sexually aggressive male. The film *Anatomy of a Murder* (1959), a courtroom drama, hinges almost entirely on the term "wolf" when describing a man accused of sexually assaulting a woman. The witness cycles through several different terms of increasing intensity: a "ladies' man," "woman chaser," "masher," and finally, "wolf." The word the attorney and witness sought already had a definition: "a man with an insatiable penchant for women." Bernhardt-House is quick to note that "the wolf is universally a sexual creature, as is its canine domesticated counterpart" (161).

2. At the start of *The Undying Monster*, the Hammond house is pictured overlooking almost everything else, and the camera reminds the viewer of the family's inherited wealth as it scans from item to item before eventually settling on a napping Helga. A few moments later, when the screams start, Helga immediately thinks that some of the lowly townspeople have attacked Oliver and Kate, mentioning that Oliver had caught a poacher on his land and had given him a "thrashing," for which the man was now seeking revenge.

3. In fact, as we will see throughout this volume, the "queering" of the werewolf and werewolf lore has been primarily critic- and fan-driven. In these perspectives, the "fear of atavistic sexuality" (Elliott 94) is read as an individual coping with their hidden or closeted selves, represented by the werewolf. Of course, the werewolf's unrelenting appearances coupled with the individual's shame and fear over the next appearance of the wolf would be symbolic of a society or an individual attempting to repress an individual's homosexuality.

4. Karen's unusual end—an effort to expose the "reality" of the werewolf in a rather dramatic fashion—can be read as a 1980s-style rebuttal of sexuality in women (du Coudray 118). When compared with the sexually aggressive werewolf Marsha, Karen comes across as intensely repressed. In that regard, the 1970s-style sexual liberation embodied by Marsha is rejected by the buttoned-down 1980s-style Karen (118). In a word, Karen rejects in the most public way possible, all insinuations associated with being a werewolf, even if it means sexuality and femininity (and enjoyment of those aspects of her character). Karen simply refuses to exist while carrying the "curse" that Marsha enjoyed—and employed—so well.

5. It should be noted that this isn't the "protective" hegemony mentioned at the start of the book. Duncan's primary concern isn't protecting his family from supposedly outside sources. He wants them sent away because *he* doesn't want to harm them.

The 1960s and 1970s

1. In a deft bit of foreshadowing, Caroline asks Newcliffe at the start of the film about his plans. She asks him what would happen if she turned out to be a werewolf. "POW!" is Newcliffe's less-than-politic response. Caroline sighs and grimaces as he leaves the room.

2. This overlong chase sequence occurs when Jan simply hops into his luxury car and drives away, without Davinia. Newcliffe climbs into his Land Rover, and the chase begins, with Jan's refined car struggling to keep ahead of Newcliffe's rugged, and far more masculinized, vehicle. Indeed, much of the chase is shot through the window of

the Land Rover, placing the viewer squarely in the passenger seat alongside Newcliffe. Newcliffe, slyly grinning, outmaneuvers Jan by going off-road and cutting off his path of escape. Jan claims to be going to a local town to visit, but Newcliffe insists that Jan ride back to the estate ... in the Land Rover.

The 1980s Onwards

1. In many ways, Dr. Hirsch's story arc closely resembles Dr. Mannering in *Frankenstein Meets the Wolf Man*. Both doctors feel that the discussion about being a "werewolf" doesn't mean that the person is actually changing into a wolf, but that the supposedly "cursed" individual is, in Dr. Hirsch's words, "deranged." They both theorize that the victim's mental illness means that they do, indeed, think they are wolves, and that, in turn, does not lead to transformation, but to violent actions. Both Hirsch and Mannering also further their theory by travelling to the small town where the "curse" originates.

2. Scott's potentially latent homosexuality also makes an appearance in *Teen Wolf*. In one sequence, Scott is ready to confess being a werewolf to his friend Stiles, who says "if you're gonna tell me you're a fag, I can't handle it." Stiles's concern about Scott being gay may have some basis in reality: after all, when Scott is finally "out" as a werewolf, it's at the basketball game, where, during a scuffle over the ball, he turns into a wolf while under a group of male players.

3. In *The Simpsons* episode "Treehouse of Horror X," Homer pokes the recently deceased Ned Flanders with a sharp stick after the family, lost in the fog, runs over Flanders as he walks down the middle of the road on a "fog walk." The offscreen squishing noise that Flanders's body makes is possibly a homage to the effects in *Wolf*.

4. *Wolf* never uses the word "werewolf" to describe Randall's wolf form; instead using the term "demon wolf."

5. Along with the "mystic" Indian who gives Randall the amulet designed to prevent him from turning into a wolf, these characters are the only underrepresented people who appear in the film. As much of the film's action is set in New York City, the whiteness of the film is striking.

6. It is worthwhile to note that over two decades separate Michelle Pfeiffer and Jack Nicholson. The film definitely places Raymond Alden and Will Randall in the same age category, thus heightening the difference in age between Laura and Randall.

7. The ostensible head of this group of feral werewolves, William, doesn't appear until *Underworld: Evolutions*, which is so sparse on werewolves in general as to earn only this brief mention in this volume. William is so uncontrollable and feral that he has completely lost the last vestiges of humanity and is unable to revert from his werewolf form. For much of the film, William the werewolf is essentially a mindless weapon of mass destruction. Thus, Lucien's concerns about finding the balance of his masculinity—and by extension, his humanity—play out in *Evolutions*.

8. In an attempt to put a unique spin on the werewolf legend, *Wer*'s writers posit that a form of porphyria is the cause of werewolf-ism. This is a creative nod to theories posited that sought to explain "real" werewolves, with the condition of porphyria being a culprit (Otten 195–198). There are numerous issues with the theory as presented in *Wer*, of course, but the greatest one is, that if porphyria is a potential reason for Talan's madness, it doesn't explain how he became strong enough to throw fully armored, fully grown men several yards, and to jump out of buildings and land on the nearby pavement before outrunning the police.

9. After Kate gets shot, she disappears from the film. During the closing interview, Gavin states that Kate is recovering nicely from her gunshot wound. This could mean many things. Kate and Gavin could have rekindled their romantic relationship, but this would most likely run counter to most werewolf films: the woman never seems to be able to tame the beast, at least not without killing him. A more distinct possibility is that Kate, having seen Gavin's "wolf" form, has kept her distance.

10. After Cayden discovers that he is a werewolf, he has a bit of a bad time: he's framed for murdering his parents and, in a fit of lust, attacks his girlfriend in wolf form. In his voiceover narration, he says "all the books" agree that suicide is the only way to end the life of a wolf. However, the books are wrong: as the film progresses, werewolves

of all types are shot, beheaded, slashed, and blown up.

11. *Wolves* was released in 2014, riding the wave of the *Twilight* series in book and film.

12. Just over ten years separates Lucas Till (Cayden) and Jason Momoa (Connor).

13. Even by 1980s action film standards, the antagonist's end in *Cobra* is particularly brutal: he is hung on a meathook and burned alive.

Under Siege

1. Jack Donovan is no doubt a controversial author. In many ways, his inclusion in this volume is primarily because of his view of masculinity—that one has to be sexually and physically dominant over everyone in order to be an "alpha male"—so closely mimics the equation of many male characters in werewolf cinema. Donovan's ideas, of course, in order to become theoretically possible, create a series of wide-ranging movements—including his own version and interpretation of feminism—that supposedly seek to strip men of their masculinity. It is also important to note that, in this decidedly non-academic treatise, Donovan's own descriptions would place himself at the top of the masculine hierarchy. Donovan, whose musculature seems to necessitate more photos with his shirt off rather than on, is almost stereotypically hegemonic in his outlook. In fact, Donovan's works often feel like a plot device in a werewolf film, something that a young and fragile male would read just before getting bitten by a werewolf and becoming a supposedly empowered and "real" man. The inclusion of this very small chunk of Donovan's work is therefore useful in illustrating the hegemonic, male-centered perspective.

2. *Howl* (2015) doesn't deal much in proper names. Although Adrian is listed in the credits, he and many of the other passengers don't give their names during the course of the film. Interestingly, whenever Adrian speaks, he is introduced in the subtitles as "assertive man."

3. In many of the "under siege" storylines, there is someone within the group of people who are being accosted that is as dangerous as whatever is attacking them—or more so. This trope appears frequently, from the earliest episodes of *Doctor Who* to the zombie actioner *Train to Busan*. Most of the time, the male who causes problems is slowly revealed to be a negative version of masculinity, one that is presented as an "incorrect" definition of a man. Concerned only for his well-being, a philanderer, an emotionally detached businessman, and one who is a disruptive presence to any attempts on the part of the group to cooperate, Adrian fits the trope nicely.

4. In fact, the 2008 film *Rambo* and the 2019 *Rambo: Last Blood* focus on an aged Rambo, who only reluctantly engages in combat and, for the first time, shows signs of mortality—wounds slow him down, and he has to rely on others to help him. Even so, Rambo is still clearly dangerous, if only for his tactical acumen.

Enemy, Mother, Lover, Object

1. As noted previously, franchises focusing on vampires or Frankenstein's monster have been long-lasting and featured multiple films. This may be due to the canonical literary origins of both works. In this regard, the ideas surrounding lesbian vampires also have a literary origin themselves: *Carmilla* by J. Sheridan Le Fanu, in which the titular female vampire provokes in her female victims a mixture of attraction alongside "something of repulsion" (Le Fanu). *Carmilla*, released several years before *Dracula*, has most likely been the starting point for numerous depictions of lesbian vampires, including the films of Paul Naschy, Jess Franco, and Jean Rollin.

2. April Miller also writes that the "familiar silver bullet cure" in *Ginger Snaps* is rejected, resulting in a "strident critique of Hollywood representations" (286). The issue, however, is that many Hollywood films released prior to *Ginger Snaps* didn't use the silver bullet as a way of dispatching the wolf; as a matter of fact, it is possible that a relative minority of werewolf films used this trope. *Werewolf of London, The Undying Monster, An American Werewolf in London* all featured wolves that died in a hail of (regular) gunfire. The wolf in *Bad Moon* is severely injured by gunfire, and later finished off by a German Shepherd, after laboriously

dispelling the silver bullet myth earlier in the film. Other than *The Wolf Man* (which didn't feature a silver bullet, but a bludgeoning with a silver cane), *Curse of the Werewolf*, *The Howling*, and the appropriately named *Silver Bullet*, numerous werewolf films feature wolves who meet a variety of demises. In this regard, *Ginger Snaps* isn't necessarily breaking new ground.

3. Barbara Creed is right to note that "despite the range of subjects" regarding women in film, "[i]t is to the horror film that we must turn for any direct reference to the woman's monthly cycle" (77).

4. For American audiences, Shout! has distributed two Paul Naschy collections. The first has *Night of the Werewolf*, the second *The Werewolf and the Yeti*. Like many foreign horror films in the 1980s, Naschy's films are often poorly dubbed, haphazardly edited, and poorly distributed. As such, the Shout! versions are as close to "definitive" Naschy werewolf as viewers can get, so these are the two films I will explore.

5. Another Naschy film, *The Werewolf Versus the Vampire Woman*, features a scene in which "the younger sister of Daninsky's girlfriend seduces him. She tricks him into meeting her in an isolated spot [...], removes her clothes, and insistently approaches him until he submits and they have sex" (Hartson 131).

6. As if to emphasize the nudity in the film (including the nudity to come), as Naschy wrestles with a female vampire, he pauses the struggle just long enough to tug her chiffon robe free, exposing her breasts.

7. The scene shows Wandesa from the back dropping her robe, Daninsky looking her up and down, a line or two of dialogue, and then a poorly-lit and oddly edited close up of a pair of breasts, before returning to the scene proper.

8. Again, the camera tells the viewer that these women are objects first. In their initial appearance in *Night of the Werewolf*, they are poolside, talking with a group of males. All three are wearing bathing suits, and, as they talk to the men, the camera slowly pans around them to emphasize their bodies.

9. When Erika is bitten by Bathory, she is dressed in slacks and a sensible 1980s blouse. After becoming a vampire, however, she changes into a more revealing black nightgown.

10. And, like a Naschy film, Marsha is fully nude for the cameras during her initial sex scene with Bill. She also wears skintight leather outfits.

11. What makes this doubly uncomfortable is that Harvey Weinstein—who has been convicted of sexual assault—is one of the producers for *Cursed*.

12. Much of the irony found in *Trick 'r Treat* can be found in the costumes the characters are wearing. A young woman dressed as an angel plays a cruel trick on someone else. Another young woman who is an "idiot savant" is dressed as a witch, and is the only one to understand the supernatural happenings around her.

13. Soon after Kelly Ann gives up her baby for adoption, we see her sitting in her bedroom, pumping breast milk to sell to the adoptive parents. In some rather hamfisted moralizing, we hear a radio playing in the background, which notes that young Scottish women living in poverty are more likely to have unwanted pregnancies.

Works Cited

Abbott, Stacey. *Celluloid Vampires: Life After Death in the Modern World.* U of Texas P, 2007.

Appignanesi, Lisa. *Mad, Bad, and Sad: Women and the Mind Doctors.* Norton, 2008.

Benshoff, Harry M. *Monsters in the Closet: Homosexuality and the Horror Film.* Manchester UP, 1997.

Bernhardt-House, Philip. "The Werewolf as Queer, the Queer as Werewolf, and Queer Werewolves." *Queering the Non/Human.* Edited by Noreen Giffney and Myra Hind, Ashgate Publishing, 2008, 159–183.

Bly, Robert. *Iron John: A Book About Men.* Vintage, 1990.

Boss, Pete. "Vile Bodies and Bad Medicine." *Screen,* vol. 27, no. 1.1, January 1986, pp. 14–25.

Braudy, Leo. *Haunted: On Ghosts, Witches, Vampires, Zombies, and Other Monsters of the Natural and Supernatural Worlds.* Yale UP, 2016.

Carrigan, Tim, Bob Connell and John Lee. "Toward a New Sociology of Masculinity." *The Masculinity Studies Reader,* edited by Rachel Adams and David Savran, Blackwell Publishers, 2002, 99–118.

Carter, Angela. *The Bloody Chamber.* Penguin, 2015.

Clover, Carol J. "Her Body, Himself: Gender in the Slasher Film." *The Dread of Difference.* U of Texas P, 1996, 66–113.

Connell, R.W., and James W. Messerschmidt. "Hegemonic Masculinity: Rethinking the Concept." *Gender and Society,* vol. 19, no. 6, pp. 829–859.

Covey, Russell D. "Criminal Madness: Cultural Iconography and Insanity. *Stanford Law Review,* Vol. 61, No. 6, 2009. Pp 1375-1427.

Creed, Barbara. *The Monstrous-Feminine:* *Film, Feminism, Psychoanalysis.* Routledge, 1993.

Donovan, Jack. *The Way of Men.* Dissonant Hum, 2012.

du Coudray, Chantal Bourgault. *The Curse of the Werewolf: Fantasy, Horror, and the Beast Within.* I.B. Tauris, 2006.

Eagleton, Terry. *Sweet Violence: The Idea of the Tragic.* Blackwell Publishing, 2003.

Eisler, Robert. *Man Into Wolf: An Anthropological Interpretation of Sadism, Masochism, and Lycanthropy.* Greenwood Press, 1951.

Elliott, Jaquelin. "Becoming the Monster: Queer Monstrosity and the Reclamation of the Werewolf in Slash Fandom." *The Revenant,* 2, 91–110. Retrieved from: http://www.revenantjournal.com/issues/werewolves-studies-in-transformation-guest-editors-kaja-franck-and-janine-hatter/#sthash.O4U0U4Rh.dpbs

Elliott-Smith, Darren. *Queer Horror: Film and Television.* I.B. Tauris, 2016.

Erwin, Elizabeth. "How Horror Thwarted 'The Code." *Gay & Lesbian Review Worldwide,* 22:6, November 2015, 18–20.

Gates, Philippa. "Cop Action Films." *American Masculinities: A Historical Encyclopedia,* edited by Brett E. Carroll, SAGE, 2003, 110–112.

Gill, Pat. "The Monstrous Years: Teens, Slasher Films, and the Family." *Journal of Film and Video,* vol. 54, no. 4, Winter 2002, pp. 16–30.

Gracey, James. *The Company of Wolves.* Auteur, 2017.

Halberstam, Judith. "An Introduction to Female Masculinity." *The Masculinity Studies Reader,* edited by Rachel Adams and David Savran, Blackwell Publishers, 2002, 355–374.

Hartson, Mary T. "Voracious Vampires and

Other Monsters: Masculinity and the Terror Genre in Spanish Cinema of the Transición." *Romance Notes*, vol. 55, no. 1, Jan. 2015, pp. 125–136. EBSCO*host*, doi:10.1353/rmc.2015.0010.

Hawley, Erin. "The Bride and Her Afterlife: Female Frankenstein Monsters on Page and Screen." *Literature Film Quarterly*, 43:3, July 2015, 218–231.

Hodgon, Tim. "Counterculture." *American Masculinities: A Historical Encyclopedia*, edited by Brett E. Carroll, SAGE, 2003, 112–114.

Hutchings, Peter. "Masculinity and the Horror Film." *You Tarzan: Masculinity, Movies and Men*. Ed. Pat Kirkham and Janet Thumim. St. Martin's Press, 1993. 84–94. Print.

Kimmel, "The Birth of the Self-Made Man." *The Masculinity Studies Reader*, edited by Rachel Adams and David Savran, Blackwell Publishers, 2002, 135–152.

King, Stephen. *Danse Macabre*. Gallery Books, 2010.

Le Fanu, J. Sheridan. *Carmilla*. Retrieved from http://www.gutenberg.org/files/10007/10007-h/10007-h.htm

Lynch, Michael. "'Here Is Adhesiveness': From Friendship to Homosexuality." *Victorian Studies*, vol. 29, no. 1, 1985, pp. 67–96. *JSTOR*, JSTOR, www.jstor.org/stable/3827566.

Mank, Gregory William. *It's Alive!* A.S. Barnes and Company, 1981.

Messerschmidt, James. *Hegemonic Masculinity: Formulation, Reformulation, and Amplification*. Rowman and Littlefield, 2018.

Miller, April. "'The Hair That Wasn't There Before': Demystifying Monstrosity and Enstruation in Ginger Snaps and Ginger Snaps Unleashed." *Western Folklore*, vol. 64, no. 3/4, Summer/Fall2005, pp. 281–303. EBSCO*host*, ezproxy.vccs.edu:2048/login?url=http://search.ebscohost.com/login.aspx?direct=true&db=a9h&AN=21216989&site=ehost-live.

Otten, Charlotte. *A Lycanthropy Reader: Werewolves in Western Culture*. Syracuse UP, 1986.

Pinedo, Isabel. "Recreational Terror: Postmodern Elements of the Contemporary Horror Film." *Journal of Film and Video*, vol. 48, no. 1–2, Spring-Summer 1996, pp. 17–31.

Rehling, Nicola. "Everyman and No Man: White, Heterosexual Masculinity in Contemporary Serial Killer Movies." *Jump Cut* 49 (2007): 1–22. Web.

Rieser, Klaus. "Masculinity and Monstrosity: Characterization and Identification in the Slasher Film." *Men & Masculinities*, vol. 3, no. 4, Apr. 2001, p. 370. EBSCO*host*, ezproxy.vccs.edu:2048/login?url=http://search.ebscohost.com/login.aspx?direct=true&db=a9h&AN=4583706&site=ehost-live.

Savran, David. *Taking It Like a Man: White Masculinity, Masochism, and Contemporary American Culture*. Princeton UP, 1998.

Senn, Bryan. *The Werewolf Filmography*. McFarland, 2017.

Siodmak, Curtis. *Wolf Man's Maker: Memoir of a Hollywood Writer*. Scarecrow Press, 2001.

Smith, Don G. *Lon Chaney, Jr.: Horror Film Star, 1906–1973*, McFarland, 1996.

Spadoni, Robert. "Old Times in Werewolf of London." *Journal of Film & Video*, vol. 63, no. 4, Winter2011, pp. 3–20. EBSCO*host*, ezproxy.vccs.edu:2048/login?url=http://search.ebscohost.com/login.aspx?direct=true&db=a9h&AN=67148690&site=ehost-live.

Summers, Montague. *The Werewolf*. University Books, 1966.

Thompson, Harold. " Sssssss' and 'Werewolf' Blend Horror." *New York Times*. August 2, 1973. Retrieved from: http://www.nytimes.com/movie/review?res=9D02E1DF103DE63ABC4A53DFBE668388669EDE&mcubz=0

Wallerstein, Hannah. "Real Gender: Identity, Loss, and the Capacity to Feel Real." *Studies in Gender & Sexuality*, vol. 18, no. 1, Jan. 2017, pp. 62–71. EBSCO*host*, doi:10.1080/15240657.2016.1238684.

Wasik, Bill, and Monica Murphy. *Rabid: A Cultural History of the World's Most Diabolical Virus*. Viking, 2012.

Winter, Thomas. "Cult of Domesticity." *American Masculinities: A Historical Encyclopedia*, edited by Brett E. Carroll, SAGE, 2003, 120–122.

Index

An American Werewolf in London 4-5, 6, 7, 9, 12, 13-14, 15, 17, 18, 20, 21, 22, 27, 33, 34, 36, 46, 48, 57, 67, 72, 73-77, 101, 104, 139, 144, 147, 148, 149, 154, 155, 163*n*, 165*n*
An American Werewolf in Paris 14, 22, 55, 103, 119, 147-148
Amicus Productions 69-72
Another Wolf Cop 100-103

Bad Moon 82-84, 165*n*
The Beast Must Die 33-34, 68-72
Bly, Robert 77, 78, 85, 112
The Boy Who Cried Werewolf 12, 25, 65-68
Bram Stoker's Dracula 15
Braudy, Leo 13, 14
Bride of Frankenstein 114-115
Bubba the Redneck Werewolf 8, 19

Capaldi, Peter 150, 152
Chaney, Lon, Jr.: as Larry Talbot 39-49, 115, 154, 163*n*; personal life 162*n*
The Company of Wolves 21, 22, 117, 119, 130-134, 147, 152, 156
The Creature from the Black Lagoon 115
Creed, Barbara 119, 166*n*
Curse of the Werewolf 7, 61-65
Cursed 89-91, 97, 135-137

Dog Soldiers 2, 7, 14, 17, 18-19, 35, 104-106, 116, 119, 134-135, 151, 154, 156
Donovan, Jack 105, 165*n*
du Coudray, Chantal Bourgault 2, 21, 29, 30, 31, 32, 78, 85, 117, 118, 163*n*
Dracula 114, 116
Dracula's Daughter 114, 116

Eastwood, Clint 102

Frankenstein Meets the Wolf Man 32-33, 36, 41-44, 74, 127, 162*n*, 164*n*

Grevioux, Kevin 33, 36
The Grey 1-5
Ginger Snaps 8, 16, 18, 35, 73, 79, 88, 101, 116, 117, 118-120, 130, 134, 135, 137-142, 143-145, 152, 154, 155, 156-157, 165*n*-166*n*

Ginger Snaps Back: The Beginning 144-147
Ginger Snaps 2: Unleashed 142-145

Hammer Film Productions, Ltd. 61
The Haunted Strangler 13
Hemlock Grove 21
House of Dracula 45, 47, 116, 162*n*
House of Frankenstein 43-45, 129
Howl 5, 23, 35, 95, 107-110, 154, 156, 165*n*
The Howling 6, 8, 9, 14, 15, 17, 22, 27, 32, 33, 34, 55, 72, 77-79, 82, 98, 103, 120, 129-130, 153-154, 155, 156, 162*n*, 166*n*

I Was a Teenage Werewolf 25, 52-56, 57, 58, 59, 77, 79, 80, 90, 98, 137, 153, 156
Interview with a Vampire 15
Iron John 11, 17, 25

King, Stephen 11, 13

Landon, Michael 52
Late Phases 5, 7, 14, 17, 22, 104, 110-113, 154, 156
Lauter, Harry 57

masculinity: hard 8, 16, 23, 24-26, 27, 29-30, 52, 61, 64, 70, 79-80, 81, 85-88, 92-93, 97, 99-100, 105-106, 112, 154; hegemonic 5, 16, 25-27, 43-45, 57, 61, 64-67, 68, 73-77, 82, 90-91, 92, 94-95, 99, 100-101, 105-106, 112-113, 121, 124-125, 131-133, 137, 156-157, 165*n*; soft 2, 5, 8, 16, 23, 25-27, 29-30, 34-35, 45, 51-52, 71, 75-78, 79-81, 85-88, 90, 92-93, 96, 98-99, 103, 105-109, 112, 125, 154; toxic 5, 8-9, 16 22, 25-27, 39, 44-45, 52, 55-60, 61, 64, 71, 73-75, 78, 82, 84, 87-89, 90, 92, 93, 95-98, 101-102, 105-106, 108-110, 112, 128, 132-134, 137, 144, 149-150, 154, 156-157
Megowan, Don 57
The Mummy 115, 116

Naschy, Paul 30, 35, 63, 75, 120, 161*n*; as Waldemar Daninsky 123-129
Nicholson, Jack 85

169

Index

Night of the Werewolf 12, 124-126, 127, 129, 166*n*

porphyria 164*n*

Rambo, John 34, 105, 161*n*

Schwarzenegger, Arnold 2, 29, 34
Senn, Bryan 81, 114, 121. 123, 161*n*, 163*n*
She Wolf of London 21, 23
Silver Bullet 116, 166*n*
Sleepaway Camp 118
Stallone, Sylvester 2, 29, 34, 102

Teen Wolf 3, 8, 22, 23, 35, 79-82, 90, 100, 117, 153, 164*n*
Teen Wolf (television show) 20
Teen Wolf Too 3, 8, 79-82, 90
The Thing 69
"tragic" male 2-5, 6-9, 16, 42, 48, 64-65, 68, 71-72, 77, 96-97, 137, 154, 155
Trick 'r Treat 18, 116, 117, 118-120. 135, 146, 166*n*
Twilight (film series) 20, 23, 116, 165*n*

Underworld 14, 36, 116; franchise 23, 33, 36
Underworld: Evolutions 164*n*
Underworld: Rise of the Lycans 92-93
The Undying Monster 21, 22, 35, 51-52, 55, 58, 59, 67, 77, 83, 137, 162*n*

Wagner the Wehr-Wolf 116
Wer 7, 19, 23, 93-96, 154, 156, 164*n*
The Werewolf 24, 25, 56-60, 61, 153, 156

The Werewolf and the Yeti 126-128, 166*n*
werewolf films: and family heritage 3, 24-25, 39-42, 46-49, 51-52, 61-62, 67, 81-82, 97-98, 150, 153; and heteronormativity 154-155, 161*n*; and homophobia 89-91; and homosexuality 50, 54, 88, 90, 155, 162*n*, 164*n*; and homosocial relationships 90, 162*n*; and juvenile delinquency 52-54, 98-99, 153; and mental illness 42, 45-48, 75, 82-83, 126-130, 143-144, 162*n*, 164*n*; and race 29-38; and science 21, 31, 43, 48 52-60, 161*n*, 164*n*; and sexual virility 11, 16, 98-99, 101-102, 107-108, 139-140, 145, 147-148, 163*n*; and symbolism of transformation 12-14, 16-17, 18, 19-22; and vampires 8-9, 14-15, 43, 45-46, 114-116, 124-129, 154, 162*n*, 165*n*; and xenophobia 32-33, 36-38
A Werewolf in Slovenia 19
Werewolf of London 18, 21, 30-33, 35, 38, 50, 54, 90, 162*n*, 165*n*
Werewolf: The Beast Among Us 2, 23
What We Do in the Shadows 3, 8-9, 18, 92, 100, 116, 156
Wild Country 22, 35, 134, 138, 149-152, 166*n*
Wolf 85-89, 99, 117, 164*n*
Wolf Cop 21, 22, 100-102, 156
The Wolf Man (1941) 6, 7, 14, 17, 21, 30, 32-33, 35, 39-41, 42, 44, 45, 48, 49, 50, 51, 57, 58, 59, 73, 77, 81, 84, 104, 114, 116, 120, 146, 161*n*, 162*n*, 163*n*, 166*n*
Wolfen 36-38
The Wolfman (2010) 46-49, 162*n*-163*n*
Wolves 5, 12, 21, 27, 96-100, 156, 165*n*

www.ingramcontent.com/pod-product-compliance
Lightning Source LLC
Chambersburg PA
CBHW032048300426
44117CB00009B/1228